P9-DJV-355

NO LONGER THE PROPERTY OF
BALDWIN PUBLIC LIBRARY

AT

FENWAY

► ◄ ♦ ♦ ♦ ♦ ◄ ► ◄

ALSO BY DAN SHAUGHNESSY

The Curse of the Bambino
Ever Green
One Strike Away
Seeing Red: The Red Auerbach Story

AT FENWAY

DISPATCHES FROM RED SOX NATION

DAN SHAUGHNESSY

CROWN PUBLISHERS, INC.
NEW YORK

BALDWIN PUBLIC LIBRARY

Copyright © 1996 by Dan Shaughnessy

All rights reserved. No part of this book may be reproduced or transmitted in
any form or by any means, electronic or mechanical, including photocopying,
recording, or by any information storage and retrieval system, without
permission in writing from the publisher.

Published by Crown Publishers, Inc., 201 East 50th Street, New York, New York
10022. Member of the Crown Publishing Group.

Random House, Inc. New York, Toronto, London, Sydney, Auckland

CROWN is a trademark of Crown Publishers, Inc.

Printed in the U.S.A.
Design by Karen Minster

Library of Congress Cataloging-in-Publication Data
Shaughnessy, Dan.
At Fenway : dispatches from Red Sox Nation / Dan Shaughnessy.—
1st ed.
p.   cm.
Includes bibliographical references (p.   ) and index.
1. Boston Red Sox (Baseball team)—History.   2. Fenway Park
(Boston, Mass.)—History.   I. Title.
GV875.B62S518   1996
796.357'64'0974461—dc20   96-281
CIP

ISBN 0-517-70104-9

1   3   5   7   9   10   8   6   4   2

First Edition

To beautiful Sarah, who has joy in her heart

ACKNOWLEDGMENTS

Thanks to agent/friend Meg Blackstone, editor Peter Ginna, Ed Kleven, Peter Gammons, Dave Smith, Ken Nigro, Dave O'Hara, Kevin Dupont, Lesley Visser, Tim Kurkjian, John Lowe, Laurel Prieb, Wendy Selig, Phyllis Merhige, Bob Ryan, Jackie MacMullan, Gerry Callahan, Mike Barnicle, Bud Collins, Bill Griffith, Joe Sullivan, Peter May, Nick Cafardo, Larry Whiteside, Will McDonough, Joe Giuliotti, Guy Spina, Clark Booth, George Sullivan, Eddie Andelman, Bob Lobel, Alan Miller, David Halberstam, Clif Keane, Glenn Stout, Stan Grossfeld, Stephen Stills, Steve Sheppard, Dick Johnson, Ken Coleman, Mike Andrews, Christina Zwart, all the good folks at the *Globe* library, John Iannacci, John Horn, Dick Bresciani, Kevin Shea, Helen Robinson, Mary Jane Ryan, Bill Tanton, Vince Doria, Don Skwar, Matt Storin, Tom Mulvoy, Clemson Smith. Lynda Gorov saved me with her edits, and Sean Mullin again proved to be the computer MVP. Thanks to Jonny Miller.

On a more personal note in a very personal book, thanks go out to all family members, especially Lou and Mary, brother Bill, sisters Mary, Joan, and Ann, my mom, and the home team of Sarah, Kate, Sam, and Marilou, who is the Franchise.

NANTUCKET, 1995

CONTENTS

◆ ◆ ◆ ◆ ◆ ◆ ◆

AT

FENWAY

▸ ◦ ◆ ◦ ◦ ◆ ◦ ◆ ◦ ◆ ◦ ◆ ◦ ◀

TANGLED UP IN GREEN

◄ ◆ ◆ ◆ ◆ ◆ ◆ ◆ ◆ ◆ ►

◆ As you read this, there are base-ball fans sitting in wide, cushy seats, watching a game in a spacious, state-of-the-art stadium with sprawling parking lots, polished bathrooms, and international food courts. Those spoiled fans might even be sitting in a climate-controlled dome, enjoying all the comforts of the twentieth century. Their hometown ballpark, like most new parks today, is a palace of awakening desire. Going to the game is like going to a new shopping mall.

Not me. I'm sitting in the press box, high atop Fenway Park. From my second-row seat, I can look beyond Fenway's outfield walls and see the Massachusetts Institute of Technology, the Bunker Hill Monument, the golden dome of the Massachusetts State House, the old and new Hancock towers, and the Christian Science Center's Mother Church. I can see the former Hotel Shelton, where Eugene O'Neill died (it's now a Boston University dorm). I can see a piece of Bunker Hill Community College, where Sacco and Vanzetti were executed when it was Charlestown State Prison. I can see Massachusetts Avenue, where Martin Luther King Jr. lived when he studied at the BU Divinity School. And I can see all the green splendor of Fenway Park.

To get here, I have battled bad weather, bad roads, and cowboy drivers. I have paid $10 for the privilege of having my car blocked in a tiny parking lot. I have walked on pigeon dung and smelled propane-heated sausages on the frost-heaved sidewalks. I have climbed the ten long ramps to the press box that sits atop the 600 Club in ancient Fenway. I feel as if I am in my dusty old den, reading a favorite book in my dad's overstuffed, dog-eared chair.

Folks at General Motors several years back introduced a campaign to sell Oldsmobiles. The slogan was, "This is not your father's Oldsmobile."

The charm of Fenway is that it *is* your father's ballpark.

The rest of baseball is George Jetson. Boston is Miss Havisham.

Fenway Park is where young Rose Fitzgerald sat in the box seats while her father, Mayor John "Honey Fitz" Fitzgerald, threw out the first ball before a 1912 World Series game. It's where Babe Ruth pitched the Sox to a World Championship in 1918. It's where Tom Yawkey and his young bride, Jean, would sit on the outfield grass and have a picnic while listening to Sox road games on the radio. This is where Ted Williams homered in his final at bat in the big leagues, Curt Gowdy making the call, Brooks Robinson at third, John Updike in the grandstand. This is where Dick Stuart chugged around the bases for an inside-the-park homer after his fly ball clanged off the head of Cleveland outfielder Vic Davillio. This is where Jim Lonborg laid down the bunt in the bottom of the sixth to ignite the rally that won the 1967 American League pennant. This is where organist John Kiley played the "Hallelujah Chorus" after Carlton Fisk clanged one off the foul pole. This is where Yaz leaned against The Wall as Bucky Dent's pop fly feathered into the netting atop the Wall. This is where fuzzy-cheeked Roger Clemens struck out twenty on a cold April night in 1986. This is where Tom Brunansky made a sliding catch near the right-field foul pole, clinching the 1990 American League East flag. This is where the triangular eye of the Citgo sign looks down on fans like the eyes of Dr. Eckelberg in F. Scott Fitzgerald's *The Great Gatsby*. This is where things happened. We take comfort in that.

These are perilous days for old Fenway. The late Boston Garden, built in 1928, was closed in 1995 and is scheduled to be disassembled in 1996. Ever the home of the Celtics and Bruins, the Garden was replaced by a building named after a Rhode Island bank. Today, Boston basketball and hockey fans see their games at the FleetCenter, where you're never more than a few feet from an ATM. The Celtics, Bruins, and their fans love Boston's new indoor sports palace. Meanwhile, the current Red Sox ownership talks about structural problems, pouring good money after bad, and the inevitability of a new baseball park for Boston. The wrecking ball may soon dangle over Fenway's green walls. Memories of the ballpark may someday be all we've got. I have a hard time being rational about any of this. I say Save the Whales, Save Our Cities, and Save Fenway Park.

This is a book about the unique experience of being a Red Sox fan and attending baseball games at Fenway. Hopefully it will serve as a companion for the long-suffering legion of Sox watchers; an almanac for Boston baseball fans. Warning, readers: Prepare to hear the dreaded first-person pronoun from time to time in this book. *At Fenway* is a decidedly personal story.

I was born in Groton, Massachusetts, in the summer of 1953, the year the Braves left for Milwaukee and Boston became a one-team town. The Red Sox in '53 were managed by Lou Boudreau (typical Sox: Boudreau is the man who beat Boston in the '48 play-off game, and the Red Sox have a habit of acquiring former Sox-killers just when their careers are on the downside). Boudreau's '53 edition went 84–69, good for fourth place, a tidy sixteen games behind the New York Yankees. Ted Williams spent most of the '53 season flying planes in Korea and played only thirty-seven games for the Sox.

When Ted was hitting .388 at the age of thirty-nine in 1957, I was involved with toy soldiers, fire trucks, and "Big Brother" Bob Emery's television show. With regret, I must admit that I had just learned how to say hello when "Hub Fans Bid Kid Adieu." This is a lasting pain for one who grew up with the Boston Red Sox and has spent much of his adult life writing about them. I never saw Teddy Ballgame hit.

My father was born in 1914, grew up in Cambridge, Massachusetts, and told wonderful stories of jumping on moving trolley cars and watching major-league ball games through holes in the fences at Braves Field. He said he saw Babe Ruth, which made him seem impossibly old. He was thirty-nine years older than I, overweight, had a bad ticker, and was a prototype stationary father of the fifties. I never saw him in sneakers and I never saw him run. He was the adult and I was the child and that was that. Very serious.

Dad was good with words and had a wonderful sense of humor. I still remember sitting in the backseat of his four-door sedan—

groovin' to the Tokens' bombastic "The Lion Sleeps Tonight," when my dad asked, "How can the lion sleep with all that racket?" Then there was the time he was giving us a tour of his adolescent Cambridge neighborhood and announced that one of his old girlfriends had lived in a house just around the corner. He turned and pointed to a brown three-decker, and we all howled when we saw a sign out front reading, Beware of Dog.

William J. Shaughnessy was an executive for a paper bag company. He met my mother at Cambridge City Hospital when he was recovering from an appendectomy. Legend holds that he kept asking one of the pretty nurses for backrubs. She rejected his advances, claiming nurses don't date patients, but finally caved in when she needed a ride to the wake of a roommate's parent. So my parents' first date was a wake. Like I said, Dad was one funny guy.

He was not much of a ballplayer by the time I came along. Yard-work was the extent of his exercise. In his early years, Dad had played some baseball, thrown the hammer, and rowed on the Charles River; by the time I came along he'd closed his locker for good. My father wasn't a hands-on baseball dad. There'll be no Ken Burns–esque fathers playing catch with sons in this essay. But I remember my dad religiously saving, cutting, and pasting S & H Green Stamps to get me my first glove, a Tito Francona model.

One day, on his way into the house after coming home from work, my tired dad took time to offer batting tips. I was in my eighth or ninth hour of a one-man (nonstop narration) World Series, and Dad stopped to offer some advice. He took my bat and told me that he'd been a pretty fair slugger in his day. He said he once interrupted a picnic with a young lady to play a little baseball—then scattered picnic sandwiches with a long drive that almost conked his girlfriend on the head. I liked the story. It was good Dad folklore. Anyway, he showed me how he hit the longball. He said he would step toward the pitcher as the pitcher wound up. He demonstrated: sidestep left foot, sidestep right foot, then swing. He was actually moving toward the pitcher when the ball crossed the plate. He said the momentum added distance to his hits. I might have been only nine years old, and I had never studied under Walter Hriniak, but even I knew this was ridiculous. Hitting the ball on the move? Sure, Dad.

On weekends my father would mow the lawn wearing black shoes. He'd pick up sticks in the yard, always bending at the back, instead of at the knees. Then he might crack open a can of Miller High Life and we'd watch the Sox on TV. What can I say? We were white-bread Americans of the early 1960s. Dad was Hugh Beaumont as Ward Cleaver. And I was Jerry Mathers as the Beaver.

Watching baseball games on television, he explained intentional walks and infield-fly rules. He'd yell at the announcers when they used incorrect grammar. He told me that the ballplayers were better in his day. His teams became my teams. Of course, there are still folks in greater Boston who are Atlanta Braves fans because their dads were Braves fans before the team left Boston for Milwaukee. Those people remind me of the Japanese warriors who roamed the jungles of the South Pacific long after Japan surrendered.

The fact is, while dads and kids at one time or another collide on most social, cultural, and economic issues, we accept dad's team as our own. Red Sox are like green eyes. It's in the genes. We get 'em from dad.

My hometown of Groton is a Rockwellian, apple town, forty miles northwest of Boston. Groton in the 1950s had about four thousand people, no stoplights, and five-digit telephone numbers (ours was 8–6430). People today think of forty miles as an easy commute. It wasn't like that for my family in Groton in the 1950s. Boston might as well have been Paris. The Hub of the Universe was a faraway place, a big city where you could easily get lost and never be found. Boston had the big hospitals if you got really sick. It was where Mom might go shopping once every couple of years if she needed a fancy hat. Boston never was at our fingertips. It took well over an hour to get there by car, people drove crazily around rotaries, and sometimes you had to *pay* to park. A trip to Boston was a pilgrimmage. You earned it, anticipated it, then you sat in the backseat with your mouth open and looked at the tall buildings and the congestion. It was loud, busy, and gray, nothing like Groton.

Most of my early baseball memories are fuzzy. My brother was six years older than I, and naturally adept at all sports, especially baseball. He was the star pitcher and hitter of all of his Little League, Pony League, Police Athletic League, and Babe Ruth League teams. I went to his games to watch him play, but it was impossible for us to play together. He was too much bigger, stronger, and faster, and no seven-year-old could keep up with Bill Shaughnessy's pack of ballplaying teens.

My first trip to Fenway Park was not the religious experience that we so often hear and read about. But it was pretty good. It was during the spring of Carl Yastrzemski's rookie year (1961), a night game against the Orioles in early June. I was in the second grade and my dad had four tickets in the upper grandstand on the first-base side. The tickets probably represented a once-a-year favor from a client in the rail freight or paper industry. My brother was allowed to invite a friend. Bill invited Fred Porter, a fourteen-year-old pal from down the street. Fred was Bill's catcher.

We went to my first Fenway game on a school night. That killed me. You knew this was important. I mean, the way my parents casually waived the bedtime curfew was enough to make a seven-year-old realize this was an important event. I remember getting lost on the drive to Boston. It never failed. My father grew up on the banks of the Charles River, went to Boston College High School and Boston College, but never seemed able to find his way around the streets of his youth. I came to expect that when we went to Boston, we got lost.

We parked in one of those lots where they take your money, then block you in for the night. We carried our jackets and bought peanuts outside the ballpark. The cheaper, sidewalk peanuts came in tightly packed brown bags. Put me anywhere on the planet, close my eyes, and hold one of those brown peanut bags up to my nose and I am seven years old, wide-eyed, gazing at the Fenway greenery. That is one of the great things about Fenway and the area around Fenway. It smells like baseball.

I had my hat and my glove. We went through the Yawkey Way turnstiles and down the ramp under the third-base grandstands. The cement floor was grimy, reeked of stale beer, and was covered with cigar butts and flattened gum. Still, it was great. This was where major league ball was played, and I was walking on the same dirty ramps that the men in straw hats had walked on when they went to see the Babe. Even at the age of seven, I had that old-timey feeling. It was like being in my aunt Catherine's old house in Medford. The ballpark felt lived-in—a place where a lot of great and weird things had happened over the years. Fenway Park had been hardball home to Cy Young, Tris Speaker, and Babe Ruth. But we were there to see Frank Malzone and Chuck Schilling, Jim Pagliaroni and this rookie left fielder, the great young Yastrzemski.

The best entrance to the open-air Fenway yard is the portal just to the right of home plate. This is an absolute. We can debate the best place to watch the sunrise on Cape Cod or the best place to see New England's leaves turn in October, but there's no room for argument when it comes to your first sight of Fenway. If you're beneath the grandstand, walk until you come to the overhead sign that reads, "Lower boxes 37–44, upper boxes 122–130, reserved sections 17–21."

Dad wasn't lost this time. We went up that ramp, and the majesty of Fenway's green unfolded before my eyes. Children today probably wouldn't have the same reaction, but after years of seeing everything in black and white on our twenty-four-inch Zenith, it was the color of green that got my attention. Think of *The Wizard of Oz* when a young Judy Garland wanders out of her storm-shattered house and into the lush land of Oz. It's the first splash of color in the classic film, and this scene often comes to mind when baby boomer Bostonians speak of their first glimpse of the venerable Boston ballyard.

The green gets your attention. It makes the Red Sox tuxedo-white uniforms stand out. It is the backdrop that put everything into focus.

Tangled up in green for the very first time, I was struck by what seemed like the huge dimensions of the park. We always speak of Fenway today as a "small" ballpark, but when you are seven and have never been far from Groton, Fenway seems very big. The left-field fence is enormous, and the lawn in right field stretches to a fence that appears quite unreachable for even the mightiest of clouters.

The rush of one's first glimpse of a big-league park is not exclusive to Fenway. In the fall of 1994, New England Patriots coach Bill Parcells was asked to recount his greatest thrill in sports. Winner of two Super Bowls, and an NFL lifer, Parcells answered, "It was when I was six years old. I walked into Yankee Stadium for the first time. My father took me to the place, and when I walked up the ramp and saw that field, that was the biggest thrill. I remember the feeling of exhilaration that I felt. Batting practice was going on and I saw those players on that field for the first time. We were sitting in the left-field box seats. That was it, my biggest sports thrill."

Pity. I can only wonder what the young men and women of Minneapolis–St. Paul will say when they speak of their first look at the interior of the Hubert H. Humphrey Metrodome. Somehow one's introduction to the Hefty Bag in right field lacks soul.

Finally in Fenway, I peeled some paint from a rusty rail and put it in my pocket. Maybe Ted Williams had once laid his hand on this flake of paint. It was my piece of history, something I could touch when listening to the next game while lying in bed. It was comforting and commemorative, my Fenway autograph.

Our seats for this mundane game were in the upper grandstand, under the roof, probably around Section 12 between first base and right field. The Red Sox were playing the Baltimore Orioles, who had a slugging first baseman named Jim Gentile, and a rising star at third named Brooks Robinson. What did I know? Brooks looked like he was okay, but he was no Frank Malzone. Second base appeared to be the easiest position: the one with the shortest throw. Sox rookie Chuck Schilling became my favorite player. I think the Red Sox won. It didn't matter. I can't say for sure if we got lost on our way home. I was in the backseat of Dad's company car, warm with sleep, and no doubt had to be carried to my room, glove in hand, hat on head.

Later that year, I remember sitting down to watch some of the 1961 World Series on television with my dad. It was the powerful Yankees against the Cincinnati Reds, who wore white hats with red pinstripes. I got bored after a couple of innings and got up to leave the room. All in all, it wasn't a bad instinct. Television enriches football and basketball, but it suffocates baseball.

A year later, I never walked out on a baseball game. The 1962 Red Sox were terrible, but it didn't matter. Between 1961 and 1962, sometime between the wonder years of eight and nine, I became addicted. That is no exaggeration. From 1962 through the World Series of 1967—that is, from third grade until high school—the Red Sox were the most important thing in my life. They were more important than family, friends, school, church, food, television, or swimming. The Sox came first. When they won, life was good. When they lost, which was more often than not in those years, I'd storm up the stairs, sometimes in tears. Maturity has many virtues, but I'm not sure I could, or would want to, ever again be as single-minded about anything as I was about the Red Sox and baseball in those six seasons of my youth. It was total immersion. I waited for each month's *Sport* magazine, then inhaled the pulp pages, committing cornball sports stories to long-term memory. I knew the names of all of the Houston Colt 45s. Whenever there was a new glove for Christmas, I'd put a ball in the webbing and tie a string around the glove to form a pocket for the first spring outings. Watching television, or listening to Sox broadcasts on the radio, I'd fire my ball into my mitt to soften the pocket. I kept scrapbooks. I memorized the lineups of all twenty big-league teams. A sportswriter by trade since 1975, I can easily tell you that I knew more players' names when I was eight than I do today. It's not even close.

I was very inventive about my hobby. My brother taught me how to create baseball games by rolling dice. This was handy when it got dark or when inclement weather forced my one-man games to move inside. I had baseball cards, and better yet, Salada-tea baseball coins. I created leagues and rolled the dice through 162-game seasons, logging each player's statistics.

My love of Salada-tea baseball coins led me into a brief life of crime. The coins were plastic and came in orange, red, blue, black, and white. Inside each coin was a paper image of a major league ballplayer. The Salada series featured ten players from each team in the majors, a total of two hundred coins. Each box of tea bags came with three coins. Through the mail, for a price, you could order sets of twenty-five coins, plus green plastic shields to store the coins. We didn't have much extra money to "waste" on mail-order baseball coins, so my supply was directly related to my parents' consumption of Salada tea. Then I found another way.

Inspection of the tea boxes revealed that occasionally, in shipping and stocking, a box would be slit at one end. The seal was broken, the tea couldn't be sold, and the coins just spilled out of the clean seam. Joe Mitchell, our grocery store manager and a tough Irishman we saw at church every Sunday, was a friend of my father's and only too happy to give me the coins from any damaged boxes. In time, I took to checking the boxes myself, and . . . with a sharp fingernail I learned how to "accidentally" slice open the boxes. Suddenly, there were a lot of boxes with slices in the side. And a lot of baseball coins in my pocket. One day after school, Mr. Mitchell saw me "checking out" the new shipment of Salada tea on his store shelf. He walked over, told me to empty my pockets, and discovered three baseball coins. I think he caught me with Leon Wagner, Rich Rollins, and Don Hoak. Mr. Mitchell took the coins, told me to go home, and—God bless him— never said a word about it to my father.

My backyard was my field of dreams. Every young boy should have one. We lived in a fifty-year-old rambling farmhouse, and our back-yard was one hundred feet long (I measured it myself with a yardstick), about fifty feet wide, bordered on the right by a pebblestone driveway and on the left by Mr. Woods's fence. Like just about every backyard, it was a home field marked by asymmetry and odd features. The field sloped downward from home plate, giving grounders an extra few feet of roll. The street at the far end, little-traveled Wood Lane, made for a perfect warning track. Mr. Woods's corn, squash, and tomatoes grew on the outside of my left-field wall, and woe was the little kid who traipsed into our neighbor's garden to find a worn baseball. (To my knowledge, Frank Woods never once gave any thought to plowing his corn under in order to build a ballfield that would bring Joe Jackson back from the dead.) There were evergreen trees down my right-field line, which made nasty traps for pop-ups on the first-base side. When a ball got stuck in the upper half of an evergreen, I'd put on a football helmet and climb the tree—smashing my helmet head skyward through the sticky needles. In between Mr. Woods's corn and our row of evergreens was my home field, a narrow slope of bumpy turf. I learned to live with the bad hops. It made me a better fielder when it came time for organized ball on more manicured diamonds.

Laundry days compounded my home-field groundskeeping woes. When my mother used the washing machine in our basement, the rinse water drained into foul territory on the third-base side. It was soggy and smelly. We had special ground rules on wash day.

But in every way, the field was perfect. And I think many of us today love Fenway because it has the irregularities that make it feel like the cockeyed backyard fields where we learned our baseball. Fen-way Park's left-field wall is adorned with a ladder. Yes, a ladder. Members of the Fenway ground crew climb the ladder to get up to the screen to retrieve home run balls nestled atop the wall. The ladder has come into play numerous times. Ted Williams one day camped under a high fly ball, which hit the ladder, ricocheted toward center field, past Jimmy Piersall, who'd come over to back up Williams. Jim Lemon wound up with a ladder-aided, inside-the-park home run. This is something that could have happened in our games at home. Our ground rules covered the possibilities of Mr. Woods's cornfield and Mom's laundry. The Sox had a ladder in fair territory.

In our Groton neighborhood, houses were spaced apart and there weren't a lot of kids nearby. This led to a lot of solo practice and absorbing mind games. One would think that batting practice would require other participants, but not when I had a bumper crop of crab apples and rocks to smash with a splintered Louisville Slugger. Our wooden back-porch stoop was my backstop, and I could invent an entire championship season by just throwing a rubber ball off the steps and making the plays when it bounced back to me. Thankfully, my dad didn't complain the first time I hit a line drive through the basement window. He went to the hardware store, bought the glass and putty, and had a laugh with the clerk. He seemed kind of proud of the whole thing.

I should point out that my solitary backyard games of baseball were accompanied by constant narration. The play-by-play somehow made it seem as if it were really happening. Curt Gowdy was the voice of the Red Sox in those days, so probably I was one of a generation of small boys who did their voice-overs with a little Wyoming accent. My sisters found my backyard broadcasts amusing. It must have been a kick to stand at the kitchen window, drying dishes, and watching little Danny playing ball, talking to himself. Mary, Joan, and Ann, those teenager older sisters who are now in their forties and fifties, still like to joke that I was the only person they knew who could get upset when I lost games I was playing against myself.

"It's you against you out there," Joan would remind me. "Why don't you just let yourself win?"

I don't know. It was not an age of reason.

Little League was a wonderful experience. In subsequent summers I have witnessed and chronicled some of the horrors of organized youth baseball, but in Groton in 1964–66 we weren't concerned with parental pressure, player safety, overemphasis on winning, or our supposedly fragile self-esteem. We loved to play ball, and if the grown-ups wanted to help us organize and buy us T-shirts and hats, that was a good thing. In 1964, when I was in the fifth grade for my first year of organized team ball, I was traded from one Little League team to another. I still remember getting the call from coach Andre VanHoogen. He told me that they were trying to even up the teams. Our team was too strong and he'd been forced to submit the names of three players, one of whom could be selected by one of the weaker teams. I was left "unprotected" by my Dodger manager and was quickly snapped up by the Braves. I had only one question—"Do I get to keep my Dodger hat?" The answer was yes, and just like that, I was a member of the Braves. It was not traumatic. I have never once been compelled to rob a convenience store because I was traded during my Little League days.

Little League was great fun for those of us who'd honed our skills in our backyards and on our porches. In my first two years of Little League, I was a nifty second baseman and a reliable singles hitter who rarely struck out. Physical maturity is a very big deal when you are a young baseball player, and in my final year of Little League, as a strong seventh-grader, I could finally put the ball over the fence.

One never forgets one's first home run.

It was a perfect May Sunday, one of those days when the air is clean and dry, and your clothes feel good against your skin. Our Little League field had an outfield fence, one of those rollaway fences that was stored in a shed during the off-season. The fence was probably 150 feet from home plate, but in 1966, it looked as if it were nine miles from the batter's box.

My game-day ritual was fairly standard: put on sneakers, jeans, my green Braves shirt, and my cap; hook my glove over the handlebars of my twenty-four-inch Rollfast bike; and peddle half a mile to Dixon's Drug Store for my pregame meal. The Dan Shaughnessy Training Table consisted of one twenty-five-cent chocolate-chip ice cream cone. It was a good day if the ever-tanned Carol Tedesco was behind the counter at Dixon's because she liked my older brother and always gave me a mountain of ice cream for my quarter. As she handed me a cone as big as a wad of cotton candy, Carol would say, "Get out of here before Mr. Dixon sees it." After inhaling the minimountain of chocolate chip, I'd ride another half mile to the Groton town field.

My parents were at the 1966 Groton Little League season opener. They always sat in their blue Ford Galaxy (Dad's company car, but don't tell anyone he sometimes used it for private purposes), parked up on the hill high above right field. I wouldn't guess they kept a box score, but my dad would politely hit the horn if something good happened.

On this first Sunday of the 1966 Groton Little League, I had a brand-new bat, a game bat. For a couple of months, I'd been eyeing this perfect piece of wood in the rack at Moison's Hardware Store. It was a thirty-inch Al Kaline model, with a good-sized barrel and lots of wood between the grain. It was not a small bat, but felt incredibly light. It had a gleaming finish, like those shiny wooden checkerboards on the shelves of souvenir shops at Hampton Beach. The bat cost $5 or $6, which was about half of my Christmas money and paper-route savings, but I had to have it.

Buzzy Lanni was the first pitcher I faced. He was a grade behind me but much bigger than everyone else in the league. Buzz came from a family of big people. *Big-boned* was the polite expression my parents used. Buzz could never wear standard batting helmets. He had a huge dome. In the spring of '66 everybody knew that old Buzz could really bring it: straight and fast. Today we would say he "challenges" you. Back then, he just threw fast.

When I walked to the plate for my first at bat of the season, Buzz was holding a white ball, white as a Chiclet's. That told us the game was for real. In the backyard, in batting practice, and in all other forms of baseball, we never played with a new white ball. Hitting this game ball was like making the first sled marks on a hill of fresh December snow.

My heart was pounding as I walked to the plate. That never changed. Through summer leagues, high school competition, and occasional softball games of adult life, there has been an element of fright and anticipation every time it's my turn at bat. I often wonder if it's still like that for Wade Boggs after all these years.

There was nobody on base. The first pitch was a knee-high fastball, right where I like 'em. I did not put anything extra into my swing; I simply did what I'd done a thousand times in my backyard. I followed the flight of the pitch, opened my hips, and swung at the ball.

Click.

Carl Yastrzemski once talked about the feeling a hitter gets when he does everything perfectly. He takes a perfect swing, hits the fat part of the ball with the fat part of the bat, and feels nothing. The ball just goes. This ball went—on a line, straight over the fence in center. Thank God for fences. Is there anything uglier than a playground home run? You hit a routine double into the gap, but there's no fence and you hustle all the way around the bases. It's like sinking a 3-pointer through a basketball hoop with no net. What good is a home run if you have to work after you've hit the ball? What fun is a home run without a home run trot?

I have never dunked a basketball, driven a race car, or skied down a mountain with my hair flapping in the wind. But let me tell you this: When you are twelve years old and you've spent hundreds of hours listening to Curt Gowdy and watching Dick Stuart and Tony Conigliaro round the bases, there is something magical about your first home-run trot. Not too fast, not too slow. No need to show up old Buzz. Just listen to the applause, round second, and watch a kid vault the fence and retrieve the ball. Make the bend at third and shake the hand of the man in the coach's box, just like they do in the majors. Same deal at home plate.

Jonathan Davis was the on-deck hitter, and he knew enough to be there with his bat over his shoulder and his hand outstretched. These were the days before slapping fives, high fives, low fives, crotch-grabbing, Bash Brothers, and Icky Shuffles. We just shook hands as I crossed the plate. Dignity. Class. Just like those pictures of Jim Gentile and Brooks Robinson, pictures I'd studied in the *Lowell Sun*.

I heard the sound of a car horn. One polite tap. I couldn't say for sure, but I think it came from the blue Ford Galaxy.

Baseball never was easy. There were plenty of strikeouts, losses, and disappointments. I played the game through my high school years, then spent the rest of my life writing about it. Looking back, I think my dad had a good attitude about the whole thing. He told me not to gloat when I won. When we lost, he took me out for ice cream and told me that losing a game or getting cut from the team is not the worst thing that can happen in life. His was an intentional distance, designed to make sure I didn't worry too much about being the best ballplayer in town. He was sculpting my soul and I never felt him chipping away.

He seemed to lose his good sense when I was in my teens. Too often he elaborated on the obvious and was forever issuing warnings and lectures. All I wanted were the keys to the car. Baseball was our common ground during those blunder years. I no longer liked Dad's cornball music, his politics, or his clothes, but I still liked the Red Sox. We'd argue about the Vietnam War, but we remained in total agreement when it came to Eddie Kasko's bullpen deployment. While Walter Cronkite and Dan Rather divided us, Curt Gowdy and Ned Martin brought us together.

In 1979, I was twenty-six years old, traveling with the Baltimore Orioles, covering big-league baseball for the *Washington Star.* I wasn't a major-league ballplayer, but I was a professional baseball writer, seeing America, living the big-league life, finally able to pick up the tab when my mom and dad met me for breakfast.

In the fall of '79, Earl Weaver's Orioles were going to the World Series, and the Red Sox were going nowhere. Baltimore played a weekend series in Boston in September. On Sunday, September 9, I left tickets for my parents in Section 27—under the roof, third-base side. They were a little late getting to Fenway because Dad had trouble finding a place to park. I didn't ask, but he probably got a little lost trying to locate the hotel. At the end of the eighth inning, in what was shaping up as an easy victory for the powerful Orioles, I made my way through the stands to get down near the clubhouse entrance. In major-league baseball, Sunday is getaway day, and it occurred to me that I would not see my folks again until sometime after the World Series. With this in mind, I stopped by Section 27 to say good-bye to my mother and father.

It was the last time I saw my father. He died in his sleep the night before the first game of the 1979 World Series.

Dad was not a baseball guy, far from it, but his blood flows through my fingers every time I write about the best game there is. He's buried in Pepperell, Massachusetts, in a cemetery adjacent to a Little League ballfield. It has always pleased me that our last handshake was at Fenway.

CHAPTER ONE

THE BALLPARK

▶ ◆ ◆ ◆ ◆ ◆ ◆ ◆ ◆ ◀

◆ In 1742 an entrepreneurial colonist named Peter Faneuil built a market house down by the Boston waterfront. Shorefront warehouses were constructed and occupied by merchants selling meat, poultry, produce, and dairy products. In time, a dining room opened on the second floor of one of the warehouses. In this large, loud place, sailors, merchants, and farmers ate meals quickly. Strangers sat side by side at long wooden tables. On July 4, 1874, more than one hundred years after the first meals were served, men named John Durgin, Eldredge Park, and John Chandler bought the dining room. Messrs. Durgin and Park were dead within a few years, but the Chandler family held the Durgin-Park restaurant until it was sold to James Hallet in 1945. In the early 1960s, Durgin-Park was one of the few businesses on Boston's decaying waterfront. When the area was polished and overhauled, giving birth to the trendy Faneuil Hall Marketplace in the mid-1970s, Durgin-Park stood as one of the original landmarks in a mall overrun with fried-dough stands and shops selling cookies for a dollar. While the rest of the modern market targets tourists, Durgin-Park still draws from old Boston. The dining room is untouched, almost exactly as it was a century ago. Diners are still seated "family style" at long wooden tables covered with red-checkered cloths. During dinner, you share ketchup and rub elbows with strangers. It's noisy and informal—that's part of the charm. Rude waitresses slam the food down and rush you through dinner so they can clear the table and make way for the people who line the stairway in anticipation of a hearty meal at a fair price. If you grew up in a big household and like boiled food, Durgin-Park is your kind of place.

Durgin-Park is old Boston. It's not convenient. There's no place to park. The bathrooms are rusty, not rustic. It's something that would never work if it were built today. It sells nostalgia. It sells an America we used to know. It sells our parents and our grandparents. When you walk into Durgin-Park, you see a sign that reads, "Your grandfather, and perhaps your great-grandfather, dined with us, too." It is very much like . . .

Fenway Park.

It's the culinary cousin of Durgin-Park. Fenway merely satisfies a different kind of appetite; a hunger of the heart and mind.

Situated within walking distance of the Museum of Fine Arts, Harvard Medical School, and Symphony Hall, Fenway Park is another Boston landmark. There is nothing trendy or hip about Fenway. It is NPR in an MTV world.

The key word is *park*. Boston's American League baseball franchise never played home games in a *stadium*. Fenway Park is not many things. It is not a multiplex. It is not a sports and convention center. It is not attached to a shopping mall or a Hard Rock Cafe. It is not covered by a dome with a retractable roof. It is not climate-controlled, and it does not have artificial turf. It is a park, in every sense of the word. It has green grass, fresh air, and is a fine place to take the family for an afternoon. Any list of America's best-known parks (Central, Yellowstone, Jellystone, Menlow, Yosemite, McArthur, Jurassic) has to include Fenway.

"I saw it for the first time in 1983, just after I was drafted out of the University of Texas," recalls Sox pitcher Roger Clemens. "I got in a cab at Logan Airport and told the driver that I had to go to Fenway Park. While he was driving, I started reading the paper. Suddenly, we pulled up and he said, 'Here you go,' and I looked out and there was this warehouse. I said to the driver, 'No, Fenway Park. It's a baseball stadium. It's a stadium.' And he said, 'Yeah, this is it.' And I said, 'No, this is a warehouse.' He told me to look up, so I stuck my head out the window and looked up and saw the lights.

"It was Fenway."

Fenway Park opened in April 1912, the same week the *Titanic* sank. The first two official major league games at Fenway were rained out. It's long been rumored that the park sits on the site of ancient Indian burial grounds. Some might view these elements as harbingers of misfortune.

Fenway has been canonized by scores of fans, ballplayers, politicians, and poet laureates. Literary giant John Updike started the flood of sportswriter syrup when he visited Fenway for Ted Williams's final game in September 1960. In his classic "Hub Fans Bid Kid Adieu," Updike held that Fenway represented "a compromise between Man's Euclidean determinations and Nature's beguiling irregularities." Since Updike's description of Fenway as "a lyric little bandbox of a ballpark," Boston's baseball theater has inspired heaps of purple prose (hello, self).

In 1975, inimitable left-hander Bill Lee called Fenway a shrine for religious rites. A Harvard professor compared the park to the bullring of Knossos on the island of Crete. Poet Donald Hall wrote, "It's like a huge pinball machine designed by a mad sculptor." The *Boston Globe*'s Marty Nolan said, "A crazy-quilt violation of city planning principles, an irregular pile of architecture, a menace to marketing consultants, Fenway Park works. It works as a symbol of New England's pride, as a repository of evergreen hopes, as a tabernacle of lost innocence. It works as a place to watch baseball."

Sometimes, even more. Baseball bard Roger Angell pointed out in 1975 that in Cincinnati fifty thousand fans *watched* the World Series games, while in Fenway, thirty-five thousand *participated* in the fall classic.

Tip O'Neill, the late, great Speaker of the U.S. House of Representatives, put it this way in 1989: "One of the reasons Sox fans are so good is the chumminess of the ballpark. It's like being in an English theatre. You're right on top of the stage. It's intimate, it's homey, it's chummy. You feel as though you're in your own living room."

Yankee manager Buck Showalter noticed something unique in the summer of 1994, when he requested that the Fenway public address system not play rock music during batting practice. Showalter told the *Globe*'s Peter Gammons, "This is the day of all days to enjoy all the senses of Fenway. This is one of those moments one never should forget, because it's not this way anywhere else. Listen to the game, damnit. It's completely still, everything echoes off all the walls and roofs here, and every fan is so close he hears it perfectly. I don't know anything about classical music, but if there's a baseball symphony, this is it."

In 1995, *Globe* columnist Mike Barnicle wrote, "Anybody looking for lots of free parking or convenient freeway off-ramps running toward a stadium better move to Texas, Kansas City, or Anaheim. Here, you saddle up and hoof it past peanut vendors, through air thick with the smell of sausage and loud with a hawker's clamor. Once inside, you sit in seats made for a hostage. No matter what shape you might be in physically, the place is so small you feel as if you just ate Spain as you struggle to find a spot for your elbow. Ted Kennedy sits in front of you and you won't even see The Wall. Yet that doesn't matter. Comfort is not the index people use to measure a day at Fenway. The place is a quaint cemetery where memories are stored, section by section, seat by seat. So much around us has changed over the years while this ballpark remains a time capsule."

Clark Booth, a renowned reporter in Boston for more than thirty years, says, "We love Fenway Park because we love antiques, be they rocking chairs or ballparks. But we love it even more because the eccentricities of the place mirror our own. It is, like us, difficult and cranky. And this makes it a mighty hard place for a player to play in. Too bad. Players come and go, but Fenway Park may become an American pyramid."

There. Fenway is a religious shrine, a pinball machine, a living room, a symphony, a cemetery of memory, and an American pyramid.

Some ballpark history:

Boston's first American League baseball team, known as the Pilgrims, was formed in 1901 and played its first eleven seasons at the Huntington Avenue Grounds, at the corner of Huntington and Rogers Avenues, a short toss from the trolley tracks. Work on the Grounds began on March 12, 1901, and the Pilgrims opened the park in front of 11,500 fans less than two months later (May 8) with a 12–4 victory over Connie Mack's Athletics. Cy Young picked up the win for Boston, one of his 511 victories.

The Huntington Grounds were often covered with soot from the nearby train yards. The stands were made of wood, there was constant fear of fire because of sparks from the coal-burning railroad engines, and it was impossible to stem the flow of gate-crashers. A saloon was next door, and most of the players lived at the Putnam Hotel, about three blocks from the ballpark, next door to the Boston Conservatory of Music. It was there that the Pilgrims defeated the Pittsburgh Pirates in 1903 to win the first World Series; tickets to the games cost fifty cents apiece. A statue of Cy Young was dedicated in 1993 and today stands in the middle of the Northeastern University campus, on the same spot where Cy threw the first pitch of the first World Series. Today Northeastern's biology premed majors and future electronics engineers stroll grounds once patrolled by Tris Speaker and the rest of the Red Sox.

In 1904, with some encouragement from American League president Ban Johnson, Gen. Charles Taylor—a Civil War veteran (wounded at Port Hudson, Louisiana, in 1863) and publisher of the *Boston Globe* newspaper—purchased the Red Sox from Henry Killilea. Taylor signed a seven-year lease for the Huntington Avenue Grounds (the ball club owned the ballpark, but the land beneath it was owned by the New York, New Haven and Hartford Railroad). Other bidders included John F. "Honey Fitz" Fitzgerald, later Boston mayor and grandfather of Pres. John Fitzgerald Kennedy.

Charles Taylor was born in 1846 and grew up in Charlestown, a fact of no small irony given the anti-*Globe* sentiment of citizens in Charlestown today. Taylor served as a private secretary to Massachusetts governor William Claflin and was considered one of New England's top publicists when he joined the one-year-old *Boston Globe* at the age of twenty-seven in 1873. Historians characterize the general as a "Cleveland Democrat," an odd fusion of reformers, Yankee Democrats, and Irish. Cleveland Democrats tended to be cautious and conservative. When Taylor took over the *Globe*, the paper was losing $60,000 a year. He realized that Boston's Irish community needed a voice, so he hired Irish editor E. C. Bailey, cut the price of the paper to two cents, and changed the *Globe*'s editorial slant from Republican to Democrat. When Bailey retired in 1880, General Taylor became editor and publisher, positions he held for forty-one years. General

Taylor had five children, including three sons—Charles H. Taylor Jr., William O. Taylor (who took over the *Globe* after a bitter battle with Charles, Jr.), and John I. Taylor, the man who named the Red Sox and built Fenway Park.

John I., as he was known, was something of a loose cannon in the Taylor family, and turn-of-the-century Bostonians assumed Charles Taylor bought the Red Sox as a toy for his sports-minded, hard-drinking, playboy son. John I. had worked in the paper's advertising and editorial departments, but when his dad gave him the Red Sox, he announced his retirement from journalism, saying, "I intend to give up newspaper work, which has been my business, and devote myself entirely to the advancement and interests of the team. I have the utmost confidence in Jim Collins and consider him as good a manager as there is in the country, and shall cooperate with him so far as it lies in my power to give Boston as good ball as it has had in the past, and will spare neither money nor effort in that direction. Boston is a great baseball city and deserves the best there is in the market. I want another pennant to fly from the top of that pole at the close of the season, and I see no reason why there shouldn't be another world's pennant as well."

Young Taylor was a forerunner to George Steinbrenner. When things were good, he glowed. Sometimes he bought suits for players who had had a solid day at the plate or on the mound. But when the team started to lose, he was temperamental and outspoken. He ridiculed overweight ballplayers.

Taylor took over the team on April 18, 1904. The 1904 Red Sox won the American League pennant and were named World Champs when the New York Giants refused to play them in the World Series. The National League club did not want to risk losing to the upstart team from the junior circuit. Taylor spent money and made deals in the next few years, but there were no more championships during his reign.

William Davis Taylor, born in 1908, was John I. Taylor's nephew and remembers the flamboyant Red Sox owner.

"He was one of the most wonderful guys," says Davis Taylor. "He used to take all of us kids to baseball games. He'd take us into the press box and we'd watch the games in the rafters. He had millions of friends. He was always immaculately dressed and was loads of fun. I think everyone in Boston thought he was a sport."

It was John I. Taylor who in 1907 changed the name of his team to Red Sox. Since their inception, they'd been known as the Somersets, Puritans, Plymouth Rocks, Speed Boys, and Pilgrims. The original Boston Red Stockings were the Hub's National League entry, beginning as early as 1871, but the name didn't stick. By the turn of the century, even traditionalists called Boston's National League team the Beaneaters. In 1907, Fred Tenney, the manager of the Boston Nationals, announced that the team was abandoning their carmine hose and switching to white stockings. After reading about this in the *Boston Journal*, John I. Taylor called Peter F. Kelly of the *Journal* and said, "Pete, I've got a scoop for you. I'm going to grab that name Red Sox, and from now on we'll wear red stockings."

Perfect. The Red Sox were named by a Yankee.

It's been written that Taylor preferred Speed Boys to Red Sox, but we can only imagine the latter-day ridicule that would have been showered on the Boston ball club if they'd remained the Speed Boys. For most of this century, the Red Sox have more closely resembled the Clydesdales, annually finishing last in stolen bases. Meanwhile, it's fascinating to contemplate the literary possibilities had the Sox been called Pilgrims for all these long years. Comparing the woes of Boston's baseball Pilgrims to the odyssey of Bunyan's lost soul would have made for great sportswriter spins through the decades.

Taylor was something of an innovator. Only twenty-nine years old when he took over the Red Sox in 1904, he was one of the first baseball owners to host "ladies' days," admitting women for free. He was also the first owner to separate the press from the spectators. Fans remain thankful for this courtesy.

By 1910, the Taylors had decided not to renew their seven-year lease at the Huntington Grounds, and on June 24, 1911, John I. Taylor announced his intention to build a new baseball park between Lansdowne and Jersey Streets, a half mile from the Charles River and less than a mile from the Huntington Avenue Grounds. New streetcar lines connected the area to the rest of Boston. Situated near suburban

Brookline on the city's cheaper western wetlands, the plot was owned by the Fenway Realty Company. Not coincidentally, General Taylor was a major stockholder in Fenway Realty.

The Fenway site was also in the heart of the Fens—a crown jewel in Frederick Law Olmsted's chain of parks known as the Emerald Necklace. A planned ring of parks and brooks, the Necklace put fields of green in the middle of a major Northeast city.

Asked about a name for the new ballpark, Taylor said, "It's in the Fenway section, isn't it? Then call it Fenway Park."

This oft-repeated line sounds cute and logical, but it should not be forgotten that the name Fenway Park would no doubt benefit the Fenway Realty Company, enhancing the value of other properties Taylor owned in the surrounding area. No one has ever accused the Taylors of being stupid.

Throughout the decades, the site of the Boston ballpark has proved beneficial for the ball club, the fans, and the city of Boston. For all of its inconveniences, a ballpark in the city is a huge addition to the urban landscape. Fans can walk to games or take public transportation. There is immediate access for those without a lot of money. City merchants profit. Young people studying in the region have a chance to see their hometown teams when they visit Boston. The park helped make the Fenway a more appealing commercial and residential district.

Late in 1911, while the new park was under construction, Taylor sold 50 percent of the family's interest to James McAleer of Washington and Robert McRoy of Chicago. McAleer had managed the Washington team in 1911, and McRoy was secretary of the American League. McAleer was named team president, McRoy treasurer, and John I. Taylor stayed on as club vice president, and the new ballpark was owned by the Taylors. It's possible that American League president Ban Johnson orchestrated the transition because he'd grown tired of John I. Taylor's personality and his problems. Taylor's expensive tastes and playboy reputation conflicted with the image Johnson wanted to project. It's even more possible that the Taylors built Fenway to make it easier to sell the ball club.

On the day he sold his interest in the team, Taylor said, "Plans for a new ballpark which will be a credit to Boston will now be formulated and the work pushed ahead at a rapid rate."

Taylor broke ground for the new park on September 25, 1911. A sketch of the future ballpark appeared in the October 15 (1911) *Globe*. The headline read: "New Home of the Red Sox; Plant Ideal in Equipment and Location." The subhead read, "Baseball Park Will Contain 365,308 Square Feet of Land With Stands of the Most Approved Type, Providing Seating Accommodations for 28,000. Completed Product, It Is Understood, Will Represent an Outlay of $1,000,000."

The 1911 newspaper drawing by architect James E. McLaughlin looks remarkably similar to the Fenway we know today.

Prior to 1909, most baseball parks—seats, stands, and walls—were built of wood. Wood was cheap and plentiful and it was all that was needed to enclose the field and keep the fans comfortable. Unfortunately, wood burned easily and quickly. Since most fans smoked, wooden stands created a fire hazard. In the first decade of the American League, there were so many ballpark fires that owners began to have trouble getting insurance. That is why the new ballparks were built with the wondrous nonflammable materials of concrete and steel. At the time Fenway was being planned, new concrete-and-steel parks had recently been built in Pittsburgh (Forbes Field) and Philadelphia (Shibe Park).

Fenway was built by the Charles Logue Building Company. Logue also built the Tower Building at Boston College and the Beaven Hall residence house at Holy Cross during this period. The Logue Company began construction in 1911 and built Boston a state-of-the-art, steel-and-concrete ballpark. The Cleveland-based Osborn Engineering Company (Osborn also designed Yankee Stadium, the Polo Grounds, and Braves Field in Boston) served as civil engineers on the Boston ballpark project, and the chief architect was McLaughlin. The park cost $650,000, was built without public funds, and there was no municipal interference. The park was initially accessed at $420,000, the land at $344,000.

The fact that the ballpark was a totally private enterprise meant that the Sox have never been beholden to city or state taxpayers. This in some ways accounts for the organization's dubious history regarding race relations, nepotism, and allegiance to the old-boy network. In many ways, Fenway was for years a whites-only, private country club.

Fronted with red brick, modeled after Philly's Shibe, the Jersey Street entrance to new Fenway Park was a magnificent sight. The outer wall featured a tapestried red brick in Boston Colonial style, with decorative diamonds, mosaics, and keystone arches. Inside, there was a roofed pavilion, wooden bleachers in center and right fields, and a ten-foot-high embankment in front of a tall wooden wall in left. There were eight different wall angles in fair territory; this was done not to make the park cute or cozy, but to conform to the property's unusual (cramped) boundaries. Fenway was shoehorned into a small parcel of land, framed by Brookline Avenue, Jersey, Lansdowne, Ipswich, and Van Ness Streets (ownership has its privileges; Van Ness was the maiden name of Taylor's wife). The original Fenway seats were made of oak. The infield grass was transplanted from the Huntington Grounds. The line from home to third was just a little to the left of magnetic north. That was good news for hitters. Games in 1912 often started midafternoon, and the alignment of Fenway's base paths ensured that the sun would never set in the eyes of the batters. It was the right fielders who would contend with the sun setting behind the third-base line.

It is somewhat curious that there was no upper deck on a park built in 1912. Folklore holds that Boston fans were a tad apprehensive about sitting in a top bunk, but more likely the absence of an upper tier was a cost-cutting measure taken by the Taylors. The owners were careful to remind fans that the park was built to support an upper deck should one be needed in future seasons. We're still waiting. In 1967, when the St. Louis Cardinals came to Boston for the World Series, ace righty Bob Gibson's first reaction to Fenway was, "Where's the upper deck?" (a small park meant smaller Series shares, and in '67, postseason money still meant something to major league baseball players).

The most interesting feature of the new ballpark was the small embankment in front of the tall wall in left field. The wall and the cliff were necessitated by the cozy presence of Lansdowne Street. A mere 325 feet from Fenway's home plate, Lansdowne couldn't be moved or eliminated because it was banked on its far side by the Boston & Albany Railroad (today the Massachusetts Turnpike runs parallel to the rail tracks). Since they couldn't put the fence farther from home plate, they made it higher. They had to do something to keep hitters honest. Thus The Wall was born. Fenway's original left-field wall (1912–34) was considerably smaller than the one we know today. Once grass was planted, the cliff served as a picnic area for fans who preferred lawn seats. It was tough on outfielders: imagine running uphill to snatch a long fly ball. The original master of the hill, Sox left fielder Duffy Lewis, said, "I used to go out and practice in the morning. You had to take one good look at the ball. Go up if you had a chance to get it. You couldn't keep looking at the ball. If you did, down you went when you hit the bank." In honor of Lewis, the hill became known as Duffy's Cliff.

The day it opened, Fenway was the third-largest ballpark in the major leagues. Nineteen twelve was an eventful year. President William Howard Taft, Woodrow Wilson, and Teddy "Bull Moose" Roosevelt ran for the White House. The summer Olympics were being held in Stockholm. We were still two years away from "The Great War," but there was a revolution in Mexico, war in the Balkans, and an invasion of Nicaragua by U.S. Marines. Closer to home, workers in the cotton and wool mills of Lawrence, Massachusetts, went on strike, causing angry clashes between pickets and police. The workers were protesting fifty-four-hour workweeks, at hourly wages of sixteen cents.

The Sox played their first exhibition in a still-incomplete Fenway on April 9, beating Harvard, 2–0. About three thousands fans went to the game, which was halted by snow flurries after six and a half innings. A newspaper cartoon depicted the curious left-field wall under a headline, "Higher than the Cost of Living." Baseball experts theorized that it might be years before anybody cleared that wall. In those days, walls were something to keep fans out of the park. As photos show, it was not unusual to use the perimeter of the field for overflow crowds. There are numerous pictures of fans standing behind ropes in the outfield at Fenway. During the dead-ball era, nobody was expected to hit the ball beyond the fence.

The day after the Red Sox–Harvard exhibition, the *Titanic* left

Southampton, England, for its maiden voyage to New York. On board were 2,340 people, and only 745 were saved when the White Star liner struck an iceberg and sank in the darkness. In the days after the disastrous episode, Boston newspapers scrambled for names of survivors, victims, and any other information. There was little else to talk about or write about. Like everything else that happened in Boston that week, the opening of Fenway was trivial, dwarfed by the horror of the *Titanic*.

Fenway's first American League game was scheduled for April 18, but three days of rain postponed Boston's American League opener until April 20. When the Sox finally got to show off their park, Boston mayor "Honey Fitz" threw out the ceremonial first ball, and the Letter Carriers Band entertained between innings. Boston defeated the New York Highlanders, 7–6, in eleven innings in front of twenty-seven thousands fans. The Sox made seven errors on the new, muddy field.

According to newspaper accounts of the day, nobody complained about the girders and posts that obstructed views. All ballparks of the day had posts. How else could you put a roof over the fans' heads? There was interest in the screen behind home plate and the electric scoreboard in left field. Eighteen turnstyles eased some of the customary crush at the gate. Admission was twenty-five cents for bleachers and fifty cents for the pavilion.

But voices of dissent were heard. Surprisingly, given today's cuddly image of Fenway, some people said the park was too big. The bleachers were far from home plate, and one scribe concluded, "It's too big for fans to exchange pleasantries about the weather." Another wrote, "On the account of the size of the ballpark, and the entrances being on two widely separated ends of the grounds, I find much of the old sociability gone." Many of the Sox regular fans objected to the ballpark's location. Compared with the Huntington Avenue Grounds, Fenway was out in the sticks. Most spectators got to the park on the Ipswich Street line. There weren't many cars in 1912, but Fenway had ample parking beyond its right-field boundary—much more than is available today.

"My uncle loved Fenway," remembers Davis Taylor. "My grandfather [Charles H. Taylor] is the one who really built it. I think Uncle

John sort of walked in. He thought it was a homey park. He loved the crowds in center field, all the gamblers in Boston. I went out there one time with him when I was a kid. He said, 'You've got to see all this going on. This is what they call gambling in baseball.' "

It's an interesting memory. In 1989, Pete Rose was banished for life from the sport because of his gambling on baseball. But in 1912, a team official could take his nephew to the grandstand and point at gamblers plying their trade in the stands—the way today we'd see sausage vendors selling their wares on the sidewalks outside Fenway.

Six days after Fenway's first game, Red Sox backup first baseman Hugh Bradley became the first player to clear the wall in left field. It was one of Bradley's two career homers.

A month after the park opened, there was an official dedication game against the Chicago White Sox. On May 17, league president Johnson came to Boston and raised the flag before Chicago's 5–2 victory. John I. Logue, grandson of builder Charles Logue, says, "In the family records we have a picture of Charles Logue with John Taylor and the Comiskey brothers, visiting from Chicago, at the opening-day luncheon."

In its early years, Fenway Park was a magic hardball house where it seemed the home team could never lose. The 1912 Red Sox won a team record 105 games, losing only 47, for a franchise-best percentage of .691. They went 57–20 in their new park and 48–27 on the road. Smoky Joe Wood went 34–5 with a 1.91 ERA. On September 6, Wood won his fourteenth straight, beating Walter Johnson, 1–0, in front of thirty thousand fans, thousands of whom watched while sitting in roped-off sections of the outfield and foul territory. The Red Sox finished fourteen games ahead of the rest of the pack and—backed by two brass bands and their Royal Rooters—took the World Series in seven games against the New York Giants. To accommodate World Series crowds, a bleacher section was added in the right-field area.

Fenway's magic lasted until the end of the decade. In 1914 the crosstown Boston Braves won the World Series in Fenway Park. (Boston's Braves Field was under construction, so the Braves played host to the Philadelphia Athletics, winning games three and four of their four-game sweep, in the Red Sox ballpark.) In 1915 the Sox went 2–0 in World Series games at Fenway, then clinched the championship at home again in game five of the 1916 World Series against the Brooklyn Dodgers. In 1918, the Sox beat the Cubs in six games, winning the World Series at Fenway Park. From 1912 to 1918, Boston baseball teams played in five World Series at Fenway, winning each time, taking the final game in Fenway four times. The Sox and Braves from 1912 to 1918 were a combined 11–3 in Fenway World Series games. The place was just plain good luck.

Fire first struck Fenway after a game on May 8, 1926, when bleachers along the left-field foul line burned down. Cash-strapped owner Bob Quinn had the charred timbers taken away but he collected the insurance (there's always been suspicion that Quinn might have been responsible for the fire) and did not replace the seats in the barren section. It made for some interesting ground rules. In those seven goofy seasons when the bleachers were gone, fielders could run down pop-ups behind the third-base grandstand.

The city of Boston wouldn't allow Sunday baseball until 1929, but for three years after that the Sox had to continue to play their Sunday games at Braves Field because of Fenway's proximity to a Back Bay church. The first Fenway Sunday game was played between the Red Sox and Yankees on July 3, 1932. Even with Sunday ball in his own park, Quinn still lost money. The Red Sox were terrible and they played in the skeleton frame of a burned-out ballpark.

Thirty-year-old millionaire Thomas A. Yawkey bought the Red Sox and Fenway from Quinn on February 25, 1933. When Yawkey bought the Sox, he assumed a hefty mortgage on his new/old ballpark. In the most infamous transaction in sports history, Harry Frazee, the Sox owner before Quinn, had sold Babe Ruth to the Yankees in 1920. In exchange for Ruth, Yankee owner Jacob Ruppert gave Frazee $100,000 in cash, plus a $300,000 loan for a mortgage on Fenway. So it wasn't just Ruth that went to New York. The hated Yankees took Boston's best player and held a note on Fenway. Yawkey assumed the mortgage when the club changed hands. He asked the Yankee owner to carry the note into the next season. Ruppert agreed, but when the Sox beat the Yankees five straight times in 1933, the Colonel demanded his money. "I sent the SOB a check the next day," Yawkey said. Since that moment, Fenway Park has been owned by the Yawkeys or the Yawkey family trust.

After the 1933 season, Yawkey spent about 1.25 million Depression-era dollars to renovate his ballpark. The Osborn Company returned to the scene and worked with the Boston-based Coleman Brothers Corp. Reconstruction was stalled by a four-hour, five-alarm blaze on January 5, 1934 (the fourteenth anniversary of the announcement of the sale of Babe Ruth to the Yankees). It was Boston's worst fire in twelve years. Afterward, six thousand grandstand seats were added and wooden stands in center field were replaced by concrete bleachers. Duffy's Cliff was dug up, hauled away, and replaced with a thirty-seven-foot-high sheet-metal-and-steel fence. Yawkey bought the new backstop netting from former Sox pitcher Howard Ehmke. When the park reopened in '34, *Boston Post* columnist Bill Cunningham declared the color scheme "a good Dartmouth green." He also noted, "The walks from the dugouts up to the plate are graveled after the fashion of most driveways in Newton." In 1934, Fenway's box seats cost $1.65, grandstand $1.10, and bleachers 55 cents. Most of the laborers who'd rebuilt Fenway bought tickets for opening day, '34. Original Red Stocking George Wright attended the grand reopening, too.

Ed Burns of the *Chicago Tribune* wrote, "Nathaniel Hawthorne's famed House of Seven Gables stands some twenty miles from Fenway Park, home of the Boston Red Sox. Although Nathaniel never played any major league ball, that seven-gable influence was felt strongly in the erection of the modern Fenway Park. The wall bounding the field has seventeen facets, just eleven more than Shibe Park, Philadelphia. . . . Its only phoney aspect is its short left field, and an honest effort was made to correct this with the rebuilding of the park. A thirty-five-foot wall now stands in left field."

The Wall.

Fenway's famous facade was built with thirty thousand pounds of Toncan iron. The April 1934 Republic Steel Corp. house newsletter, *Toncan Topics*, explained the details of the construction: "The wall's reinforced steel-and-concrete foundation extends twenty-two feet below the field level. Counterfort construction was employed. Sixteen-inch steel columns placed ten feet on centers were cast three feet into concrete. Horizontally, 3½-inch by 2½-inch ¼-inch angles were riveted four feet on centers. Three-quarter rods were used for sway bracing every fifth panel. Two-by-six nailer boards were clipped to the angles. To these boards were nailed the 18-gauge galvanized Toncan sheets."

The official color of the wall today is *field* green. It's a custom blend made for the Red Sox by the California Paint Co. John Smith, a commercial painter from Wilmington, Massachusetts, says he's painted the wall fifteen times since inheriting the task from his father, the late Ken Smith.

So much for the technical description of the wall. When we come around to discussing the most famous walls in the world, we think of the Great Wall of China, the Wailing Wall, the Berlin Wall, the Vietnam Veterans Memorial Wall, Phil Spector's Wall of Sound, Pink Floyd's *The Wall*, and Fenway's Green Monster. In most Boston newspapers and magazines, Fenway's left-field structure is The Wall. Strictly upper case. To speak of Fenway Park is to speak of The Wall. It is what makes Fenway special. Baseball in the 1990s has seen a return to the ballparks of earlier generations. Camden Yards in Baltimore, The Ballpark at Arlington (Texas), and Jacobs Field in Cleveland have successfully merged nostalgia with modern convenience, but nobody's found a stadium signature that can match Fenway's Wall.

Rico Petrocelli, who hit 40 homers while playing shortstop for the Red Sox in 1969 (he hit 210 in his career) recalls, "Growing up in New York, I knew very little of Fenway Park. When I first came here, I'll never forget it, I went up the ramp from under the stands, and when The Wall became visible, it was unbelievable. It looked so close you could reach out and touch it. I said, 'Wow. This is fantastic.' "

It may not have been accidental that the big new wall was billboard size. Ads for whiskey, razor blades, and soap were plastered from the left-field foul pole to the center-field flag pole. A generation of Sox fans grew up mocking the ad that read, "The Red Sox use Lifebuoy soap." Boston kids joked, "The Red Sox use Lifebuoy, but they still stink." Green paint covered the ads starting in 1947. This is when the wall truly became "The Green Monster."

Two years after the new wall went up, a 23½-foot screen was added to the top of the fence. It was designed to save the windows on buildings across Lansdowne Street, but it also saved Yawkey money he'd have spent buying new baseballs. The initials of Thomas and

Jean Yawkey can be seen in Morse code on the left-field scoreboard. In 1958, Yawkey asked Red Sox general manager Joe Cronin to see if the city of Boston would let the team buy Lansdowne Street so the Red Sox could tear down the wall and build another grandstand.

Today the famous Citgo sign looms behind the giant green door. In the rest of America, Citgo is where you buy gas; in Boston, it's the neon sign that stares in from the horizon. The sign was built in 1965 and sits atop 660 Beacon Street in Kenmore Square. It was shut off to save energy in the late 1970s, but citizens petitioned the Boston Landmarks Commission to save it. It is no less a city landmark than the Bunker Hill Monument, Ironsides, or the Old North Church. Citgo renovated the sign in 1983 and it was turned on during the seventh-inning stretch of a Red Sox game on August 10, 1983.

A few blocks from the Citgo sign stands the old John Hancock tower—once the tallest building in Boston. A light at the top of the tower serves as a weather reporter for Bostonians. A steady red signal means rain. Steady blue means fair. Flashing blue means cloudy. In winter, flashing red means snow. In summer, flashing red means the Red Sox game at Fenway has been postponed due to inclement weather.

For decades, the sign at the base of Fenway's left-field wall indicated it was 315 feet from home plate to the left-field fence. Three hundred and fifteen feet is not far for major league hitters. From the time the 315 sign was posted, batters insisted that The Wall was less than 315 feet from home plate. No doubt some of this skepticism was due to the height and breadth of The Wall. Its imposing dimensions make it appear closer than it is.

Citing national security and other silly concerns, the Red Sox for years refused to let anyone measure the distance from home plate to the left-field fence. It was part of the Fenway mystique. Author George Sullivan once used a yardstick and came up with a distance of 309 feet 5 inches. In 1975, *Boston Globe* sports editor Dave Smith was presented with aerial photos of Fenway, accompanied by the report of an expert who flew reconnaissance missions in World War II. The military man concluded that the distance from home to the fence was 304 feet. Armed with the goods, sports editor Smith made a formal request to have someone from the *Globe* measure the Fenway foul line.

He told the Sox that the paper had proof that the dimensions were not as advertised. The Sox refused, and the next day it was page-one news in the newspaper. Original blueprints from the Osborn Engineering Company indicate that The Wall is 308 feet from home plate.

In April of 1995, I measured it myself (in broad daylight, without the blessings of Red Sox management) with a hundred-foot Stanley Steelmaster Long Tape. The distance from home plate to the wall was 309 feet 3 inches. Case closed. In mid-May of that season, after my story appeared in the *Globe*, the Sox put up a new sign—310 feet. "That's about what it is," admits groundskeeper Joe Mooney. "We rounded it off. It came out in that story, so why hide it?"

Those dimensions would not work today. There's a league rule stipulating that all fences must be at least 325 feet from home plate.

Inside The Wall, a human being operates baseball's last true scoreboard. Fans who sometimes see a left fielder talking to himself should know that the ballplayer might not be crazy; he might be talking to Richie Maloney, who operates the board with Chris Elias. Maloney is twenty-six years old and grew up in Newton, one of three children of Moe and Marion Maloney. Moe Maloney is the varsity baseball coach at Boston College, and Richie has been working inside The Wall for four seasons. By day, he's a mutual-fund representative, wearing a three-piece suit. At night, he ducks behind the green door and puts the numbers in the slots every time he gets a call from scoreboard headquarters in the press box. The rectangular numbers measure twelve by sixteen inches and weigh two pounds each.

"We used to call out there from the dugout phone and give them phony numbers," says Sox equipment manager Joe Cochran, laughing. "We'd tell them Detroit scored ten in the first, then laugh when we saw the big ten go up on the board."

Maloney and Elias make $40 per game and endure a lot of discomfort. The area inside The Wall is an icebox in the spring and fall, and a microwave in the middle of summer. The cramped area is lit by six bare light bulbs. The game on the field is a rumor. Maloney and Elias are simply too far inside old Fenway to know what's going on inside old Fenway. They get their orders via telephone or radio. Their workspace is dark and dirty, and there's no bathroom.

One of the Sox ballpark employees says, "It's kind of funny that they make that spot part of the new Fenway tours. They leave that Wall door open and let everybody walk in and look around. We laugh about it all the time. There's about one hundred years of pretty rough graffiti on the walls in there. And here are people from the suburbs walking with their little kids reading that so-and-so sucks dick and so-and-so blows. And the people don't care. They're so happy to be at Fenway they just giggle and keep on walking the tour."

For decades, The Wall has inspired debate among baseball fans. Is it an advantage or a disadvantage for the hometown team? Red Sox teams from the 1940s through the 1980s were designed with The Wall in mind. As a result, Boston baseball fans have watched three generations of right-handed sluggers try to bash the Red Sox to World Series victory. Much of this was done at the expense of pitching, speed, and defense—elements that have brought championship teams to just about every major city from Baltimore to Los Angeles. Jimmie Foxx, Walt Dropo, Dick Gernert, Jackie Jensen, Dick Stuart, Tony Conigliaro, Ken Harrelson, Carlton Fisk, Jim Rice, Butch Hobson, Tony Perez, Tony Armas, Don Baylor, Nick Esasky, Jack Clark, Tom Brunansky, and Jose Canseco are among the big, lead-footed right-handed sluggers who've been hired to hit home runs over Fenway's left-field wall. The Green Monster seduces hitters, making them want to pull everything to left. Meanwhile, it's also blown the minds of more than a few young pitchers. It's long been held that a southpaw hurler is doomed at Fenway. All pitchers tend to stay away from the inside half of the plate. Managers also feel the impact. The Wall reminds every skipper that a big inning is always near; get a couple of walks and a windblown fly to left and you've got yourself a three-run homer. That kind thinking has kept the Red Sox from attempting to steal bases over the years: you don't want to run yourself out of the big inning.

Yawkey told *SI* in '65 that he wanted a team that could run and manufacture offense, rather than one that would stand back and try to bash the ball over The Wall. "Hit and run, steal a base, that's the way I like to play the game," said the owner. ". . . It's awfully hard to win in this park. I'm not sure if we can ever do so. It kills the young pitchers. And you can't win without pitching. . . . But damn it, that wall hurts; it has an effect on the whole organization from top to bottom. We have to go after players who have that Fenway stroke, but they get in the habit of pulling the ball and they try it on the road—in Yankee Stadium or Comiskey—and it's no good."

All of the above contributes to what's happened to the Red Sox in the years since Fenway was built and rebuilt. Boston last won a World Series in 1918, and there's plenty of evidence that Fenway Park has contributed to the long drought. Teams have been built to take advantage of the ballpark, but teams built on power eventually can be stopped. A team of slow, power hitters is entertaining, but eventually the winds will shift and the power will be shut off. Then you don't have enough left to win baseball games. Pitching, speed, and defense are ingredients better suited for the long haul of a baseball season. Those are the elements that enable a team to disguise a hitting slump.

In 1989, former Sox lefty, Bill Lee said, "They build their club around Fenway. If there is an Achilles' heel of the Red Sox, it's the left-field wall and the closeness and proximity of it that influences management's decisions."

Ferguson Jenkins, a Hall of Fame hurler who put in a short, forgettable stay with the Red Sox, recalled, "Mostly I remember that pitchers weren't meant to look good. Instead of pitching, we had a lot of singles hitters who hit home runs in that easy ballpark."

Former Sox first baseman George Scott told *Sports Illustrated*, "You hear about the Curse of the Bambino when the team doesn't win. Well, there isn't a Curse of the Bambino. The curse is the way the Red Sox develop their ball club. They're always looking for those strong guys to hit the ball over the left-field wall. Big, strong right-handed hitters. They've never looked for speed. They're still building teams for the forties, fifties, and sixties. These are the nineties. They've never changed to the modern game."

Author David Halberstam says, "It's a great ballpark, and I think it cripples the team. Not what it does to the pitchers, but it makes ordinary players, particularly right-handed batters, look better than they are. There's a tendency to get slow infielders with inflated statistics. Rico Petrocelli. It immobilizes the front office. Players are more popular than they should be. They're all hitting .320 with ninety RBIs so you can't trade them. And also, you don't go for speed. It makes ordinary ballplayers look better than they are, and it deludes the fans into believing the team is better than it is. It is both a curse and a bonus."

The 1949 Red Sox were the ultimate proof of the curse of Fenway. The '49 Sox went 61–16 at home, but couldn't win even half their games (35–42) away from Fenway. They lost the pennant by one game, to the Yankees, losing in New York on the final day of the season—on the road.

Sox reliever Bob Stanley later said, "The Wall giveth and The Wall taketh away. Most of the time, it giveth."

If there is one moment that crystallizes the love-hate relationship Sox fans have with The Wall, it would be Bucky Dent's pop-fly home run in the seventh inning of the 1978 play-off game against the Yankees. The '78 Red Sox were a team of monster mashers. Rice, Hobson, Fisk, Scott, and Dwight Evans tattooed The Wall throughout the summer, and lefty hitters Fred Lynn and Carl Yastrzemski were adept at going to the opposite field for cheesy doubles. The Sox and Yankees each won ninety-nine games, and they met on a crisp October afternoon to decide who'd go to the play-offs and who'd go home. The Red Sox led, 2–0, after six, and Boston righty Mike Torrez took a two-hitter into the seventh inning. With two outs and two on, Dent, who'd hit only four homers all year, turned on an inside fastball and lofted a fly ball toward left. Red Sox Hall of Fame left fielder Yastrzemski backed up and gazed helplessly as the ball barely cleared The Wall and feathered into the netting above the fence.

"I always loved Fenway Park," Yaz said later. "But that was the one moment when I hated the place. It was the one moment when The Wall got back at us. Jesus Christ, I still can't believe it went in the net."

The Wall is not the only unusual item in Fenway's asymmetrical outfield. In 1940, bullpens were added in front of the bleachers in right field and right-center field. Officially, it was done as a favor to pitchers; no longer would they have to warm up on the sidelines or under the stands. In reality the bullpens were added to maximize the abilities of Ted Williams, who hit .327 with 31 homers and 145 RBI in his rookie season (1939) with the Red Sox. After the bullpens were added, the right-field fence was twenty-three feet closer to home plate. A left-handed power hitter, Williams would make great use of the new, cozier dimensions (though his home run production mysteriously dropped to 23 in the 1940 season). The bullpens were unofficially dubbed Williamsburg.

After the bullpens were completed, the right-field foul pole was just 302 feet from home plate. It's a deceiving figure because the fence runs away from home plate and back to a spot in straightaway right field where the target is a formidable 380 feet from home. It's difficult to drive a ball into the small area where the sign reads 302, but infielder Johnny Pesky did it a few times in the 1940s, and pitcher Mel Parnell renamed it Pesky's Pole.

Fans seeing the park today often ask about the single red seat in the sea of green that makes up the right-field bleachers beyond the bullpens. The seat was painted red to commemorate a long homer hit by Williams off Detroit's Fred Hutchinson on June 9, 1946. Joseph A. Boucher, then fifty-six, was sitting in section 42, row 37, seat 21, when Williams's historic smash crashed down on top of his straw hat. "How far away must one sit to be safe in this park?" Boucher asked. "The sun was right in our eyes. All we could do was duck. I'm glad I didn't stand up. They say it bounced a dozen rows higher, but after it hit my head, I was no longer interested."

There is almost no foul territory in Fenway. This, as much as the cozy left-field wall, helps hitters over a season. A hitter like Wade Boggs when he played for the Red Sox might have been saved two or three outs per week by foul balls that plopped into the nearby box seats, rather than into the mitts of American League first basemen, third basemen, and catchers.

"It's especially tough for a pitcher because of The Wall and the lack of foul territory," says Hall of Fame pitcher Jim Palmer. "You make the hitter pop up, but there's almost no way the ball stays in play. There's just no foul territory. The stands are too close, so half of your pop-up outs become souvenirs. It's very frustrating."

Fenway got its first light towers in 1947. For several years, Yawkey resisted night games (the ever-progressive Sox were the fourteenth of sixteen big league teams to install lights), but the crosstown Braves were making money playing at night. Fenway's first night game drew 34,510 fans. Fenway's first televised game was on May 12, 1948. In

1953, a runway was built between the visitors' (third-base) dugout and the visitors' clubhouse. Before the addition of the second runway, both teams used the same tunnel leading to the clubhouses beneath the stands. In 1952, combustible Sox center fielder Jimmy Piersall got into a runway fistfight with Yankee infielder Billy Martin. A year later, Yawkey gave the visitors their own runway.

The triangular area of center-field seats has caused problems for hitters. Fans sitting in straightaway center field fall into the hitter's line of vision. After Tony Conigliaro was seriously beaned by a Jack Hamilton pitch in August of 1967, the "triangle" was roped off to fans for several years. But when big crowds came back to Fenway, the area was opened again, and today hitters say they are sometimes blinded by white shirts of fans, especially during day games.

"It's dangerous out there during the daylight," says Sox first baseman Mo Vaughn. "That's how guys get hurt. There's no background out there. I hate day games here. You have no chance when a pitcher's coming over the top. You can't see the ball."

The flagpole was removed from the center-field warning track in 1970. The next major changes came in 1976, when the first electronic scoreboard went up in center field and the left-field wall was rebuilt. Tin panels were removed and replaced with a smoother, Formica-like covering to produce truer caroms. The tin pieces were cut up and sold as paperweights with proceeds going to the Jimmy Fund (children's cancer research) charity. Prior to the '76 season, padding was also added to the outfield fences. The idea for the padding came in the middle of the memorable sixth game of the 1975 World Series when rookie MVP center fielder Fred Lynn crashed into the hard wall in center in pursuit of a fly ball hit by one of the Cincinnati Reds. Yawkey saw Lynn crumple to the ground and said, "We've got to pad those walls next year." A multicolor videoboard replaced the electronic messageboard in 1987.

The first twenty-one of an eventual forty-four luxury boxes were installed in 1982. Seven years later, a costly construction project gave birth to the 600 Club behind home plate. The 600 Club is an enormous, glass-enclosed theater that begins at the top of the screen behind home plate and rises several stories above the roofline of Fenway. Fans in the 600 Club dine on gourmet foods and wines. Appropriately enough, the 600 Club takes plastic only, no cash. It is a snooty, quiet place where high rollers schmooze with friends and clients. It's believed that at key moments in the game, fans do not applaud—they simply rattle their jewelry. Former Sox second baseman Marty Barrett observed, "It's weird at night. I stand out there at second base and see this giant glass window with all these people inside. Sometimes I feel like I'm at the movies, watching them . . . instead of them coming here to watch us." The 600 Club annoys broadcast and print reporters because it forces them closer to heaven. The 600 Club occupies the area that once housed the press. Today, the press box sits on top of the 600 Club, forcing the media to watch the game from an angle that makes it impossible to tell a slider from a spitter. Meanwhile, Red Sox hitters have used the 600 Club as an excuse for a decrease in power production. A moderate seventy-one feet high before the addition, the stadium structure behind home plate is now one hundred feet six inches. Wade Boggs and Mike Greenwell were the first to float the "600 Club theory."

"Ever since they put that 600 Club up, it's been harder to hit the ball out," says Greenwell. "There's no doubt about it. You could tell the first day, when we took batting practice. I think it's especially worse for left-handed hitters like myself, because something changed about the wind patterns out there."

At least one MIT scientist has validated this handy excuse.

Fenway has been the site of a limited number of nonbaseball events. On November 4, 1944, Franklin Delano Roosevelt gave his final campaign speech there. Standing on a podium on the Fenway lawn, FDR said, "Today, in this war, our fine young boys are fighting magnificently all over the world, and among those boys are the Murphys and the Kellys, the Smiths and the Joneses and Cohens, the Carusos, the Kowalskis, the Schultzes, the Olsens, the Swobodas, and—right in there with all the rest of them—the Cabots and the Lowells." FDR was dead less than six months later.

A few football teams have borrowed Fenway. With the left-field wall wiping out half of the sideline seating (temporary stands were set up in front of the wall), the Boston Redskins played at Fenway for four seasons in the mid-1930s. After the Redskins went to Washington, the Boston Yanks played in Fenway from 1944 to 1948 (they moved on to

New York, Dallas, Baltimore, and today are the Indianapolis Colts). In 1944, Frank Leahy's Fighting Irish of Notre Dame beat Dartmouth, 64–0, in front of 38,167 at Fenway. Boston College and Boston University played many home games at Fenway Park until 1956, when the Red Sox decided the damage to the grass was too severe. Football returned to Fenway in 1963 when the American Football League's Boston Patriots needed a home. The Pats stayed at Fenway until 1968, and no football games have been played in the baseball park since. Fenway seated 40,000 for football. In addition to football, the park has been used for basketball exhibitions, soccer games, revival meetings, memorial services, and a 1973 jazz festival.

The largest crowd in the park's history was 47,627 for a doubleheader against the Yankees on September 22, 1935. The third-biggest crowd came when 46,766 turned out for Babe Ruth's final Fenway game on August 12, 1934. Unless the park is expanded, these single-day attendance figures will never again be reached because of the more stringent fire laws implemented after World War II. Today, Fenway's official seating capacity is 33,871. Standing room can bring the crowd up to 36,000. Officially speaking, the largest postwar Fenway crowd was 36,228 for a game against the Cleveland Indians in 1978. Unofficially, club CEO John Harrington has said he believes there were 47,000 people in Fenway the night Luis Tiant beat Jim Palmer, 2–0, to move the Sox closer to the American League East Division flag in September of 1975.

In terms of ticket demand, a small park has benefited the Red Sox. Certainly there are nights when the Sox could draw 60,000 people or more. But it's widely believed that if seating capacity were infinite, fans would be reluctant to buy in advance, and then ticket sales would be directly linked to the success of the team. In poor seasons like '87, '89, '91–93, the Red Sox still drew approximately 2.5 million fans each year. Most of the sales were attributable to tickets bought early by fans eager to avoid being frozen out late in the season. In some recent seasons, the Sox were guaranteed attendance of close to 2 million before the first game was played. For this, the Sox can thank cozy Fenway Park.

In the name of progress, there is much talk today about the need for a new baseball park in Boston. It's an extremely emotional issue, but Sox officials insist that the shelf life of Fenway will not stretch far into the next century. The ball club may yet figure out how to preserve Fenway with a total renovation, but more likely a replacement park will be built somewhere (white suburbia perhaps?). No doubt Red Sox fans will wail at the foot of The Wall when the demolition ball dangles outside our hardball shrine.

How can we be rational? Fenway is the house where we were raised. The place always needs a paint job, the plaster is cracking, and sometimes we don't have enough room for everyone, but we love this old house of hardball. Every year when we first return, it reminds us of our parents and our home.

Baseball always promised us that we wouldn't have to grow up. Fenway is part of the promise.

CHAPTER TWO

RED SOX NATION

◆ It is a Friday night in July 1995 and there's a good crowd in the restaurant/function room of the Harbor House on Nantucket. A four-man band, the Poland Strings, plays Van Morrison and Beatles tunes from a corner stage. Vacationers and natives fill the house, sitting at tables and milling about the bar. A few couples dance. It's dark, loud, and relaxed.

At the far end of the room, a large television faces a line of barstools. The first-place Red Sox are playing the Detroit Tigers at Fenway, and the image of Red Sox relief pitcher Ken Ryan fills the big screen. It is baseball without sound. On this night, the noise in the Harbor House lounge belongs to the Poland Strings, and fans who want to watch the game have to keep pace on their own.

A few feet from the TV, Christine Sugarman, a thirty-one-year-old research analyst, sits with her husband, Rich. He is listening to the band, sipping his beer. Christine has arranged her chair to watch the baseball game while listening to the music. Her eyes rarely leave the TV.

What would compel a young woman to watch a soundless baseball game in the middle of a festive night with her husband on Nantucket?

"It's my grandfather," she says as Ryan puts the winning run on base with a walk. "His name was Urban Anderson and he was born in Worcester in 1913. His parents were from Sweden and he worked his whole life at the Norton Company as a laborer. My twin sister and I were his only grandchildren. He and my grandmother were big base-ball fans, and I would stay at their house for weeks in the summer. My grandfather and I would stay home, and the one thing we always did was watch the Red Sox games. When I was about ten or eleven, he started having problems walking, so we watched TV a lot. We never actually went to Fenway. I have all these memories of watching games on his screened-in porch. He passed away last year and I think about him all the time. He loved the Red Sox, he really did. Maybe it was the generation. Of course, he'd always talk about how the Sox break his heart. He called them the Red Slobs—'those damn Red Slobs.' He'd say it all the time. It was like he knew what was going to happen every year. They'd hook you, then kill you at the end of the season. He'd always say he wasn't going to watch them anymore, but he always came back. It's been one year since he died, and the Red Sox are doing well and maybe this is going to be the year. On a night like this my husband will sit and listen to the band, but I'll end up wander-ing off and find a TV screen. I've just got to watch them and keep rooting for them. It's like I keep my grandfather's memory alive by watching the Red Sox. When I watch the Red Sox play, my grandfa-ther is with me. Every season he hoped this would be the year, and I feel as though I need to carry on that tradition—sick as it may seem."

➤ ◆ ◄

The late Red Sox outfielder Jackie Jensen said, "Fenway Park has a voice of one."

It is the voice of Red Sox Nation.

Sox fans join with the team and the ballpark to form the unique triangle that is the Boston baseball experience. Fenway is old, small, and filled with legions of New Englanders who make the Red Sox part of their daily routine. This is where we can look at you with a straight face and tell you that baseball isn't a life-or-death issue . . . but the Red Sox are.

You can grow up in greater Boston and choose to ignore the Ameri-can League standings and box scores in your daily *Globe*. You can proudly claim that you don't know Roger Clemens from Samuel Clemens. You can click past the Red Sox when you accidently stumble across the Fenway lawn while channel surfing. But you cannot avoid the hometown team.

Try to find a New Englander born before 1976 who cannot recall precisely where they were and what they were doing when Bill Buckner let the ball creep through his legs in the infamous sixth game of the 1986 World Series. Walk down Newbury Street in the Back Bay and see how long you can go without seeing a Sox cap. Skip the sports pages and the sports reports on local television; you will still catch baseball news regularly on page one of the *Globe*, and at the top of newscasts. For the entirety of this century, weather, politics, and baseball have furnished most of the conversation in small towns and big cities of New England. Strangers can always break the ice by saying, "Hot enough for ya?" "Think the mayor is on the take?" or "How 'bout those Sox?"

Sox fans are a literate and emotional lot. They know that the anticipation is usually more fun than what actually winds up happening. Expectation is reward. The citizens of Red Sox Nation come from six New England states and parts of Canada. They are old, young, male, female, rich, and poor. The Sox fan base crosses into every group. Poets, farmers, schoolkids, and shut-ins are Red Sox fans. Horror man Stephen King is a Sox fan, as were the last two baseball commissioners, Fay Vincent and the late Bart Giamatti. All those folks have one thing in common: they break out in a rash at the very mention of Bucky Dent.

Formed in 1901, the Boston American League baseball franchise won five of the first fifteen World Series. But the Red Sox have not won the Series since 1918 and have subjected their fans to more near misses than any other team in sports history. The Chicago Cubs and Buffalo Bills have nothing on the Red Sox. The Sox since 1918 have been in four World Series and lost each in a seventh game. The 1986 Red Sox came within one strike of winning the Series, but blew it in ghoulish fashion. No team has ever come closer to winning the Fall Classic without actually winning. There have been only three one-game play-offs in American League history, and the Red Sox have lost two of them. From 1986 to 1995, Boston lost a major league record thirteen consecutive postseason games. These blown pennant races and awful Octobers have created the image that when it comes to the Red Sox . . . something will go wrong. Always.

Sox fans love being nervous. They are uneasy when they see their team in first place. They know that the Sox are the only team that can give the appearance of being mathematically eliminated when they are still in first place. Steve Sheppard, who grew up in Brockton, Massachusetts, and today is a loyal Red Sox fan living on Nantucket, says, "The Red Sox are never going to win the World Series. Never ever, ever. The sooner you realize that, the happier you are."

Today it's been fashionable to bash Red Sox fans. Boston baseball boosters have been characterized as a whiny, self-indulgent lot. Outsiders constantly remind New Englanders that we ought to shut up and enjoy the product. It's pointed out that fans in some cities (like Cleveland and Seattle before last year) never get a sniff of a championship. Boston fans have no monopoly on losers. That is fair criticism, but only when leveled by lifelong New Englanders. Those who can't stomach the self-pity of Red Sox Nation tend to be people who've come here from other shores. My *Globe* colleague and friend Bob Ryan is a harsh critic of Sox fans. In 1990, Ryan wrote, "What has come to distinguish Red Sox fans is astonishing self-absorption. Woe is me. Woe is you. Woe is us. Bull, you will pardon my French, bleep. Among the intelligentsia, there is no letup. The Weeping and Wailing Season never ends. One after the other, they troop to the word processor for yet another narcissistic account of how frustrating, how painful, how ultimately Sisyphean it is to root for this team. They always let me down in the end. I'm Charlie Brown; they're Lucy. Boo-hoo. Bring me, meanwhile, the barf bag. Large economy size."

So what does Ryan know? The guy grew up in Trenton, for gosh sakes. He didn't arrive in Boston until his freshman year at Boston College in the mid-1960s. He's been a Bostonian for just three decades. He's not even sure where he saw his first big-league ball game. Might have been Shibe Park, might have been the Polo Grounds. Small wonder he'll never know what it was like to grow up with the Red Sox. You are not from here unless you were born and raised here. The outsiders, they'll never know. But the natives, they understand.

From Miami to Seattle, the continental United States is populated by twenty-eight major league baseball franchises. Each team has a base of core constituents. There are Cubs fans, Yankees fans, Mets fans, Cardinals fans—even San Diego Padres fans. But only the Red

Sox have a citizenry that alternately pledges blind allegiance and curses the club, vowing never to care again. Sometimes this range of emotion can be deployed within the span of a single half inning of a meaningless Tuesday-night game against the Seattle Mariners in April.

Clemens, who grew up in Ohio and Texas and first came to the Red Sox in 1984, says, "I've come to know that no matter what happens, the town is Boston Red Sox. I understand the tradition behind the Celtics and what they have. Same thing with the Patriots and the Bruins, but everybody talks about the Boston Red Sox. In watching and reading about all the history and the past, it's just a fact. I was prepared for the tradition of it all, but I wasn't prepared for the entire season and how important it is, and how people watch it so closely. It's an event, the way everything unfolds every season. There's always a story behind each one. I've had major league friends, guys who've never played in the American League, and sometimes they come to Boston at the end of their careers and they can't believe it."

The founding fathers of Red Sox Nation were the Royal Rooters, a gang of about three hundred rowdy fans founded just before the turn of the century. The leader of the Rooters was Michael T. McGreevey, a legendary Boston barkeep who went by the name of Nuff Ced. McGreevey was a raconteur, a gambler, a barroom barrister, a handball champion, and an original L Street Brownie. He befriended one-time heavyweight champion John L. Sullivan, Boston mayor John F. "Honey Fitz" Fitzgerald, gambler John "Sport" Sullivan (allegedly involved in the 1919 Black Sox scandal), everyone who played for the Red Sox, and the little people who populated Boston's street corners and saloons. A short Irishman with a handlebar mustache, McGreevey earned his nickname by hollering "Nuff said" to silence the patrons at his bar. Seizing an opportunity to create a nifty character for the times, members of the Boston baseball press made "Nuff Ced" a local celebrity. McGreevey went so far as having "Nuff Ced" printed on his business cards. "Nuff Ced" was even printed in mosaic tile on the tavern's floor. According to venerable baseball historian Frederick G. Lieb (*The Boston Red·Sox*, 1947), "There were some Bostonians so crass in their thinking that they believed 'Nuff Ced' used his association with the Royal Rooters to ballyhoo his grog shop."

Nuff Ced. The image is irresistible, a filmmaker's delight. Picture hundreds of red-faced gentlemen wearing suits and smoking cigars, hunched over their midday liquid lunches, raising their voices to be heard above the din . . . and suddenly from behind the bar, a mustachioed man wearing a vest and drying a glass with a hand towel bellows, "Nuff said!" abruptly halting all conversation. McGreevey conducts a bit of small business, perhaps placing an order with the kitchen, then nods, allowing customers to return to their drinks and chatter.

A ubiquitous, Zelig-like figure, likely to show up in the background of newspaper photographs, McGreevey was known across Boston and eventually became famous throughout the American League. He attended spring training with the team, had his own uniform, and sometimes took infield with the real ballplayers. Legend holds that a minor-league ball club once bought McGreevey's rights after watching him practice with the Sox. In 1908, Nuff Ced was asked to pose for the official Red Sox team picture. In 1909, he presented Red Sox second baseman Amby McConnell with a $250 diamond ring—McConnell's reward for leading the team in stolen bases.

McGreevey may well be the man who invented the sports bar. Located at 940 Columbus Avenue, his joint was within shouting distance of two big league ballparks—the Walpole Street (or South End) Grounds, home of Boston's National League entry, and the Huntington Avenue Grounds, where the Boston Americans began play in 1901. Opened in the late 1890s, the saloon was called Third Base because, as every fan knows, third base is the last place you stop on your way home. In the days before satellite dishes and basketball arcades, McGreevey lined the walls of his establishment with pictures of baseball stars, and he kept a scoreboard on the outer wall. Ceiling light fixtures were made out of baseball bats, and a grandfather clock had a bat-and-ball pendulum. Above the bar was a mannequin wearing a Boston baseball uniform. There were two side doors—called first and third. Nuff Ced was Sam Malone. Cheers.

According to Dick Johnson, curator of the New England Sports Museum, "Third Base was as much a salon as it was a saloon. It was the cultural epicenter of Boston, where journalists, athletes, politicians, and gamblers plied their trade. It was the Boston equivalent of New York's Algonquin Roundtable."

McGreevey's Rooters wore black suits with high white collars. They pinned blue rosettes on their lapels and put their ticket stubs in the hatbands of their derbies. The Rooters first cast their loyalty with the Boston Red Stockings (known as the Reds and/or Beaneaters) of the original National League. The Stockings won the NL flag eight times between 1877 and 1898. The Rooters first road trip was to Baltimore for a crucial series against the Orioles in 1897. Probably the train had to restock the bar in Delaware.

Though they are remembered today as loyal fans of their ball team, the Rooters were, in fact, the original front-runners. When aligned with Mike "King" Kelly, the superstar of the Boston Nationals, the Rooters cheered pennant winners in '91, '92, '97, and '98. But when the Boston Americans (later Somersets, then Pilgrims, then Red Sox) were born as part of the new American League in 1901, the Rooters switched allegiances. The AL had taken some good players from the senior league—players like Cy Young, Chick Stahl, and Jimmy Collins. Plus, Pilgrims games were cheaper. American League games cost twenty-five cents, compared with a fifty-cent ticket at the Beaneaters' Walpole Street park. That gave the Rooters a few extra bob for a couple of drafts, and perhaps another wager. That settled it. The Royal Rooters gave their hearts to the upstart ball club.

The Rooters were at their best during the first World Series, the 1903 classic (best five of nine) that matched Pittsburgh against the Boston Americans. With Boston trailing two games to one, McGreevey announced, "Road trip," and led a contingent of two hundred Rooters to Pittsburgh.

It was during game four in Pittsburgh, that McGreevey swung into action. In mid-game, with the Sox trailing, he hired a band to sit with the Rooters and he sent club member Tom Burton to a Pittsburgh music store to find some sheet music for a new theme song. Burton chose "Tessie," a popular tune (written by Will Anderson) from a musical comedy called *The Silver*. When the Boston Americans came to the plate in the top of the ninth, trailing 5–1, McGreevey ordered the band to play. The Sox promptly rallied, but lost, 5–4. Still, McGreevey was inspired. His Rooters sang "Tessie" all the way back to their hotel, and the headline in the next day's *Boston Journal* read, "Grand Rally in the Ninth Started by Rooters."

Cy Young pitched the next day, and as McGreevey and the boys sang "Tessie," the Americans drilled the Pirates, 11–2. The *Boston Post* game story included this passage: "By this time Boston's loyal rooters acted more like escaped patients from an insane asylum while Pittsburgh rooters fumed and raged." When the Americans won again the next day, the Rooters were held tying the Series at 3–3, responsible for the Series turnaround.

Knowing that the Rooters had train reservations back to Boston, Pittsburgh's management postponed game seven, claiming it was too cold for baseball. McGreevey didn't fall for it. The Rooters convened and decided to stay in Pittsburgh until the last game was played. In game seven, Young beat the Pirates again, sending the Series back to Boston with the Americans leading four games to three. The Rooters rode the train back to Boston with their team, and some six hundred Boston fans greeted the returning heroes.

The Series resumed on October 13 at the Huntington Grounds, and the locals won it, 3–0. As the Letter Carriers Band played "Tessie," fans stormed onto the field, and everbody danced over to the Third Base Bar. The Boston Americans were World Champs. Nuff Ced.

In *The Glory of Their Times*, Pittsburgh player Tommy Leach admitted, "I think those Boston fans actually won that Series for the Red Sox . . . ["Tessie"] sort of got on your nerves after a while."

The Sox enjoyed a harmonious relationship with the thirsty, gambling Rooters until the next-to-last game of the 1912 World Series. On that tragic and fateful day, McGreevey's pub crawlers stayed at Third Base too long and arrived at Fenway to discover that, due to a box-office mix-up, their left-field grandstand seats had been sold to other fans. Outraged, the Rooters paraded around the field behind their own band, then sat down on Duffy's Cliff in left field and refused to leave. A riot ensued and McGreevey's gang had to be removed by mounted police. They were literally herded out of Fenway Park. A Boston newspaper compared the chaos to the treatment of Moscow civilians by Russian Cossacks.

This shabby treatment resulted in a boycott of the next day's World Series game. Thus, only 17,034 fans attended the final game (game eight, due to a tie in game two) of the 1912 World Series. When the

Sox won the game and the Series, Mayor "Honey Fitz" got Sox owner James McAleer to apologize to the Rooters. McGreevey and his followers accepted, then led a city parade honoring Boston's World Champions.

This passionate episode set the tone for a century of emotion and devotion from the ranks of Red Sox fans. It's been a love-hate relationship ever since Nuff Ced and his chorus line of drunks rioted on the Fenway lawn before the seventh game of the 1912 World Series. The Rooters remained a force at Fenway until 1920, the year Babe Ruth was sold to the Yankees. But the record shows that it wasn't the sale of the Babe that broke up the band of Rooters. Eleven days after Ruth was shipped to New York, the Volstead Act was passed, banning beer, wine, and liquor across America. There would be no more days quaffing lagers at Third Base. With that, the Rooters lost their thirst for baseball. It's often written that the Red Sox haven't won a World Series since Babe Ruth was sold to the Yankees, but we shouldn't forget that the Sox also haven't won since Prohibition.

How many people are Red Sox fans now? There are no available statistics. It's not like charting the number of registered Democrats in Cook County, Illinois. Baseball teams do not have *fan clubs*. Annual Fenway home attendance is a helpful barometer of the customer climate, but can't measure the true numbers or the fluctuating levels of devotion that New England sports fans shower on the local baseball team. The ball club itself relies on a season-ticket base and cable television subscriptions (the Red Sox are shown on the New England Sports Network cable channel) to gauge fan interest and furnish revenue. Television and radio rights, relative to those in other cities, usually tell a franchise what its drawing power is. But the numbers are deceptive. The Dodgers, Yankees, Mets, Cubs, and White Sox play in larger cities. More people means more potential customers, higher rights fees, and higher ratings. But advertising revenue and attendance numbers don't measure a team's saturation impact, or the passion of the fans.

The Red Sox were baseball's first regional franchise. The Yankees had New York and the Cubs had Chicago, but the Red Sox always had Boston, plus Providence, Worcester, Springfield, Portland, Rutland, parts of Nova Scotia, and the better half of Hartford.

Here's a page from the 1960 Red Sox official program and scorecard (fifteen cents): "The Boston Red Sox extend a cordial welcome to the baseball fans of New England and visitors to this area from other sections of the nation and the world. Red Sox fans are registered in our book as among the most loyal and appreciative in the country. The comfort of these people always is a prime requisite with the Red Sox management in the continual upkeep and maintenance of Fenway Park as an outstanding sports stadium. It is Red Sox policy to attempt at all times to reward the patronage and support of our fans with the best in baseball in every way."

The passage could have been penned in 1920, 1940, or 1990.

Because they have been playing since 1903, and playing in the same park since 1912, the Red Sox predate all memory of most living citizens of New England. This establishes them as a certified tradition, and New Englanders love tradition. In 1909, *Boston Post* publisher E. A. Grozier mailed gold-capped ebony canes to 431 New England towns. According to Grozier's instructions, a cane was to be given to oldest resident in each town, then duly transferred to the next-oldest citizen whenever a cane-owner died. The *Boston Post* went out of business in 1957, but there are still *Boston Post* canes in the hands of old people in many New England towns. The Red Sox are like the *Boston Post* canes. They go back to the first decade of the twentieth century, they are perpetual, and they belong to all of New England.

In his 1985 book, *Beyond the Sixth Game*, *Globe* sportswriter Peter Gammons wrote, "As one drives the back roads of northern New England and slides across the radio dial, one small station after another fades in and out with Red Sox baseball, stations that for generations have made Curt Gowdy, Ned Martin, Jim Woods, and now Ken Coleman voices as familiar as those of the ministers at the Congregational and Episcopal churches."

When New England grew into the twentieth century, baseball was the game everybody played and watched. During this proverbial "simpler time," young people played the game all day long without supervision. Little boys didn't need uniforms, $100 mitts, or loudmouthed parents carrying whistles. There were no child-nappers lurking in the parks. Kids got on their bikes, hooked their gloves over the handlebars, peddled to the town field, and played ball until it got dark, or they heard their mothers calling them for supper.

In the 1930s and 1940s, New England town teams of young and middle-aged men provided steady summer entertainment for folks who spent their days working in paper mills and railroad yards. Town baseball was a low-cost, no-travel form of recreation and socialization. The seven-inning games were played on weekends and evenings, and hundreds (sometimes thousands) of fans sat on grassy knolls in foul territory. Some towns charged a nominal admission—or a stick of gum. A lot of fans bet on the action—just the way those city slickers did in the bleachers at Fenway Park.

Author David Halberstam, a man with a vast sense of American history, says this about baseball: "It's everybody's game. I think the great thing about it is that it's inclusionary. Everybody can play it, regardless of size. And it's been a great way to Americanize. I think my father loved it because it was the first thing in America he could do. It's always been an immigrant way, the first rung of American culture that you can grasp, on the schoolyard, even when you have an accent. Baseball. You can understand it, you can play it, and you can follow it. That was a way you could connect to people. . . . The obvious thing is that if you look at the war monuments and the box scores, it's the same names. It's a great index of who's doing the heavy lifting. Who are the grunts in the society at the time? Those are the Waspy names on the Civil War monument. But there's a lot of Fernandezes on the monuments now. . . . It has serious generational problems, and it has not handled them well. If you were inventing the sport today, you would not invent a sport that takes three hours. It really is a remembrance of another America. It's rural. Country. It's an America with a lot of time on its hands."

In many ways, baseball is America's soccer. Throughout the world, soccer is the most popular sport. It is a game played on grass, with little equipment, and one needn't be tall or muscular to play well. The game neutralizes the dominance that big kids have in basketball and football. In all of these ways, baseball is like soccer. And just as Europeans and South Americans find baseball slow and boring, most second-and third-generation Americans have a difficult time watching soccer matches. Both are games that would not do well if invented today, but both are part of the cultures in which they are played.

Nationwide, baseball is having difficulty drawing new fans. The game has done a poor job of promoting itself. World Series games are played too late for children to watch, and the electronic/video generation prefers its sports fast, violent, and flashy. The NBA and the NFL appeal to today's younger audience, and advertisers have enlisted pro basketball and football players to sell merchandise to Nintendo kids.

Allowing that baseball is lost on many young people, and that the Bill Parcells–Drew Bledsoe New England Patriots emerged for a few months of 1995 as the hot New England team, I will say that baseball continues to be the number one sport in greater Boston. At any time of the year, fan interest in the Red Sox outweighs the aggregate tonnage of that accorded the Celtics, Patriots, and Bruins. This is evident in letters to the *Globe* sports department, phone calls to all-sports radio shows, and casual conversations around town. The Red Sox are the team that never goes out of fashion. They can be stupid, boring, and contemptuous of their consumers. They can finish last three years in a row. They can be on strike for six months. They still have a choke hold on New England sports fans.

This was never more evident than in the dark, scary winter of 1994–95. It was a bleak time for baseball fans across the land. Major league ballplayers had walked out on strike on August 12, 1994, and the work stoppage forced cancellation of the World Series for the first time since 1904 (when those cowardly New York Giants refused to play the American League champion Boston Pilgrims). Negotiators for players and owners made no progress in the autumn of '94, and as the Christmas holidays approached, there was still no end in sight. Fans were hurt and wounded. Many pledged never to return once the game came back. Baseball executives recognized it as a crisis situation, but there was little anyone could do until the parties came to terms on a new agreement. Meanwhile, close to home, the Red Sox had given their fans almost nothing to look forward to. In the summers of '92, '93, and '94, Boston finished in the second division and under .500. It marked the first time the Sox had come home under .500 in three straight seasons since the years of horror and apathy that preceded the miracle of 1967. In the aborted season of 1994 the Sox were neither good nor exciting. Slugging first baseman Mo Vaughn was the lone star attraction, and teams found ways to pitch around Vaughn while taking advantage of weak Sox hitters. There was almost no reason to go out to the ballpark.

That was the plight of the citizens of Red Sox Nation in the beginning of December 1994: they were supporting a bad team with no stars and little hope for the immediate future. Worse, everyone was on strike. It read like an entry from Franz Kafka's diaries.

Then on Friday, December 9, while the stupid strike lingered and it looked as if baseball might never come back . . . Red Sox general manager Dan Duquette called an 8 P.M. press conference and announced that the ball club had acquired Texas right-handed slugger Jose Canseco in exchange for Otis Nixon and Luis Ortiz. Reaction was swift and overwhelming. Fans forgot about the walkout. Strike? What strike? The Canseco deal came down in the middle of a baseball work stoppage, in the middle of a Celtics game, and exactly two days before the Patriots most important game in six years. But suddenly the only subject Boston sports fans could talk about was the Red Sox. The December 10 *Boston Globe* sports section devoted 80 percent of its cover page to the Canseco deal.

Finally, the Sox had a star. We knew Jose was going to get caught going 120 mph on Route 95 South at three in the morning. We knew he was going to be detained at Logan when they found him packing heat as he passed through security. We knew he'd own Newbury Street, bouncing JFK Jr. and Cam Neely off the *Boston Herald*'s Inside Track gossip column. That was okay. In fact, that was great.

The message was clear: Jose was coming to town. Send lawyers guns and money. Duquette had hit the fans.

Four days after the trade was made, I traveled back to my hometown to speak to the Groton Men's Club. One of the unique aspects of my boyhood hometown is that though tiny in size, it has contributed several individuals to the Fenway scene. In the early 1990s, on a given night at the Boston ballpark, you might find as many as five Groton natives working at Fenway Park: Meg LaVigne, Heather Roberts, Robin Fogden, Gammons, and myself. LaVigne is program director of the station (Channel 38, WSBK) that produced Sox telecasts until 1996. Roberts is an assistant director for WSBK. Fogden is a freelance television cameraman who's been working games at Fenway for two decades. Gammons and I work in the press box. There have been nights at Fenway when we felt we had enough Groton natives to provide a quorum for a town meeting.

Gammons is nine years older than me, but we both attended kindergarten in the basement hall of the Unitarian Church, a drafty barn that would make a nice cover shot for *Yankee Magazine*. The church sits atop a hill across Main Street from the town library. Gammons and I like to think that in the small, feeble world of baseball writing, our attending the same Groton kindergarten is tantamount to having Bill Russell, Frank Robinson, and Curt Flood all from the same high school (McClymonds, in Oakland, California). More than once, I've earned a scowl from the great Frank Robinson by telling him that the Groton Unitarian Church basement is the McClymonds of baseball writers.

This in part explains why since the late 1970s, Gammons and I have been guest speakers at the Groton Men's Club's annual sports night. It is a night from our past, a night to feel safe and warm in a place that felt big and wooden when we were children.

On the annual Men's Club Sports Night, about sixty of the club members sit at long wooden tables and eat bowls of beef stew, prepared by Ray Tolles and his wife and daughter. It's a scene right out of Mayberry with Goober, Barney, Floyd the barber, and Howard Sprague. Many of the older gents wear their best flannel shirts. At the conclusion of the help-yourself dinner, everyone pitches in $7 for the stew, then we move the tables out of the way and rearrange the chairs to form a minitheater. For the next few hours, Gammons and I field questions from the townspeople. Even though the event takes place in December, most of the guys want to know about the Red Sox.

On December 13, 1994, four days after the Canseco deal, all the Groton old-timers wanted to talk about Jose. "I don't like it," said eighty-two-year-old Joe Mitchell. "We've been trying to do it that way for too many years."

It was freezing outside, the first snow was falling, and the Patriots were on the brink of qualifying for the play-offs for the first time in eight years. And we talked about Jose Canseco and Frankie Rodriguez and Dan Duquette and Lou Gorman. In the terrible work-stoppage winter of 1994–95, it was a wonderful night of hot-stove baseball.

The warmth lasted into the strike-torn spring of 1995. For all of March and part of April, big league teams gave fans a spring training with "replacement players." It was a joke. These were plumbers, carpenters, truck drivers, and men who'd been released from minor league teams years ago. But for one false spring they wore big league uniforms and pretended to be Yankees, Phillies, Tigers, and Red Sox. Coupled with the cancellation of the 1994 World Series, these were baseball's darkest hours since the Black Sox scandal of 1919.

But while twenty-seven major league teams worried about selling tickets for "replacement baseball," the Sox announced that 94 percent of season-ticket holders had renewed their packages. To watch Fraudball. At Fenway.

"What can I say," said Sox CEO John Harrington. "These are Boston fans. They're the greatest. In normal times, our renewal rate is about ninety-six percent, so this is remarkable."

Ultimately, the strike ended and the players returned to work. In early April, they reported for an abbreviated spring training. The day Canseco finally arrived in Fort Myers, he was asked about Boston's baseball tradition.

Though he'd spent his career in Oakland and Texas, Canseco had some feel for Boston and its fans, saying, "The fans in Boston are so educated in baseball. They've been to games thirty, forty years. It's a way of life there. Baseball is everything in Boston. I've heard about their traditions and conflicts with the New York Yankees. The fans know the game so well, they can pick up a balk from the pitcher. And in Fenway, there's no foul territory. So they can reach out and grab you—choke you or shake your hand. It makes them that much more involved."

After a hideous spring training with replacement players, baseball's ownership and labor forces called a truce and agreed to start an abbreviated (144-game) season in the final week of April. Fans across the country were skeptical. Many threatened to boycott baseball. Thousands did. The Pittsburgh Pirates drew fewer than 8,000 fans for their second game of the season. Milwaukee had crowds under 10,000. Fans in Kansas City stayed home. But in Boston, there was little fallout.

The Sox had their usual opening-day sellout, then drew 23,199 for game two, over 27,000 for their third game, and 30,658 for game four. Scalpers outside Fenway Park were ecstatic. "This is the only city in the country where it's happening," a happy ticket broker told the *Globe*. "The fans don't care about the strike; they just want to get into Fenway."

Ted Williams says, "It's so easy to stimulate them in Boston. I think the Boston fans are a little different. They're closer knitted to the team itself. It just seems like the Boston people get their feelings behind them so much. They're supersensitive and I like that."

Across America, baseball attendance in the first week of the 1995 season was down 15 percent. In Boston, the Red Sox were up more than 4,000 fans per game from the same point in 1995. By the end of May, baseball attendance around the country was down 20 percent, an average of 5,900 fewer fans per game.

The Red Sox bucked the trend all season long. In 1995, the Sox averaged 30,061 fans per game, a higher average than they had in 1994. When play-off tickets went on sale, the Sox held a lottery and more than 40,000 fans mailed in postcards in an attempt to score tickets. Few where chosen. Meanwhile, in Cincinnati, there were more than 14,000 empty seats for the Reds first League Championship Series game against the Atlanta Braves.

Boston University professor John Cheffers, an authority on the study of crowd behavior in America, told the *Globe*, "Boston fans love going to Fenway. A baseball game at Fenway is an event. The game is second. It's not the baseball they enjoy as much as the entire event. Boston fans are much more sophisticated than most sporting audiences."

Oriole pitching coach Mike Flanagan was asked why he thought Boston was insulated against the fan backlash that plagued the rest of baseball. "Because the fans here think this is the year," said Flanagan. "They always do."

Flanagan grew up in Manchester, New Hampshire, and attended the University of Massachusetts. His father, Ed, was a pitcher in the Red Sox system in the 1940s, and his grandfather, Ed senior, was a professional ambidextrous hurler who was known to pitch double-headers, one with each arm. Mike Flanagan won a Cy Young Award with the Orioles in 1979 and pitched in postseason play with both the Orioles and Blue Jays. But he's a New Englander and he knows what keeps the Sox fans going.

This is the year.

On May 15, 1995, a cold, rainy Monday afternoon during a school week, the Sox held their first-ever Friendly Fenway Fan Festival. More than twenty-five thousand fans lined up for a free tour of Fenway, free autographs, and a chance to chat with Sox players, coaches, and manager Kevin Kennedy. In a national climate of baseball bashing, it was another indication that Boston is different. Fans waited as long as three and a half hours to get a Canseco autograph. At one point the line stretched into Kenmore Square. Inside Fenway, the souvenir-hunting citizens of Red Sox Nation scraped white paint from the giant *K* on the left-field scoreboard. It was an event. Only in Boston.

Eddie Andelman, a sports talk-radio host in Boston for more than twenty-five years, says, "Red Sox fans think of the team the way parents think of children. They forgive them all the time and continue to give to them because they really care about the team. They think they're part of the Red Sox, and they really feel that they're the tenth player on the team."

Dick Radatz pitched only five seasons for the Red Sox in the mid-1960s. His big league career also took him to Cleveland, Detroit, Chicago, and Montreal. It's been more than three decades since Radatz hurled for the Townies, but he lives in Greater Boston and still gets recognized almost daily. He's a local businessman and his Red Sox connection is good for business. Any New England businessman over the age of forty will return a phone call from Dick Radatz.

"I'm from the great sports town of Detroit," says Radatz. "But I find the fans here a little more knowledgeable. One reason I'm living and working here is the memories that people have of me. I appreciate that and I think most of the players here do. People still remember certain instances like the night I struck out Mickey Mantle, Roger Maris, and Elston Howard here with the bases loaded. People also still remember me giving up a homer to Johnny Callison in the 1964 All-Star game. There's a lot of games they bring up, certain situations, and I would not get that in any other town. I still hear about the night that I threw my glove into the stands in Detroit after I gave up a home run to Al Kaline. I bet I hear about that once or twice a month, and it happened thirty years ago."

Rico Petrocelli played twelve seasons for the Red Sox. When the Red Sox clinched the 1967 pennant, defeating Minnesota on the final day of the season, Petrocelli caught Rich Rollins's pop-up for the final out. He says, "When you go out to sign autographs or something about here, they come up with new things. They remember things. The Rollins ball is something I'm known for, I guess. But I also played in the 1975 World Series, and that's something I'll always be proud of."

Bernie Carbo hit the second-most-famous, but most-crucial home run of the '75 World Series. His pinch-hit, three-run blast enabled Carlton Fisk to win game six for Boston. Here's what Carbo has to say about Sox fans: "I think the Red Sox fans are a lot different. They're the greatest fans that I ever played in front of, and I played all over. One of the reasons is that they know the game. They know the little things about the game. When you slide into second to break up the double play, or hit a fly ball to score a run from third base, or bunt somebody into scoring position, they applaud you. Those are things that maybe an ordinary fan would not cheer for, and some will boo you for them. But those are things about Boston Red Sox fans. They're not afraid to applaud or cheer when you're doing good, and they'll boo you when you're doing bad. And that's what gives you the incentive to work harder and play harder and do as much as you possibly can because you want that applause. I loved playing here because I knew if I did well, they'd put you on a pedestal. And the fans here have always loved me. In the 1975 World Series, that home run I hit was my gift to the Boston Red Sox fans. Every time I come to this area, when people hear my name, they'll tell me where they were and what they were doing when I hit that home run. It's really nice to be able to be remembered for something good. I was really blessed to be able to hit that home run. And I still like to talk about it. I don't think I'll ever get tired of it."

The 1975 Series ended in game seven when Red Sox manager Darrell Johnson lifted reliever Jim Willoughby for a pinch hitter in the bottom of the eighth, only to have nervous rookie Jim Burton surrender the winning run in the top of the ninth. Three months after the Series was over, the *Globe*'s Gammons and Mike Barnicle were enjoying a brew with Boston television journalist Clark Booth at a now defunct pub in Cambridge. A Bruins game was on the TV, and Gammons, Barnicle, and Booth noticed an elderly gentleman sitting at the end of the bar, staring into space, and drowning himself in twenty-five-cent lagers. When the Bruins game ended, the man turned to the trio of reporters, said, "How the hell could he have taken out Willoughby?"—then passed out.

The late Bill Veeck, a Hall of Fame owner, said in 1980, "Boston fans are pro–Red Sox, but can change their minds in two minutes. The Red Sox only have to fall three runs behind before the front row gives them the thumbs-down. It's a reconstruction of the old Colosseum. In the [1948] play-off game when Lou Boudreau hit the two homers for us [Cleveland Indians], they were cheering for us."

Sportswriters and sportscasters from greater Boston know that, even in lean times, the Red Sox fan base is larger than that of any of the other Boston professional sports teams.

The Boston baseball fan is loud and sophisticated. He recognizes a balk when he sees it, and he cheers when he peeks at the out-of-town scoreboard and sees that the Yankees have fallen behind. He appreciates a well-pitched game by the opponent. He doesn't need a scorecard because he knows all the players on both teams. He might even know the names of the umpires. He saves his wrath for local managers who stay on the job too long, and for overpaid, underachieving, and/or out-of-shape Sox players. He sometimes gets very quiet when the Red Sox are doing well; this is when he sits on his hands and waits for something bad to happen. He is likely to be a she. The Red Sox have more female fans, particularly older women, than any other Boston sports team.

Red Sox vice president in charge of public relations Dick Bresciani says, "I think the Red Sox fans are the longtime New Englanders who go back through generations of following the Red Sox. I think we have more women fans than ever. We have more families and kids groups, and I think that's because it's more affordable [than pro basketball, football, or hockey]."

Johnny Pesky, born in Oregon in 1919, has served the Red Sox since signing his first professional baseball contract in 1939. He's been a Sox player, manager, coach, broadcaster, and assistant general manager. He's never stopped hitting fungoes to Sox infielders. He says, "I think Red Sox fans are great. You take people the way you find 'em. Boston is just the greatest place to play. In Boston, each person has an opinion. When we were playing, if you played well, they applauded, and if you played poorly, they let you know. But they should. There's nothing wrong with that. And if you're thin-skinned about it, you'd better grab a lunch pail and go to work. It never bothered us. You didn't like to hear it, but it just made you run on the field a little harder.

"I wouldn't live anywhere else. Bobby Doerr always asks me how I could not go back to live in Oregon, and I tell him that the people here have been great to me and my family. I'd be a darn fool to go somewhere else."

"The fans here are great," says Lou Gorman, a former general manager who was often harpooned in the local media. "Even when things were going bad for me, when I'd walk through the stands, they were very supportive. When we had our Fan Appreciation Day [May 1995], I couldn't even walk across the street. People stopped me, taking pictures. I was holding babies and signing autographs. I made some mistakes, sure, but the fans were always great. They're the best fans in baseball."

There is a charming continuity about Red Sox Nation. In the 1930s, perhaps the Red Sox's most loyal fan was a young woman from Providence named Lolly Hopkins. Ms. Hopkins was a season-ticket holder who cheered the Sox with a megaphone from her box seat. She adopted second baseman (and future Hall of Famer) Doerr as her favorite player and was often seen giving ballplayers taffy kisses during batting practice. The young girls who accompanied Ms. Hopkins to games became known as the Lollypop Gang. They collected autographs. In the spring of 1992, a member of the Lollypop Gang, a woman born the day the Red Sox played the second game of the 1918 World Series, got Roger Clemens to sign an autograph book she'd been keeping for fifty years. Seventy-three years old, she had Clemens sign the same page where Cy Young had signed when she was a teenager. She said she had no plans to sell the autographs. She said,

"When my time comes, all this stuff goes to my baby." Her "baby" is a forty-something Boston radio personality.

Author Ellery Clark, who wrote three books on the Red Sox, held that one of the obligations of a Red Sox fan is "propagation of the species."

The Red Sox fan is most likely to call a sports talk show and to subscribe to a sports periodical. He rarely bets games. He violently defends the American League. He has been to Cooperstown, and his wife doesn't mind spending money for sports cable. He reads the sports page first. He thinks the baseball box scores are one of the four basic food groups. He owns at least one piece of clothing that has a Red Sox logo. He has a casual interest in the other sports, but the Red Sox are his passion.

Legend holds that there's a devout Red Sox fan who has moved to Thailand yet continues to purchase a pair of bleacher season seats so that he'll have World Series tickets in the event the Red Sox make it back to the World Series. That is faith.

Longtime fan Steve Sheppard says, "Red Sox fans are everywhere. This is a baseball area and we all know that. There's hope every spring. We always think we might be able to do it again. It's like hoping the locusts won't come this year and I won't have to pay the IRS."

Sheppard has good reason for his convictions. Sheppard and Karin Ganga were married at St. Mary's Church in Nantucket on April 19, 1986. They concluded their wedding vows with, "Till death do us part —or until the Red Sox win the World Series." Six months later, with the Red Sox leading the New York Mets, three games to two, Steve and Karin watched game six of the World Series with a group of Nantucket friends. When the Sox took a 5–3 lead into the bottom of the tenth, then retired the first two Mets, there was some tension in the island air. But Sheppard says, "Knowing in my heart of hearts they couldn't do it, I could bet my marriage on it. We were willing to sacrifice our marriage for the good of the team. But even that didn't work. They get you every time. They always find a way to blow it."

Sheppard's cousin, Paul Comerford of Quincy, Massachusetts, is an even bigger baseball nut. Paul and his wife, Marilee Lintner, met at Fenway Park, and their wedding had a distinct baseball theme. There was a replica of home plate at the altar. After the bridal processional, the national anthem was played. Then the best man dusted off home plate and yelled, "Play ball." Comerford claims he was not inspired by the Baltimore Colt fan who made football the theme of his wedding in the classic film *Diner*.

"We actually met because of the Red Sox," says Comerford. "Marilee was supposed to go to Fenway with a friend, but the friend canceled on her, so she went alone. I was living in Boston, and on that night I decided to pop over to the game myself. It was a rainy April night. I was on the way to my seat and she was sitting behind home plate in the grandstand. She had a scorebook in her hands. I was impressed, so I went over and asked her if Rod Carew was playing tonight. What an opening line. I proceeded to sit down in the row behind her. We had our first fight when I said that Dewey [Dwight Evans] was a stiff. Three nights later we started going out, and two and a half years later we were engaged."

When Paul and Marilee had their first child, a daughter, Paige, in the summer of 1995, Paul called the Red Sox and requested an opportunity to have the baby baptized at home plate—"maybe sometime quiet after the World Series is over."

There are Sox nuptial nuts who are not related to Sheppard or Comerford. In 1989, Lori Barrington and Douglas Matthew Green sent out wedding invitations that featured a cover shot of Carlton Fisk celebrating his 1975 game-six World Series homer against the Cincinnati Reds. Fisk's historic clout came on October 21, 1975. Barrington and Green were married on the fourteenth anniversary of the famous homer and used the baseball theme as a hook for their wedding. Their wedding invitation cover, showing Fisk celebrating, read, "October 21, 1975—A Great Moment." Inside the invitation, the headline read, "October 21, 1989, Another Great Moment." This was followed by the traditional notice of the parents of the bride and groom requesting the honor of your presence at the marriage of their children. In another part of the country, the invitation might have been considered bizarre. In New England in 1989, it was evidence of one more Red Sox couple unable to let go of the past or dream about any future without including the Boston ball club.

In the days after Boston's horrific loss in the 1978 American League one-game play-off game, the late John Cheever told the *Globe*'s Diane

White, "All literary men are Red Sox fans. To be a Yankee fan in literary society is to endanger your life." That might explain why the *Boston Globe* in the fall of 1986 was able to put together a special section featuring baseball essays from George Will, John Updike, Stephen King, Robert Parker, David Halberstam, George V. Higgens, Martin F. Nolan, Doris Kearns Goodwin, A. Bartlett Giamatti, Geoffrey Wolff, and Ward Just. Updike admitted, "The Red Sox were the team I had chosen, and one's choices, once made, generate a self-justifying and self-sustaining inertia. . . . The memoirs of a Red Sox fan tend to sound sour, a litany of disappointments and mistakes going back to the day when Babe Ruth was traded."

In the summer of '95, the Red Sox got a lot of support from the rock-'n'-roll community. On a Friday night in June, Bob Dylan performed for a crowd at Boston's Harborlights Pavilion and said, "I hear the Red Sox will win the World Series." In front of a sellout crowd at Great Woods, Elton John dedicated "Rocket Man" to Roger Clemens. When the Sox played in Cleveland, Clemens was the guest of Meat Loaf at the Rock Hall of Fame.

The Red Sox even inspire verse from those who are not literary men. I first became aware of this when opening mail sent to the *Globe* after the 1975 World Series. It seemed that every bleacher creature was inspired to write sonnets about the Sox romantic near-miss in the fall of '75. Of all the unsolicited, creative correspondence, my personal favorite was "A Week on the Concord and Merrimack Rivers with Ned Martin."

In 1990, a loyal *Globe* reader sent me a transcript of a Roger Clemens press conference. My correspondent broke a rambling Clemens answer (the only kind Roger knows) into thirty lines of verse, then explained, "Little did we know that Roger—a longtime student of T. S. Eliot's poetry—speaks in blank verse."

The BoSox Club, the Sox official booster club of more than five hundred members, gets together for lunch at Anthony's Pier 4 about ten times per year. Visiting players and coaches are encouraged to attend these meetings. The club holds an awards luncheon every September. Yankee manager Bob Lemon once remarked, "The Red Sox get more people for a weekday lunch than the Oakland A's get for a ball game."

Frank Geishecker, former BoSox Club president, says, "I joined in 1967, the year the club started. Technically, the club started in the fall of 1966 under Dom DiMaggio, Ken Coleman, and [former Sox public relations director] Bill Crowley. In 1966, attendance was atrocious. That was the purpose of the club—to get the business community involved in supporting the team. I came on the board of directors in 1975. I was president in 1989. It's been a lot of fun. The BoSox Club was patterned after the Wahoo Club in Cleveland. It is said that we are the largest sports booster club in the country. For the most part, the team is receptive."

In addition to the BoSox Club, there is a New York-based organization known as BLOHARDS—Benevolent Loyal Order of Honorable Ancient Red Sox Diehard Sufferers. There are plenty of other informal fan clubs, including one that honors the Red Sox Hall of Shame and a Washington-based Willie Tasby Club. Tasby is distinct because he played for the Washington Senators, Baltimore Orioles, and Red Sox. The Tasby Club's insignia is a lightning bolt because Willie once removed his spikes while playing center field during a thunderstorm. Sox fans also support an underground scorecard (sold outside Fenway on game days), and there's a healthy subscription for a monthly publication entitled *Diehard*.

Red Sox CEO John Harrington says, "I do have to say that ours are the most loyal and intense fans. We have fans that have been brought up on one hundred years of tradition, passed down from prior generations. Because of ever seeking the gonfalon, it becomes a Don Quixote–type search for the grail. I think it adds another dimension to the intensity. It's unlike what you have with the newer franchises. In other cities, the fans believe they are as loyal and intense and knowledgeable. But I believe the New England fans are more knowledgeable, intense, and loyal than anywhere else."

For all of its broad-based appeal, Red Sox Nation comes up short in the minority community. Earlier in this chapter, Halberstam spoke of baseball as "inclusionary." Unfortunately, this hasn't held for Sox fans. Few people of color are in Red Sox Nation, and there are some good reasons for the Sox lack of a minority fans.

In the late 1920s and early 1930s, the Negro leagues provided real competition for the Red Sox and Braves. Black semipro teams attracted crowds of ten thousand for games in the South End and Roxbury sections of Boston. One of the top attractions was a submarine right-handed pitcher named Will Jackman. Black semipro ball began to disappear after Jackie Robinson broke the color barrier in major league baseball in 1947, but the Red Sox did not pick up a larger portion of the baseball fans from Boston's black community. There is ample evidence that the Sox were a racist organization throughout the forties, fifties, and sixties. Jackie Robinson, Sam Jethroe, and Marvin Williamson, three black players, were given a phony tryout at Fenway in 1945, and veteran reporter Clif Keane remembers, "Somebody up in the back of the building yelled, 'Get those niggers off the field.' " The Sox rejected an opportunity to sign a young Willie Mays for $5,000 in 1949. Boston was the last big league team to bring a black player to the major leagues (Pumpsie Green, 1959). Sox owner Tom Yawkey, a plantation owner from South Carolina, hired several Southerners who were decidedly racist, including two-time manager Mike Higgins. In the early 1980s, the Sox allowed members of the Winter Haven Elks Club to give courtesy passes to all white members of the Red Sox team. Coach Tommy Harper spoke out, was fired, and eventually collected an out-of-court settlement after filing a racial discrimination suit against the team. At the start of the 1991 season, the Red Sox had just one black player on the team, outfielder Ellis Burks.

All this left its mark in what is historically a racially divided city. Fenway has never been a place where minorities feel welcome or comfortable, even today. Sox management in recent years has made efforts in the minority community, but that hasn't translated into attendance at the ballpark. It's been said that a Fenway gathering resembles the crowd at a rugby match in Pretoria. In 1991, *Globe* interns counted the number of blacks in the house during a Red Sox home stand and found no more than 80 black fans at any game. On a Friday night against the Blue Jays, Globe reporters counted 71 black faces out of a crowd of 34,032. That's .2 percent of the crowd.

Just as there are few minorities, there are few high rollers at Fenway. The Sox have a lot of fans with political and financial clout, but the Fenway stands are not cluttered with the chic elite. Celebrity Sox fans tend to be low-key. A day at Fenway is not like a night at the LA

Forum where Dyan Cannon and Jack Nicholson applaud from the front row. Boston has no time or tolerance for trendy fans, and the ballpark has something to do with this. Fenway is a great equalizer. The rich and powerful fight the same traffic, eat the same soggy hot dogs, and endure the same Sox pain as everyone else. Sox celebrity regulars are Stephen Jay Gould (author and Harvard professor), Donnie Wahlberg (of New Kids on the Block), and Seiji Ozawa, conductor of the Boston Symphony. Not exactly Woody Allen, Arnold Schwarzenegger, and Madonna.

Author Stephen King is a Sox season-ticket holder and sits behind home plate. King's got a scraggly look that would provoke bookstore owners to make him empty his bag if he walked into their shops. He's a diligent scorekeeper and enjoys total anonymity in the Fenway stands. There is nothing casual or trendy about King's interest in the Red Sox. Listen to his recollection of the infamous Sox-Yankee playoff game: "Dent, '78. I was teaching college and gave everybody the day off. It was like getting a Big Mac and finding a dead rat inside. After that game I put a sign on the office door: 'No class, no office hours, on account of depression.' It was the worst year of my life. I went out and wrote *Pet Sematary*, my gloomiest book. I loathe the Yankees. . . . I was stuck with the Red Sox from birth. I'm used to all the chokes and all the folds. I think Red Sox fans have been athletically molested. We have a tremendous complex."

The Sox even have a voice on the Supreme Court. Five days before he was sworn in as a justice, New Hampshire native David Souter said, "After 1967 I said I'm never going to let myself get excited again about the Red Sox, and I have not done so." Souter's mother, Helen, saw Babe Ruth play for the Red Sox.

In 1994, *Washington Post* columnist E. J. Dionne Jr. wrote, "Being a Democrat is like being a Red Sox fan: it means being affiliated with a glorious institution that always contrives to self-destruct and disappoint."

Robert Reich, secretary of labor in the Clinton administration, got involved in the great baseball strike of 1994 and tried not to take sides. He said, "I've always been a Red Sox fan. I was born a Red Sox fan; I will die a Red Sox fan. You have to be a certain kind of masochist to be a Red Sox fan."

The Red Sox have always been part of pop culture. Ali MacGraw talked about Carl Yastrzemski in *Goodbye, Columbus*. In the box-office hit *A Few Good Men*, starring Jack Nicholson, Demi Moore, and Tom Cruise, Cruise wears a Red Sox hat while taking batting practice. In real life, on March 25, 1995, Nicholson attended the West Regional Final between Connecticut and UCLA, wearing . . . a Boston Red Sox cap.

One of the most beloved characters on American TV was Sam Malone, the barkeep on *Cheers* played by Ted Danson. Everybody at the bar knew how Sammy became famous. He was a pitcher for the Red Sox, a guy who gave up the long home runs. His nickname was "Mayday Malone." In 1993, *Sports Illustrated* ran a cover story on Sam Malone, (fictional) former Red Sox pitcher. John Harrington, Red Sox de facto owner, participated in a taping for the 275th and final episode of *Cheers*. In the taping, Harrington was asked what bizarre ending he'd like for the show: "Bring Sam Malone out of retirement, come out of the bullpen, and save the seventh game of the 1993 World Series . . . ending the Curse of the Bambino."

Author Halberstam says, "I started out with the Yankees because I grew up in the Bronx, seven blocks from the stadium, and that was the first thing I saw. But in World War Two we lived in Winsted, Connecticut, and it is really in the crease in the zone. We had Mel Allen and Curt Gowdy both. There were different spots in our house where we could pick up the Yankees or the Red Sox. I had an uncle who'd come up from Tennessee, and he had a commercial paint store in Boston. And he bought season's tickets to the Red Sox. And he came down and visited us in Winsted. I could not believe that someone in our family had season's tickets to the Red Sox. And he could not believe that he had this ten-year-old nephew that knew every batting average. He really did have season's tickets, right behind first base. How could you not root for Pesky, Doerr, Williams, Dominic DiMaggio? They just jumped out at you. So I was this Yankee fan with an odd ambivalence of liking the Red Sox as well. I'm a half-breed. Baseball, who you root for is not a choice. It's where you grew up. You don't have any choice over your genes, and you don't have any choice over who you root for."

The clergy have always been aligned with the Red Sox, and why not? Father Gerard Barry, a seventy-something priest raised in South Boston and now parish priest at Saint Bernard's in West Newton, says, "Those who deserve love the least need it the most. Our Red Sox."

In 1978, the College of Cardinals assembled at the Vatican to elect a new pope. Boston television journalist Clark Booth (WCVB) covered the event and was mildly surprised when the late Humberto Cardinal Medeiros sought him out to ask how the Red Sox had done the previous day. Booth remembers, "I was standing in a courtyard next to St. Peter's. I was waiting for them to come out. Finally, there was a recess and Medeiros came out and asked, 'How are the Red Sox doing?' Then he picked up his robe, like a woman would pull up her skirt, and he revealed his red socks. He said, 'Look, I've got my red socks on. I'm with the Red Sox.'"

Fay Vincent, the last commissioner of baseball, is a Red Sox fan, just like his predecessor, A. Bartlett Giamatti. In the summer of 1991, when Vincent was still commissioner, he came to Fenway Park and told a story about going to a Catholic mass in Cooperstown, New York. "The priest pulled out a Red Sox cap and put it on after the service," Vincent said. "And he told me, 'See, I've learned about suffering and the meaning of the cross in more ways than one.'"

More than any other group of fans, Sox watchers are obsessed with the hereafter.

Mark Scott of Lincoln, Massachusetts, says, "My mother was born on the twenty eighth of July in 1918, the summer that the Red Sox last won the World Series. My brothers and I all said it would be like Mark Twain and Halley's comet, that they'd win again . . . the year our mother decided to die. In 1990, three days after my mom's seventy-second birthday, my brother Stan fell to his death in a climbing accident. The last thing he had said to me was 'How 'bout those Red Sox!'"

Scott pledges that when the Sox finally win it, "I'm going to sneak into that seventh game of the World Series. . . . I'm going to take a small matchbox of my brother Stan's ashes and spread them on his field of dreams."

Comedian Ray Goulding of Bob and Ray declared, "On my tombstone it is going to say 'Cause of Death, Boston Red Sox.'"

Steve Nazro, director of events for the new FleetCenter, says; "My father, Frank Nazro, died on December first, 1993. He loved baseball so much. He was a salesman for Blue Cross and drove more than one hundred miles a day. Those were the days when it was all day games, so he always listened to the Sox broadcasts. After he retired, his sight deteriorated and he was practically blind. He was living in Peterborough, New Hampshire, and I'd go up to visit him every other week— always on a Saturday or Sunday. When I came into the house, I would see him, in his rocker, with his nose pressed up against the television screen, trying to watch the game. Eventually, no matter what size the screen, he couldn't see. But he never missed a game. It was important to him because he liked the pace of baseball. He had knowledge. If the announcer said somebody hit a home run off the second deck in Detroit, he could visualize that. I knew I had to listen to the game so I could talk with him about it."

Sportswriter Kevin Dupont, now with the *Boston Globe*, formerly with the *Boston Herald*, wrote these words about his dad in September of 1978: "My father sits at night with one light on, listening to what he has heard for years, what he has grown to accept . . . listening to Ned Martin and Jim Woods tell him how, once again, it isn't going to happen. The Red Sox aren't going to win a world championship. . . . The radio is relaxation. The cigarette, ever-glowing, is more relaxation. In some ways, losing is relaxation. . . . The season comes. The season goes."

Mel Dupont died in 1989. Still waiting.

On March 15, 1992, Lulu E. Royce of Roslindale, Massachusetts, died at the age of seventy-nine. According to her obituary in the *Boston Globe*, she had eight children, seventeen grandchildren, and ten great-grandchildren. Her obit concluded with these two lines: "A devoted Red Sox fan. Maybe my boys will do it this year, Lulu."

Lulu's boys did not do it. In 1992 the Red Sox finished last.

CHAPTER THREE

OCTOBER IS THE CRUELEST MONTH

▶ ◆ ◆ ◆ ◆ ◆ ◆ ◆ ◆ ◀

◆ New England is about seasons. Few other parts of America experience such diverse weather. Local television stations across the country put "weathermen" on the evening news. In greater Boston, the TV stations hire *meteorologists*. New England is where snowbound winter gives way to rainy spring, which yields a summer of blazing heat and humidity, followed by the golden glow and dry air of autumn. It makes life hard in many ways. New Englanders need clothes for every possible outdoor situation. We need bathing suits, ski boots, tweed jackets, raincoats, down parkas, short-sleeve shirts, corduroys, rubbers, sweaters, T-shirts, cutoffs, and a pair of thongs. We learn to drive on snow, ice, wet leaves, frost heaves, and pothole/minefield roadways. Our weather is subject to constant change, meaning we automatically prepare to cancel picnics, ball games, and every other outdoor activity. We grow accustomed to disappointment. We learn to cope when we don't get our way. We become cynical, but we also respect the good days. We enjoy the sunshine when it's here because it might be raining a half hour from now. We take nothing for granted.

The seasons are what make New England a special place to live. Watching our trees and gardens, we see the circle of life unfold annually. True New Englanders, those who endure the hard times in exchange for the stimulus of the seasons, would not trade our goofy climate for others that are more comfortable and predictable, yet less rigorous. Traveling in Florida in October, we miss our rainbow foliage. Flying west to Pasadena in December, we miss our white Christmas. Too much good, warm weather lulls the mind into a sleepy state of unmotivated mellow. Has any creative idea ever been spawned in regions of perfect predictable weather? No. We believe it is better to experience the highs and lows that come with the hot and cold. We believe one should *earn* the good days. There is no entitlement.

The Red Sox are a perfect fit for the region because the Boston baseball year can be divided into quadrants, one for each New England season.

Spring training is good for the Red Sox because there's infinite warm weather and hope. Sox fans find great comfort when the team is 0–0 throughout February and March. Red Sox summers are like New England summers: some are warm and wonderful, and others are hot, humid, and rainy. In this sense, a Red Sox season ticket is the same gamble as a deposit on a $3,000-a-week beach house in Nantucket; it could be a bargain or an infuriating waste of money. Traditionally, autumn has been cruel to the Red Sox. Sad but true, the Sox fall in the fall. There's irony here. In terms of weather, September and October provide the reward for weather-beaten Bostonians, but the fall is a miserable season for Red Sox fans. It is the season of the witch. The Red Sox and the foliage haven't peaked simultaneously since 1918. Red Sox winter starts the minute the previous season ends, usually in early October. In most years, Sox fans are anxious to finish the season because, once again, the Townies have not lived up to expectations. By late September and early October, Boston fans are already thinking about next year. As the Red Sox play out the string, citizens of Red Sox Nation debate which players are worth bringing back for next season. The Red Sox always look better on paper than they do on the field, and in winter there is no reality to dampen next year's prospects.

All of which brings us back to spring. The beginning. The long hello. Spring training is unique to baseball. No other sport insists on a massive franchise airlift to prepare for a new season. In an age of fitness awareness and year-round conditioning, there's something redundant about baseball's lengthy rehearsal. Most of today's players stay in shape in the off-season. Millions of dollars are at stake and hundreds of hungry young players are ready to take jobs from the veterans. Established ballplayers can't let their bodies melt to mush during the winter banquet circuit. It's doubtful that today's baseball players need six weeks and 32 practice games to prepare for a six-month, 162-game season. When a labor dispute shortened spring training to three weeks in 1990, the regular season was unaffected; games went on without any drop in the quality of play. Ditto for 1995 when the "real" ballplayers reported April 5 and started the season three weeks later.

Although it is established that spring training is too long and slow, these elements make baseball's preseason special. The diamond game has no twenty four-second clock, no overtime, no two-minute drill, no five-minute major, and no twenty-second time-out. Baseball is not governed by the man-made timepiece, and springtime in Florida is the slowest time for our slowest game. Young ballplayers mingle with old fans. It is nothing like the big-city, luxury-hotel, airport-to-ballpark, autograph-for-sale atmosphere that pollutes the regular season. In Florida, the game is slow, the traffic is slow, even the fast food is slow. Boston baseball reporters always took some small delight noting that the Winter Haven (Florida) Taco Bell franchise was perhaps the only fast-food joint in America where the drive-through window was on the *passenger* side of the car.

In July and August, your favorite ballplayers have no time and little patience. They're getting ripped in the newspapers and booed by the fans. There is the daily pressure of the pennant chase, and a weariness brought on by nonstop travel and games. A moat separates participants from customers. But fans find a completely different set of rules in Fort Myers in March. On the Gulf of Mexico, diehards who escape the slush and rush of the North encounter athletes unencumbered by the demands of July's Fenway. Autographs are easy to get, and it's not unusual to bump into your favorite player at the airport or the pool. You might find yourself standing next to Mo Vaughn in the eight-items-or-less aisle at the Winn-Dixie checkout counter. You might wind up playing miniature golf next to Tim Naehring. This is the time of year when no one is in a hurry. Ballplayers and fans share the sense that there is nowhere else to be, nothing else to do.

Before the start of the spring games, fans come to the park to watch still-life workouts. They watch the ballplayers stretch. They watch pickoff plays and pitchers covering first base. They watch batting practice. They watch the ospreys build nests in the light towers. It sounds boring, but for those who love hardball, it is enough. During the spring lockout of 1990, devout fans came to Winter Haven's Chain o' Lakes Park just to watch the sprinklers soak the field. Perhaps, like Kevin Costner in *Field of Dreams*, they were able to see a game that the unwashed masses could not.

Traditionally, food has been a staple of spring-training conversation. Since there is so little to do, most players, fans, and scribes are constantly in search of good places to eat. Much of the patter around the pool and the batting cage concerns last night's dinner. *How was the service? What did you order? Were the prices okay? Do they take reservations?* It is the backbeat of spring baseball in Florida. Everyone wants to know where you ate last night and where you'll be dining tonight.

Baseball's preseason is a public relations bonanza for major-league ball clubs. Optimistic reports from Florida and Arizona promote hope and sell tickets back home in the frozen North. In New England, we are convinced anew that this is the year. The Red Sox have not won a World Series since 1918, but when the Sox start spring training, it's easy to dismiss reality in the name of potential. When you watch the Red Sox, the best time is the time of anticipation. Longtime fans know that the Sox are never better than they are in spring training—they are infinite before the games begin. It is when the games start that the Sox find trouble.

Elsewhere in New England, February and March are quiet days for Boston's pro sports fans. The Patriots are out of season. There are no NFL play-off games on which to wager. The Bruins skate in circles for one more interminable month before the games start to mean something. In the 1990s, the Celtics have been adrift in a sea of mediocrity, either missing the play-offs or bowing out in the first round. The annual Beanpot hockey tourney (Boston College, Northeastern, Harvard, and Boston University in a round-robin) is over in mid-February, and in the weeks before the college basketball tournament gets going, there's no good material for sports talk czars.

This is when the Red Sox provide.

In New England, the Sox simply never go out of style. The Sox are news. And in late February and all of March, finally the Sox are back in uniform, back on Florida's fields of green. For those who starve without box scores, there is nothing more fulfilling than the newspaper containing the first preseason summary. Springtime boxes are filled with the names of has-beens and wanna-bes. Star players sometimes shower and go golfing after three innings of work, but the absence of a regular lineup doesn't diminish the thrill of seeing that Roger Clemens fanned five in his first three-inning test of 1995. And did new acquisition Jose Canseco hit any home runs?

Since 1920, the Sox have held spring training in Hot Springs, Arkansas; Tampa, Florida; San Antonio; New Orleans; Bradenton, Florida; Pensacola, Florida; Savannah, Georgia; Sarasota, Florida; Medford (that was during World War II); Baltimore; Pleasantville, New Jersey; Scottsdale, Arizona; Winter Haven, Florida; and Fort Myers, Florida.

The spring season has its share of generic stories, guaranteed to fill columns of the *Globe* and log airtime on local television stations. Baseball readers brace themselves for the well-worn, time-tested "He's late because of visa problems" story. Everyone knows that ballplayers from Venezuela and the Dominican Republic have had since October to plan their return, but there's always at least one fellow who uses government red tape as an excuse for tardiness. In 1992, the Red Sox waited so long for Dominican pitcher Cecilio Guante that it became something of a joke. He was a baseball Godot. In the final week of spring training, Cecilio finally appeared in Florida. But by then, the Sox had no place for him.

Other annual spring staples include the player who comes to camp overweight and is put on a diet; the aging player coming off a bad season who announces that he worked out all winter and is—at the age of forty—"in the best shape of my career"; the contract dispute/holdout story; the manager-in-the-hot-seat story; the "play-me-or-trade-me" story; and the can't-miss-phenom story.

Throughout the years, the Red Sox have produced some extraordinary springtime entertainment. Leave it to the Sox to put their unique spin on typical spring yarns.

The first great Red Sox spring story involved none other than Babe Ruth. In the winter of 1918–19, Sox owner Harry Frazee switched the team's training site from Hot Springs, Arkansas, to Tampa, Flor-ida. Because of postwar complications, spring training was delayed until mid-March, and most of the Sox made the trip south on a coastal steamer that sailed from New York. Ruth wasn't on the boat because he was holding out for more money. A pitching hero with Boston's 1918 World Champs, the Bambino was threatening to leave baseball and become a professional boxer. He claimed he had a $5,000 offer to fight a heavyweight contender named Gunboat Smith. The threat and the holdout won Ruth a three-year, $30,000 contract. Only after sign-ing the deal did the Babe take a midnight train from New York to Tampa.

In the Sox's first exhibition game at the Tampa fairgrounds dia-mond, Ruth batted against New York Giants pitcher George Smith and hit a home run that traveled between five hundred and six hun-dred feet. No one had ever seen a batted ball travel so far. Ruth already had twenty big-league homers to his credit, and it was decided that he'd be converted to a full-time outfielder. The rest is baseball history.

Not all the spring tales are happy stories. In 1932, when the Sox were training in Savannah, friends of Boston pitcher Big Ed Morris (a nineteen-game winner in 1928) held a going-away party for the hurler in Brewton, Alabama. Morris got into a fight with a gasoline-station operator, suffered a knife wound in the chest, and died in a Florida hospital.

In 1938, a skinny teenager from San Diego put on a Red Sox uniform and stepped into the batter's box for some practice swings in Sarasota. A photographer, anxious to record the moment, asked the kid to find a cap. "The people who see this are going to be told they're watching big-leaguers, not sandlotters," the photographer said. The kid pulled a cap out of his pocket, put it on his head, and replied, "Is this all it takes to be a big-leaguer? And I thought it was going to be tough." All the veterans made fun of him. The teen outfielder was a good-looking slugger, but he needed more seasoning. When he was shipped to the minors, the teenager pledged, "I'll be back. Tell that to all of them. [Joe] Vosmik, [Doc] Cramer, and [Ben] Chapman think I'm just a fresh young punk, don't they? Well, you can tell them I'll be back, and I'll make more money in a single year than the three of them put together."

And he did. Ted Williams became one of the greatest hitters who ever lived.

In 1959 the Sox moved from Sarasota to Scottsdale, and in the spring of 1964, another skinny teenager launched some long home runs. Tony Conigliaro was local. He'd played Little League ball in East Boston and starred at St. Mary's High in Lynn. In Arizona in the spring of '64, he was accompanied by his father, his mother, and his brother. The 1964 Red Sox were terrible, but Curt Gowdy kept telling us about the tape-measure shots of the local boy, Tony C. It gave Sox fans something to root for, and they were rewarded when Conigliaro came north with the team and homered in his first Fenway plate appearance.

In 1966, Thomas Yawkey moved his team's spring site from Scottsdale to Winter Haven. Veteran pitcher Earl Wilson, a black man, was turned away from two Winter Haven nightspots because of his race. Wilson told a couple of sportswriters about the incidents and later that year was traded to Detroit for Don Demeter. Wilson won forty games over the next two seasons. Demeter played twenty games for the Red Sox, hitting .279, before he retired because of a heart condition.

For twenty-seven spring seasons, Winter Haven provided Sox fans with heaping helpings of hope, hype, and hysterics. In a quirky way, there was something magical about the place. Situated in the middle of the state (we've never proven this with aerial reconnaissance, but it's probably farther from ocean waters than any other place in Florida), Winter Haven is a city of trailer parks, fast-food emporiums, and fruit stands. The trucks have gun racks and the women have tattoos. When people tell you they are from L.A., they mean Lake Alfred.

In Winter Haven in 1967, rookie manager Dick Williams predicted, "We'll win more than we lose." Everybody laughed. The Sox had lost one hundred games in '65 and finished ninth in '66, but Williams was right. He brought home a 100–1 shot, and the 1967 Red Sox, the Cardiac Kids, won Boston's first pennant since 1946.

Winter Haven is where Luis Tiant was pulled over for speeding and told the police, "I was bringing some heat." It's where Ted Williams played tennis with Carl Yastrzemski. It's where Bill Lee announced that Dennis Eckersley had been acquired from Cleveland in a six-player deal. Lee ran in from the right-field bullpen and told reporters, "Send lawyers, guns, and money, the shit has hit the fan." In 1978, a minor-league pitcher named Bobby Sprowl was shot in the arm when a doctor's gun in a next-door apartment went off.

In 1984, when Mark Fidrych was attempting his final comeback, several of Fidrych's Northborough buddies got into a brawl at the Holiday Inn hotel bar. When the fight was over, Fidrych was still standing, but the lead singer of Johnny Carro and the Flames had a busted nose.

No one could have been prepared for the strange spring sagas of Dennis "Oil Can" Boyd. A volatile young man from Mississippi, the Can was a productive right-handed pitcher for several seasons in the mid-eighties, but he made much of his news off the field. The Can bought a home in Winter Haven and spent most of his winters near Chain o' Lakes Park. Sometimes ill (he had a mysterious liver ailment in the spring of 1986), often AWOL, always controversial (through the years he fired several charges of racism at teammates and club officials), Boyd was good copy, and reporters beat a path to his Winter Haven home. One year, the Sox issued a press release stating that Boyd was undergoing psychiatric testing. In the spring of 1987, Boyd erupted when local police came to the Winter Haven ballpark to ask about some overdue video rentals. A list of the missing tapes appeared in the local newspaper, and the Can was slightly embarrassed when everybody read that his cassettes included *Nudes in Limbo* and *Sex-Cetera*. It was statistical wizard Chuck Waseleski who dubbed the event "the Can's Film Festival."

As good as the Can was, Wade Boggs has supplied more springtime excitement than any Red Sox player of the last half century. Boggs is a Florida native (Tampa) and is best known as the perennial American League batting champ. In 1988, his career was sidetracked by a $6-million palimony suit filed by his former mistress, Margo Adams. In the spring of 1989, Adams's tell-all, show-all interview/profile appeared in the pages of *Penthouse* magazine just as the Sox were landing in Winter Haven. In the article, Adams talked of the "sexual frenzy" that gripped the Sox spring site in the final week of training camp. That was news to all those who'd spent time in Winter Haven since 1966. The Sox encountered more embarrassment when Boggs and his wife agreed to an interview with Barbara Walters for a *20/20* segment.

Winter Haven folks won't soon forget the sight of Walters and her camera crew sitting in the family section behind home plate at Chain o' Lakes Park. Boggs went on live TV and said he had a sexual addiction. Boyd said, "Who needs the psychiatrist now?"

Boggs made headlines again in 1992, the team's final spring in Winter Haven. After eating dinner with his wife at the popular Nick Christy's restaurant (where a larger-than-life painting of Nick greeted each customer), Boggs somehow fell out of his Jeep while Debbie Boggs was pulling the vehicle out of the restaurant parking lot. Boggs tumbled out the passenger side onto U.S. Route 17, where his elbow was run over by the back wheel of the vehicle. Showing scars from a steel-belted radial, Boggs quipped, "I'm the white Irving Fryar."

In addition to Walters, other celebrities visited the Red Sox in Florida. In 1986, Pulitzer Prize–winning author Doris Kearns Goodwin, working on a *People* magazine profile of Boggs, played catch with her sons on the lawn of the Winter Haven Holiday Inn. In 1988, presidential candidate Michael Dukakis took batting practice against the soft serves of Red Sox pitching coach Bill Fischer. In 1992, candidate Bill Clinton introduced himself to Sox manager and fellow Southerner Butch Hobson.

The Sox relocated to swanky Fort Myers in the spring of 1993. The site is less intimate than Winter Haven, but a nice beach is thirty minutes away, and Fort Myers has its own airport. Sox outfielder Mike Greenwell owns an amusement park in town.

City of Palms Park is new and beautiful, but in the spring of 1993, Sox infielders complained that the field was too hard, and when shortstop John Valentin aired his complaint, he was critiqued by Fort Myers's mayor, Wilbur Smith. Another spring first. As far as we know, Chicago mayor/boss Richard J. Daley never ripped Ernie Banks. Mayor Smith was ubiquitous in the first years of the Sox stay in Florida, and one player pledged, "I want to be around here long enough to see him indicted."

Like Boyd and Boggs, Roger Clemens has been a perpetual spring story. He is the one who failed to report on time in 1992 for manager Butch Hobson's first day on the job. When he was supposed to be working out with his teammates, Clemens was signing autographs at the Velvet Elvis, a bar in Houston. Reached at home in Houston, he said, "Why should I go down there and stand around spitting sun-flower seeds?"

In the spring of 1987, a young Clemens (then the reigning MVP and Cy Young winner) stormed out of camp over a contract dispute. I was covering the Red Sox for the *Globe* in Winter Haven and spent a lot of time and money trying to locate Clemens and his agents, Alan and Randy Hendricks. More than a week into the holdout, reporter Steve Fainaru (then of the *Hartford Courant*) and I hatched a plan that we felt would deliver some news from the Clemens camp. The Red Sox were scheduled to play an exhibition game against the Toronto Blue Jays in Dunedin, Florida. We had reason to believe that the Hendricks Brothers ("Jimi" and "Elrod" in the eyes of *Herald* colum-nist George Kimball) were holed up in a Holiday Inn at Clearwater Beach. En route to the Sox game in Dunedin, we decided that our time would be better spent staking out the elusive Hendricks brothers. *Globe* columnist Mike Madden was going to be in Dunedin, and I figured there was no sense having two people at a boring exhibition game when there was a chance to break real news in Clearwater. Fainaru and I were pretty pleased with ourselves when we wheeled into the Beach hotel and saw a gold Town Car in the parking lot. The Hendricks brothers were traveling in a gold Town Car. Certainly, the car had to be theirs. What luck. Only the dopes had gone to Dunedin. We were sitting on the story, waiting for the brothers to deliver Clem-ens to us. I checked into the hotel, bought a pair of shorts at the gift shop, and called my boss, Vince Doria. I told Vince that Madden would be able to cover any baseball news at Dunedin. I was at Clear-water, staking out the Hendricks brothers, keeping an eye on their gold Town Car. I told the boss I'd call him as soon as we had anything.

Meanwhile, back in Dunedin, Madden bumped into American League publicist Phyllis Merhige. "Where are Dan and Steve?" she asked. "I expected to see them here with the Red Sox."

Madden whispered in her ear, "Don't tell anybody, but they're staking out the Hendricks brothers in Clearwater. They think they might get to Clemens today."

"Mike," said Phyllis, "the Hendricks brothers are right here in the press room, eating lunch with Haywood Sullivan."

Madden got the story. We got a lofty hotel bill. Only the dopes . . .

It was left to Red Sox general manager Lou Gorman to put everything in perspective the day writers informed him that Clemens had walked out of camp. We demanded an official response. Gorman thought for a moment, pondered the cloudless sky above, and said, "The sun will rise, the sun will set, and I'll have lunch."

Baseball, sunshine, relaxation, a nonstory, and food. It was the ultimate spring-training quote.

► ◆ ◄

Opening day at Fenway is the next big event of any Red Sox year. All over New England, there are empty chairs in classrooms, board rooms, and office cubicles. Phones go unanswered. There are funerals for grandmothers who may be at the game themselves. Dogs eat everybody's homework.

It's an unofficial Back Bay holiday. Around the ballpark, babies are born at Beth Israel Hospital, kids from Simmons and MIT blow their monthly allowance at Tower Records, steel wheels screech as Green Line cars roll into Kenmore Station, and Boston cabbies get a lot of short fares between Yawkey Way and Boylston Street. Gas stations and fast-food joints sublet their lots for ball-game parking. Across the street from the ticket windows on Yawkey Way, hundreds of fans browse the Twins Souvenir shop.

And when public address announcer Leslie Sterling says, "Good afternoon, ladies and gentlemen, boys and girls . . . ," Boston baseball fans take comfort in the knowledge that all is well with the universe. Boston's venerable hardball museum has opened its doors for another season. It's New Year's Day. If you're a Sox fan, it's the first day of the rest of your strife.

Opening day is the day when there's red, white, and blue bunting hanging from Fenway's walls. The bunting is reserved for the opener and for postseason play. In New York City, middle-aged men associate bunting with golden autumn afternoons at Yankee Stadium, circa 1950. At Fenway, bunting in the background means opening day. A Boston woman named Jane Alden annually delivers the patriotic linens to Fenway. She is the Betsy Ross of Fenway Park.

"She took over for her father, who worked into his eighties," says

Red Sox groundskeeper Joe Mooney. "She calls us every year and asks if we want it. A lot of the pieces have been stolen over the years. I think she had the most stolen during the '86 World Series."

In the 1990s, the Fenway opener gets the royal treatment because there have been so many of them and because there are only so many left. Fans in Michigan know that venerable Tiger Stadium is endangered. Soon it will be only Wrigley and Fenway, eyeballing one another, wondering which will be the last one standing.

Within a few weeks of the home opener, there's a game that's uniquely Fenway. On the third Monday of every April, the Red Sox play host to the only morning game played in baseball each season. It is Patriots Day, the day of the running of the Boston Marathon. Every Patriots Day for one hundred years, roadrunners have been chugging the twenty-six miles from Hopkinton to Boston. The first Red Sox Marathon Day game was played in 1902 when thirty-five-year-old Cy Young hurled the Sox to a 7–6 victory at the Huntington Avenue Grounds. For a few years the Sox played doubleheaders on Marathon Day, but in 1968 they started a tradition of playing one game, starting at 11:05 A.M. "It's early, but it's fun," said Sox outfielder Mike Greenwell. "It's part of tradition, and that makes it worth doing."

Fenway's annual Patriots Day game has confounded American League opponents for decades. Getting up for a morning baseball game makes for a drastic change in a ballplayer's routine. Big league ballplayers, like Broadway performers, stay up late and sleep late the following morning. There's a conventional wisdom that a day game following a night game is the toughest parlay in baseball.

"Not true," former Baltimore Orioles manager Earl Weaver said many years ago. "The toughest thing in baseball is a day game after a day game. The reason is simple. After a day game, you have so much more time to ruin yourself, going out to bars and staying up late. Your ballplayers have too much free time, too much drinking time. Then they have to get up early the next morning to play."

In Chicago, baseball fans have for years used the Weaver theory to explain the Cubs' annual difficulties. The Cubs have rarely contended for first place, and some believe the team's rigorous schedule may have something to do with that. The Cubs play more day games than any other team in the majors—hence more day games after day games.

Patriots Day in Boston presents the ultimate back-to-back challenge. It's a morning game after a day game. Ballplayers abuse themselves for all hours after Sunday's afternoon game in the Hub, then rise with the roosters to be ready to play at 11 A.M.

On Patriots Day at Fenway, both managers usually skip batting practice and customary infield drills. Players are still rubbing their eyes when the first pitch is thrown. One hour after the start of the morning game, the gun goes off in Hopkinton, unleashing a sea of fat-free athletes bound for downtown Boston. The marathon route takes runners down Beacon Street and through Kenmore Square. From their vantage point high above home plate, folks in Fenway's press box and the 600 Club can catch a glimpse of the leaders running through Kenmore at around 2 P.M. Fenway fans know the race is nearing conclusion when helicopters hover beyond the left-field wall.

On Patriots Day in 1992, when the Red Sox were staggering through the first month of a particularly dismal (last place) season, I watched the first few innings of a Sox-Toronto Blue Jays game, then walked to the marathon finish line on Boylston Street in time to see the winners crowned. I hung around the finish line for more than an hour, then started walking back toward Fenway. It turned out that the Red Sox and Blue Jays were engaged in an interminable, thirteen-inning, four-hour slopfest. It was one of the few times that the game outlasted most of the marathon runners. With almost no exceptions, the degrees of suffering and pain experienced by marathoners are inversely proportionate to the order of finish. The first runners to cross the line look great. Those who come in later look worse. I won't soon forget the sights, sounds, and smells that bombarded my senses walking back toward Fenway on that April day in '92. There was vomit on the pavement and people were writhing in pain on the curbstones of Kenmore Square. Imagine my surprise when it turned out that those were the Red Sox fans who'd just filed out of Fenway after seeing Toronto's 6–4 victory over Boston.

Traditionally, the Sox are slow starters. Ball clubs built on raw power tend to do better when the warm weather arrives. In years when the Celtics and Bruins are playing well, the Sox sometimes get lost in the hype of the NBA and NHL play-offs. "That's okay with us," Sox lefty Bruce Hurst said in 1986. "We always like to lie in the weeds until the Celtics got through with their play-offs."

By the time graduation gowns are hanging in closets, the Red Sox are the only sports show in town. In the early part of June, thousands of students vacate Boston, and the streets of the Back Bay start to breathe again. It becomes easier to park around Fenway. Sports fans eschew air-conditioning and spend nights at balmy Fenway. On most nights, beach balls are bouncing around the bleachers. For parents, it's okay to keep the kids out after 10 P.M.

The Red Sox are New England's boys of summer. Generally speaking, it is the time when the team plays its best, and it is the only time when real baseball weather visits Boston. April and May can be cold and rainy, but the bleachers are sunny and comfortable for most of June, July, August, and September.

In Fenway summer, the fans are finally warm, and the hitters find their power.

"It's almost impossible to hit a ball out of here in April," Mike Greenwell says every spring. "I hit a ball right on the screws and it just dies out there. It can be pretty discouraging. I've seen a lot of guys, guys from other teams, and they just shake their heads when they hit a rocket and it doesn't make it over the fence."

All this changes in June. The wind most days blows out, and baseballs start crashing off the facades of the Euroclubs that dot Lansdowne Street beyond the Green Monster.

When the Red Sox were loaded with home run hitters in 1977, George Scott took note of the rare early-season power binge and said, "Wait till July and August. It'll look like Vietnam around here."

"That's one of their problems," lefty pitcher Bill Lee noted. "Their whole attitude is predicated on offense, and that only works in the middle of the season. I always say they're horseshit in the beginning of the season and they're horseshit at the end of the season when the winds change. They're a fucking monster ball club in the middle."

New England is dotted with great summer-vacation spots including the islands of Martha's Vineyard and Nantucket, the Berkshires, the coast of Maine, Bar Harbor, Newport, Rhode Island, and Cape Cod. Whether you like fishing, sailing, or shopping in scrimshaw boutiques,

New England's got something for every prospective vacationer. In Massachusetts alone there are more than seven hundred museums. In Boston, there are eighteen outdoor cafés on Newbury Street. That said, New England summers are more enjoyable when the Boston ball team is competitive. Fans bring transistor radios to the beach. Folks listen to games at night as they sit in screened-in porches from Old Orchard Beach to Provincetown.

Roaming New England, vacationers can't go without their daily fix of Sox news. It's fine to leave the house, the dog, and the job behind, but true baseball junkies take their passion with them. On warm Cape Cod mornings, vacationing Bostonians shuffle to minimarts and convenience stores for the morning papers. It's annoying when the early editions don't have the Sox final game story or box score. The message is carried by word of mouth, and by noon most fans have a good grip on what happened in last night's game.

If baseball were strictly a summer game, the Red Sox would have a far different history. But too much disappointment has followed the joys of summers, and Sox fans have learned to temper their emotions when the team is hot in July and August. The 1946 Red Sox clinched the American League pennant on September 13, but slumped a little later and lost the World Series (despite being favored by almost 3–1) in seven games against the Cardinals. The 1974 Red Sox led the American League East by seven games on August 23, but went 14–24 the rest of the way and finished the season in third place, seven games behind the Orioles. In July of 1978, Boston was 62–28, and *Herald* reporter Jake Liston went on television during a rain delay and said, "It would be a little more fun if they weren't so far ahead of everybody." The '78 Red Sox came back to the pack in September and lost the division title in a one-game play-off in October.

In June of 1995, the Red Sox were playing .656 baseball and owned a six-and-a-half game lead over the rest of the American League East. It represented Boston's biggest first-place lead in five seasons. By August, the Sox lead was fifteen and a half games—the largest lead since Ted Williams and company shredded the American League in 1946. Sox fans enjoyed a carefree summer, knowing that no team could catch Boston in September. The summer of 1995 was one of the best ever at Fenway. Mo Vaughn enjoyed an MVP-worthy season,

John Valentin was on his way to knocking in one hundred runs, and a knuckleball pitcher named Tim Wakefield came out of nowhere and ran his record to 14–1. In one stretch in August the Red Sox won twenty of twenty-two ball games. Naturally, they were touted as serious postseason contenders. Page seventy-five of the 1995 *Old Farmer's Almanac* asked, "Am I delirious? Or are the Red Sox in the Serious?" Hearing this, Boston fans got a little nervous.

Mike Flanagan, who pitched for the Orioles and Blue Jays in more than a dozen AL East races, says, "For the Red Sox, it almost seems to be a blessing for them to be on the road in September. Nobody ever lets them forget the memories of the ones gone by."

Fall is the season of death, and year after year it's the death of hope for Boston's baseball fans. There are no Mr. Octobers in Boston baseball lore. September and October—the most splendid months on New England calendars—are Fenway's season of the witch. The Red Sox haven't won a World Series since 1918, when Babe Ruth was a crafty left-hander for the local nine, and Sox fans recite the near misses the way they can reel off the names of their children. . . . Hmm, let's see, there was 1946 when Johnny Pesky held the ball while Enos Slaughter was rounding third to score the winning run of the 1946 World Series; there was 1948 when the Sox blew the first one-game play-off in American League history; then there was 1949 when Boston went to New York needing only one win in the final two games. The Sox lost 'em both. Then there was the miracle of '67, when the Sox made it all the way to the seventh game of the World Series only to lose to the Cardinals again; there was 1972 when Luis Aparicio fell down rounding third base in Detroit and the Sox lost the division title; there was '74 when Boston blew a seven-and-a-half-game lead (losing eighteen of their last twenty-nine) in the final month, finishing seven games behind the Orioles; there was '75 when they lost yet another World Series seventh game; 1978 when they blew a nine-game lead (fourteen games over the Yanks, who eventually won) and dropped the second one-game play-off in American League history; there was 1986 when they came within one strike of winning the World Series, only to lose in the most ghastly fashion; then there was 1988 when they were swept in the play-offs by the Oakland A's; then there was 1990 when they were swept by the A's again. In October of

1995, the Sox were swept out of the play-offs in three straight games by the Cleveland Indians. Boston became the first team in big-league history to lose thirteen consecutive postseason games.

Thirteen straight. Only the Red Sox. It all started with a two-out single by the ever-annoying Gary Carter on the night/morning of October 25/26 (depending on whether you'd already turned back your clocks) in 1986. The Sox were set to win their first World Series in sixty-eight years. They had a two-run lead in the bottom of the tenth and needed only one more out to finally grasp the Holy Grail.

They never got the third out. Before the inning was over, John McNamara, Calvin Schiraldi, Bob Stanley, Rich Gedman, and poor Bill Buckner had enshrined themselves in the Red Sox Hall of Pain while hundreds of thousands of Boston fans put champagne bottles back in the fridge and cried in their beer.

Who could have known that this was only the beginning? Who could have predicted that over the next nine years, the Red Sox would set a record that may never be broken?

Baltimore has Cal Ripken and 2,131. Boston has the Fizzles of October—a baseball franchise that in a span of only nine years has lost thirteen consecutive postseason games. By any standard, what the Sox have done since 1986 amounts to a flop of epic dimension. Consider: A postseason losing streak is something of an oxymoron (and the Sox have been called much worse). To get to the play-offs, a team presumably must do well over the course of 162 (or 144) games. Only good teams are still playing in October. How, then, can anyone explain a franchise losing thirteen of these games . . . in a row?

It's not as if this Sox streak happened over a half century. The 1995 Sox broke a record set by the Philadelphia Phillies, but the Phils lost their eleven straight starting in 1915 and ending in 1976. That qualifies as a quirk. Just plain bad timing and bad luck. But the Red Sox did the baker's dozen doughnut in only nine years. Clemens and Greenwell were in Sox uniforms for the entire sorry streak. Playing in every game of the streak, Greenwell was punched out by Jesse Orosco, smothered by Dave Stewart, and frozen by Orel Hershiser. Clemens started five of the thirteen games.

Though he has won only one of nine postseason starts, the hope of winning a World Series keeps Clemens going.

"I don't like getting up at six in the morning and running four or five miles," he says. "I hate it. I want to go to the golf course, or I want to go play some hoops. I'm ready to go on and watch my boys grow and do dad's pitch and enjoy those things. And I want to come out here and sit with y'all and watch the next generations of teams. And that's what I'll do. I'll show up periodically and say hi and shake a few hands and be happy as I can be if we win. I'll be just one of the Red Sox players if we don't win a championship. And that's the only reason I'm playing right now. I just want to win. If we win this year, you won't see me next year. If I can win a World Championship, I would feel I've done everything I could possibly do and it wouldn't even be right for me to come back. I just want to see the city, how they would react, if we ever win here. . . . Now there's urgency for me. If I play another three or four years here and we don't win, then I'm just one of the guys—like Ted and Carl and Jimmy and Dewey. I'm just one of those guys that didn't win."

Memory is selective. It's said that if people could remember the pain of running a marathon or giving birth, they would never do it another time. This is what it's like if you are a Red Sox fan. If you could remember the pain of October, you'd never give the Sox your heart in July and August. But Boston baseball fans do it almost every year.

A *Washington Post* editorial concluded, "The baseball season in Boston is traditionally concluded in an atmosphere of recrimination, regret, and bitter disputation infused with a certain amount of the occult."

▶ ◆ ◀

As soon as each Red Sox nonchampionship season is concluded, the Hot Stove Season commences and New Englanders fire up their hopes for next year. And in the well-worn pages of the Red Sox almanac, next year promises to be a year of plenty, yielding a bumper crop and a flag over Fenway.

One of the most touching winter kickoffs came on the final day of the 1991 season (October 6) when manager Joe Morgan trotted his team (84–78, seven games out of first place) to the first-base line to deliver a message to the fans who had supported them all season. Normally, a team lines the first-base stripe only on opening day and before postseason games. This was different. Morgan wanted to issue a public apology to the fans of Boston, and he insisted that his tired troops stand out there with him and face the forgiving legions. Tollway Joe stepped to the microphone and said, "Have a good autumn, a good winter, and we'll have a better year next year." Morgan was fired less than two weeks later. The year after he left, the Sox went from second place to the cellar. So much for year-end resolutions.

Tickets for the upcoming Fenway season go on sale annually on the first Saturday in December. Since the late 1980s, the day has become a media event. Hard-core fans have been known to line up outside the Sox ticket offices on Yawkey Way three or four days before the doors open. The crazies live in cardboard boxes and plywood sidewalk huts. They eat doughnuts, build fires in trash barrels, and huddle under blankets as the gales of December swirl around ancient Fenway. Like ice fishermen in northern Minnesota, they sit patiently, stoically, never yielding to the elements. Day afer day. When they need to use the bathroom, they use the facilities at the bowling alley beneath Fenway, at the corner of Brookline Avenue and Lansdowne Street.

"We need three things," one of the shivering sidewalk fans said in December 1990. "We need NyQuil, women, and women. But it's kind of hard to pick up girls down here. What are you gonna say, 'Come back to my cardboard condo?' "

Even on the first day of ticket sales, it's tough to get good seats for the best games. Season-ticket holders, ticket agencies, and scalpers seem to land the primo seats. Fenway's capacity is limited and this ups demand. No doubt some of the "kids" who wait in line are hired by agencies to score good tickets for September games. But some of them are just baseball fans, trying to beat a system that freezes them out of the big games once the regular season starts. When the Sox throw open the ticket windows on the first Saturday morning in December, the ball club provides free coffee and doughnuts. . . . And to think some folks say the Red Sox don't have heart.

In January of each off-season, the Boston baseball writers host a huge dinner at the downtown Sheraton Hotel. Usually this bash is attended by Sox officials, a handful of Boston players, some old-timers, a few out-of-town baseball personalities, and about eleven hundred fans. Members of the public fork over $85 for the privilege of hearing some baseball speeches and maybe getting an autograph. It's an annual sellout. The Red Sox try to boost the event by making a deal or signing a free agent sometime just before the supper. It's a way to get baseball back in the newspapers just before the Super Bowl.

The next bookmark in the Boston baseball year is the annual newspaper photograph of the Red Sox equipment truck being loaded for the drive south. Living in Boston, one takes comfort in odd annual events that are uniquely Bostonian. April has the Boston Marathon. In July, the Pops play for free on the Esplanade and the church bells on Beacon Street peal as fireworks explode and the Pops play the "1812 Overture." In September, students' U-Hauls line the side streets of the Back Bay, and it is impossible to get the overworked phone company to make a house call. On January 1, local TV stations storm the beaches of Southie to watch the L Street Brownies splash in the surf. The photo of the Red Sox truck complements all of the above. It's one of those kooky little events that remind us where we live and what is going to happen next. Boston newspapers publish the photo to remind readers that the mountains of ice and snow will melt. In the old days, the photo featured Johnny Orlando slinging Ted Williams's equipment bag into a moving van, bound for St. Petersburg, spring home of the Red Sox. Today we have Mo Vaughn's batting gloves bound for Fort Myers. The picture provides inspiration to take the Christmas-gift mitt out of the closet and start breaking it in. There's new temptation to throw the hardball around the house, meaning that many New England windows will be broken in the dead of winter. Blame it on the picture. Blame it on the truck.

Bats, balls, and gloves are not the only items on the truck. There are also cartons of sunflower seeds, canisters of Skoal, spikes, golf clubs, strollers, baby seats, bicycles, stuff from the trainer's room, and at least one of Greenwell's toy gators. Today the players' wallets arrive under separate cover. The wallets are secured in an armored truck—a much bigger truck than the one carrying the equipment. The wallet truck has the heavier load.

When the Sox equipment truck parks on Van Ness Street in mid-February, we know it means only six more weeks of winter. The cycle is complete. Spring training is on the way. Soon the Red Sox will be back in Florida. The photo is baseball's version of the groundhog. It means there will be sunshine and green grass and hot nights and cold beer. There will be baseball.

CHAPTER FOUR

FOILED! CURSES AGAIN

▶ ◆ ◆ ◆ ◆ ◆ ◆ ◆ ◆ ◄

➤ On August 8, 1988 (which is 8/8/88, for anyone into numerology), Margaret Blackstone, then an executive editor at E. P. Dutton publishers, wrote me a letter that read:

"Dear Mr. Shaughnessy: The way that you write about baseball makes me enjoy the game even more, which I would have thought would be impossible. I am wondering if you are at work on a book. If so, I would be very interested in seeing it. If not, I have an idea for a book about the history of the Red Sox that I thought might interest you. If you would like to discuss the matter further, please feel free to give me a call. If you aren't interested, please simply consider this a fan letter."

That was the literary birth of *The Curse of the Bambino*.

Actually, the Curse began on Monday, January 5, 1920—eleven days before the start of Prohibition—when Red Sox owner Harry Frazee announced that he had sold slugger/pitcher Babe Ruth to the New York Yankees. A lot of goofy things have happened to the Red Sox since then, and, of course, Boston is still waiting to win a World Series. The Red Sox won five of the first fifteen World Series played, but it's been nothing but disappointment and frustration since Ruth was shipped to New York for cash.

Margaret Blackstone grew up in Oyster Bay, Long Island, but first learned of the Curse of the Bambino from her maternal grandfather,

Arthur Whitfield Davidson. Davidson was a Dorchester housepainter who played baseball in his youth and wore the scars that come with a lifetime of Red Sox devotion. He explained to his granddaughter, "The Red Sox will never win because they sold Babe Ruth to the Yankees. It's the Curse of the Bambino." As a young woman living in New York, Ms. Blackstone never forgot about the Curse. When the Red Sox blew the 1986 World Series in hideous fashion—to a New York team—she was reminded of her grandfather's words. She kicked the idea around in her head for a couple of years, then approached me.

My book came out in 1990. It hardly broke new ground. Throughout New England, fans had long held that the Sox were jinxed. In the 1946 *Saturday Evening Post, Globe* scribe Harold Kaese penned "What's the Matter with the Red Sox?" Years later, Walter Kelly's Pogo comic strip from New Year's Day showed a character exclaiming, "It's Leap Year—the year we elect a president, the year of decision, the year the Red Sox win the whole kaboodle." Another character responded, "You say that every year."

Long ago, Boston sports fans trained themselves to expect disaster whenever the Red Sox got close. The sale of Ruth was often cited as the beginning of the bad luck, but nobody had ever collected all the dark history and put it in book form. And to my knowledge, nobody knows who was the first Sox watcher to use the phrase "the Curse of the Bambino." There is certainly no evidence that George Herman Ruth uttered any threatening remarks toward Boston or the Red Sox after he was traded. One day after the deal was announced, the *Boston Globe* ran a story headlined, "Babe Says He Will Play in Boston or Nowhere." In the story, Ruth's agent, Johnny Igoe, said he had received a telegram from Ruth (who was in Los Angeles) that read, "Will not play anywhere but Boston." Agents have a way of manufacturing positive spins in situations like that, and there is every indication that Igoe was merely trying to make the fans of Boston feel better. Ruth knew that going to New York was a good opportunity, and he'd been frustrated by contract hassles with Frazee. The Babe knew about the pending transaction almost two weeks before it was announced. When the Yankees and Red Sox first discussed the sale of Ruth, New York owner Jacob Ruppert wisely sent Yankee manager Miller Huggins west to work things out with the Big Fella. Huggins negotiated with Ruth in Los Angeles, and the sale contract was signed the day after Christmas, 1919. Ten days later, Ruth's agent told the Boston press that the Babe would not play anywhere but Boston.

Ruth's 1948 autobiography contains no curse on the Red Sox. Recounting his conversation with Yankee manager Miller Huggins when Huggins met with Ruth to propose the deal, Ruth wrote, "I told him [Huggins] I liked Boston and always had been happy with the Red Sox, but if Frazee sent me to the Yankees I'd try to play as hard there as I ever did in Boston. . . . As for my reaction over coming to the big town, at first I was pleased, largely because it meant more money. Then I got the bad feeling we all have when we pull up our roots. My home, all my connections, affiliations and friends were in Boston. The town had been good to me. . . . Of course, as the years rode on, New York got me, the same as it gets most people who settle there. Today it is my home, and whenever I leave I am always happy to get back."

So there was no real curse. Ruth never walked out to the middle of the Fenway diamond and ordered a pox on the Sox. He did not hire Salem witches to punish the Boston ball club. He tweaked Frazee a few times over the years, but never wished ill on the Fenway franchise. Yet the theme of the Curse remains powerful. It gives Red Sox fans something to lean on. It's human nature. When asked to explain the unexplainable, it's convenient and less threatening to introduce the possibility of Larger Forces calling the shots. That way, the Curse of the Bambino becomes a salve for Red Sox fans. It would be more painful if they had to find a rational explanation for things going wrong. It's much easier to tie it up in a neat bundle. When the ball goes through Bill Buckner's legs, it's the Curse of the Bambino. Simple. Tidy.

In the summer of 1990, when the *Curse* was put out for public consumption, there was tremendous response. It was very personal with a lot of Boston fans. They told me stories and wrote me letters. It seemed that every fan had his or her spin on the Ruth jinx. I received letters from former Massachusetts governor and presidential candidate Michael Dukakis, and from Richard Darman, then-president George Bush's director of the Office of Management and Budget. A fan wrote to point out the connection between Bruce Hurst and the Babe. Hurst and Ruth rank side by side in the list of winningest Red Sox left-handed pitchers (Ruth is fifth with eighty-nine victories, Hurst sixth with eighty-eight). They are the last two lefties to win World Series games in Fenway, and the last two Sox pitchers to win Series games by a 1–0 score. Best of all, when one rearranges the letters in Bruce Hurst, one can spell B. RUTH CURSE. An anagram of evil.

The Sox saga as Greek tragedy is a time-tested theme. In June of 1990, the *Boston Globe* hired Emily Vermeule, a Harvard professor of Aegean archaeology and Greek to review *The Curse of the Bambino*. In 1978 Ms. Vermeule had written this about the Red Sox: "The Red Sox did not fail, they became immortal. The classic tale of their summer and autumn could not have matched the great dramatic literature of the past had it ended any other way. They were worthy of the Sophoclean stage, actors in traditional and poignant myth, in the long conflict between the larger-than-life hero and inexorable time, native brilliance and predestined ruin, the flukiness of luck. . . . That so few gallant, striving men on the brilliant green stage of Fenway stirring so many souls for so long, and lost by such a small, inevitable twist at the last second, made the Red Sox a theme of song for a century to come."

Whew. And I thought they were just guys who spit on the dugout floor and grabbed their crotches between innings.

Surely the Curse of the Bambino must have its roots in Greek mythology. The Yankees and Red Sox, representing New York and Boston, are the Athens and Sparta of baseball. Author George V. Higgins was first to see Sox righty Mike Torrez (signed as a free agent after he won the World Series for the Yankees) as a wooden horse gifted by the Greeks. Bill Buckner had an Achilles' heel injury, didn't he?

One of the more amusing angles on the Curse is how all Red Sox players refuse to admit it exists. That is only natural. No ballplayer wants to believe in a negative destiny, and it must be annoying to be told you can't do something because things have gone wrong in the past.

The mentality of today's Red Sox fan was established in the 1970s, when a succession of strong teams blew first-place leads. The Sox could have won the American League East in 1972 and again in 1974, but folded in the clutch. Boston won the American League pennant in 1975, but lost the World Series to the Reds in seven games. Cincinnati probably had the stronger team, but it was a Series the Sox should have won. The 1978 Boston baseball season is still recalled with horror. On July 20, the Sox were 62–28, led the second-place Brewers by nine games and led the Yankees by a whopping fourteen games. Incredibly, it wasn't enough. New York roared back, caught the slumping Sox, then won the play-off game on Bucky Dent's cheap homer into the netting above the Green Monster. Since then, no lead has been safe. Red Sox fans are convinced something bad will happen, and they let the young men who wear the Boston uniform know it.

The print media plays a major part in this mind-set. We feed the beast. We know the fans expect collapse, and it becomes a self-fulfilling prophecy. This was never more clear than in 1986, when an exciting Red Sox team took over first place in late May and never yielded the top spot. The '86 Sox were expected to finish fifth (they'd been 81–81 in '85), but roared out of the gate on the strength of twenty-four-year-old Roger Clemens. Clemens won his first fourteen decisions and set a major league record by striking out twenty batters in a nine-inning April game against the Seattle Mariners. Don Baylor joined the team just before opening day, and the Sox were a confident, happy unit throughout the summer. The only thing that bothered them was the constant nagging by fans and reporters: *When are you gonna blow it?*

In July of '86, when the Sox slipped on the West Coast but still clung to their lead, I wrote that the Red Sox were the only team in baseball that can give the appearance of being mathematically eliminated while still in first place. The story concluded with, "Sox fans know better. They have seen this play before. The cast changes and new liberties are taken with an ancient script, but Hamlet always dies in the end." In August, the *Globe* ran a page-one story that began, "A fatalistic gloom hangs over Boston. It's August and the Red Sox are in first place." Front-page photos of Babe Ruth and John Calvin accompanied the text. Meanwhile, *Sports Illustrated* weighed in with a story detailing past collapses, headlined, "Poised for Another El Foldo?"

Before the 1986 postseason, author Geoffrey Wolff wrote (in the *Globe*), "What is it with New England? What a gang of hanging judges and long-faced sad sacks. Is it the Yankee heritage? This isn't the seventeen century, or even the nineteenth; New Englanders are too various, too comfortable with pleasure to hang crepe like a corporation of gravediggers or bankers.... If a choke exists, it's nurtured rather than natured. To fail under pressure is not the most notable genetic component of a professional athlete's makeup, but to read in the newspapers and hear on radio talk shows that he will fail under pressure is surely one of the principal experiences of a New England athlete's professional destiny.... An athlete, hearing often enough that he will choke because once upon a time other athletes from the Boston area choked, which they didn't either, might come to believe such a prophecy."

In 1986, Brett Butler, then an outfielder with the Cleveland Indians, said, "I was in Boston for three days and I couldn't believe it. Everybody was knocking the Red Sox. The fans think they're going to fail. I had dinner with some friends and they were talking about the Sox already being mathematically eliminated. 'You've got to be kidding me,' I told them. It's like everybody's expecting failure. If that's the way the media and the fans are going to be—not backing them like they should—then it's going to be tough. Cubs fans aren't like that. It's different. They always pull for their club, and if you say something about the Cubs, they say, 'Want to fight?' In *Gulliver's Travels* there's a character named Glug. He's never optimistic. He's pessimistic. That's what Boston fans remind me of. They're saying, 'Oh, no, we're not going to win,' and, 'Oh, no, Toronto's going to beat us.' Back your team. Come on."

Of course, the Red Sox did go on to win the division title in '86, then produced one of the most stirring comebacks in play-off history. Boston trailed the California Angels, three games to one, and fell behind in the fifth game by a score of 5–2 in the ninth inning. Down to their final three outs, the Sox rallied to take the lead. Baylor hit a two-run homer to cut the margin to 5–4, and with all of California waiting for the Clinch Party, David Henderson turned on a Donnie Moore pitch and smacked a two-run homer to give the Red Sox a 6–5 lead. Boston won the game in extra innings, then swept two more at home to bring the American League pennant to Fenway Park. That should have wiped away the ghosts of seasons past forever. The '86

Red Sox were downright heroic as they went into the World Series against the Mets.

Lefty reliever Joe Sambito spent his career with the Astros and Mets before coming to Boston. Uncle Billy Sambito had a barbershop in Ayer, Massachusetts, and the shop gave Joe Sambito a good look inside the New England mind. When the '86 Sox kept turning back challenges, Sambito said, "If we win, it'll screw up this whole town. They'll have to start thinking positive."

Sox manager John McNamara took the heat on national television when he was interviewed the day before the first game of the 1986 World Series. *Good Morning America* host Charles Gibson chuckled and noted that Woodrow Wilson was president when the Red Sox won their last World Series. "Hey, you're not funny," snapped Mac. "Seven o'clock in the morning, that's not funny."

Those were the Changing Sox. They were the team that would spit in the face of destiny. With the energy of the innocent, they expected to be crowned World Champs of baseball.

But in the end, the weight of the Red Sox uniform was too heavy. The unthinkable happened. They did something only the Red Sox could do. They led the World Series, three games to two and took a 5–3 lead into the bottom of the tenth inning of game six in New York. Sox righty Calvin Schiraldi retired the first two batters in the inning. It appeared that there was no way the Sox could lose. But it happened. The Mets struck three straight singles against Schiraldi. Hard-luck reliever Bob Stanley came on and uncorked a wild pitch (Sox fans know it was a passed ball by catcher Rich Gedman) to bring home the tying run. Then Mookie Wilson hit the ground ball that skipped between Bill Buckner's legs and into history. It was the cataclysmic, apocalyptic moment in Red Sox history—the singular choke against which all past and future folds would be measured. It was one of those "only the Red Sox" moments. Never again will Boston fans believe their team is going to win—not until the Sox get the final third out and pour champagne over each other's head.

Days, months, and years have passed since that fateful night at Shea Stadium. The memory does not fade. The Sox loss in New York came on a Saturday night when the entire six-state region was braced for an overdue victory. The Red Sox were going to break their sixty-eight-year-old jinx, and they were going to do it against a team from New York. My unscientific polling has found that almost all residents of our region, including scores who know nothing about sports, can tell me exactly where they were and what they were doing when the baseball trickled through Bill Buckner's legs. That is no exaggeration. In New England, people remember the Sox choke—even those who don't know a forkball from a forklift.

In his autobiography, Don Baylor wrote, "He [Buckner] just did not make the routine play. If it happens in April, it's an error. If it happens in the Series, it's history. If it happens to a Boston player, well, it's the Red Sox. The fans knew, we knew, the Mets did not beat us. We beat ourselves. I know I started to wonder about that jinx. The players may have felt something could go wrong. New Englanders seemed to know that something *would* go wrong. I felt powerless to break that spell."

In the spring of 1995, I spoke to 130 members of the New England Paper Trade Association. After the brief talk, I opened the floor to questions, and the first one came from a gentleman who asked, "If Buckner had fielded the ball, do you think Stanley would have made it over to first base in time to take the throw and beat Wilson?"

Nine years had passed, and still the public wanted answers. Oliver Stone should make game six the subject of his next movie. Theories about the controversy refuse to die.

In 1995 a book entitled *One Pitch Away* hit the stores. Written by Mike Sowell, published by Macmillan, the 312-page narrative chronicled the lives of several people involved in the 1986 play-offs and World Series. There were entire chapters devoted to Buckner, Dave Stapleton, Schiraldi, and Stanley. Stapleton (the man who filled in for the hobbled Buckner at the end of every other Sox postseason victory) for the first time admitted, "All they were trying to do was leave Buckner out there so he could be on the field to celebrate when we won the game. . . . I think everybody knew it. Our manager [McNamara] knew it. He wouldn't admit it to this day, but he damn well knows that he messed up. And he very well could have cost us the World Series that year. I thought he was probably the worst manager I ever played for, from the minor leagues on up."

Baylor, now manager of the Colorado Rockies, admitted that when he sits in the visitors dugout at Shea Stadium, he thinks about game six. "I like to torture myself," he told Sowell.

It doesn't go away. In April of 1995, a band named Letters to Cleo visited Plant City, Florida, and guitarist Michael Eisenstein posed for a picture with Cincinnati Reds coach Ray Knight. Eisenstein asked Kay Hanley, the band's lead singer, to pose with them, but Hanley is from Dorchester, Massachusetts, and she refused, saying, "I'm sure Ray Knight's a nice man, but he was the one who scored the winning run when the ball went through Buckner's legs."

Just about every New Englander has a story from the night of October 25, 1986. It was the night we turned the clocks back one hour. Let's turn the clock back again and listen to some tales of woe from people whose lives were smacked, slapped, and broken by game six.

Sean Horgan covered the Red Sox for the *Hartford Courant* for five seasons. In 1986 he was a business reporter for the *Quincy Patriot Ledger*. A lifelong Sox fan who grew up in Danvers, Massachusetts, he was partying with friends in Brighton on the night of game six. He might have had a little too much to drink after the incredible finish, then was stopped by police in Wellington Circle while driving home. "It was one of those road checks they sometimes have on Saturday night," says Horgan. "The officer pulled me over and said, 'Are you sober?' I'm not sure what my blood-alcohol level was, but I said to him, 'Officer, I've just had the most sobering experience of my life.' He said, 'You saw the game, huh? Well, they might have another chance tomorrow night.' And I said, 'No, they don't.' And we started arguing at a sobriety check point. Not very smart on my part. But he let me go."

Mike LaVigne grew up in Groton, Massachusetts, one of five children of Margaret and the late Dr. Richard Joseph LaVigne. Dr. LaVigne was chief of radiology at Burbank Hospital in Fitchburg, Massachusetts. The good doctor had four sons and one daughter, and on weekends they would accompany their busy father to work, sometimes helping out by stamping the X rays. En route to the hospital, it was a family tradition to stop at the Moran Square Diner on Main Street in Fitchburg.

Mike LaVigne's story: "These guys at the diner all knew my father.

They called him 'The Doc.' One of the owners was a guy named Angie and he loved the Yankees. We were brought up to hate the Yankees. For thirty years, Angie gave my father shit about the Yankees. I think it was because he was from an Italian background and Joe DiMaggio had played for the Yankees.

"Anyway, I watched game six on television in the Forest Hills Gardens section of Queens, New York. I was with Lisa White and her mother in her mother's apartment. So I'm in New York for this and we're watching the game. And Hendu hits the home run. I'm like millions of people from New England. We'd been waiting for this moment all our lives, and all I could think about was my father. My father died of cancer on January second, 1980. I remember one of the last times I visited him when he was dying and he was lying in the bed. I said, 'Is there anything I can do?' He said, 'The one thing I wish had happened was that the Red Sox had won the World Series.' He said, 'If they ever win that World Series, I want you to go and buy the most expensive bottle of champagne you can find, and you go up to the Moran Square Diner. You go up there and put that bottle on the counter and say, 'This is from the Doc.'

"So here I am, stretched out on the bed, and the Sox go ahead. There's two outs and all I'm saying to myself is that they're going to win and I'm thinking about the bottle of champagne. Gary Carter comes up. I'm saying, 'This is perfect. Carter makes the last out—this fake pseudo-Christian. It's going to be perfect.' Then Carter gets the hit and Lisa says, 'If the next guy gets a hit, that keeps the rally going.' There's the jinx. So then everything happens and the Mets won the game. With me, it wasn't a question of being depressed. I was in this zone. I'm lying in bed. Honest to God, I thought I was having a heart attack. I got shortness of breath. My heart started to beat. I thought I was going to die. I go from being one out away to dying in bed. And of course, outside all the car horns are honking. So I had to get up and take a Valium. I never take Valium. But all I could think of was how perfect it would have been, just walking into the diner and slamming it down on the counter and saying, 'This is from the Doc!' "

Nine years after the 1986 World Series, fifteen years after Dr. LaVigne died, Michael was rummaging through the family attic and found a newspaper clipping that revealed that his father had played in an exhibition game with the great Joe DiMaggio in 1943.

"I can't believe he never even mentioned it," says Michael. "The only reason I can think of is that it must have been because he hated the Yankees so much."

Monte Dutton lives on a cattle farm in Clinton, South Carolina. He is a sportswriter for the *Greenville News*. Dutton's father was once stationed at Fort Devens in Ayer, Massachusetts, and carried a love of the Red Sox back home to Carolina. This passion was passed down to his son Monte, who loved the Sox so much that he named his dog Yaz and one of his lambs Fenway. Like most of Red Sox Nation, he watched the sixth game of the 1986 World Series at home. He was crushed. Apparently, Fenway the lamb took it pretty hard, too. Dutton recalls, "When I went out in the pasture the next morning, Fenway was lying there dead. He might have died right at the end of the game."

The Silence of the Lamb. The Curse of the Bambino.

In the first moments after the game six calamity, Red Sox manager John McNamara walked to the pressroom podium and announced, "I don't know nothin' about history and I don't want to hear anything about choking or any of that crap."

Nice try, Mac. Ever heard of George Santayana? Those who do not study history are condemned to repeat it. And he who has choked will hear about it whether he wants to or not. Nobody wants to ask the captain of the *Exxon Valdez* about all the times he brought the ship home safely.

Lou Gorman was at the side of the late Jean Yawkey when the Sox coughed up game six. The Yawkeys had owned the team since 1934, and winning a World Series was the old lady's dream.

"I can't say what she said to me," says Gorman. "I'm saving that for my book. But she was bitterly disappointed. The Mets were having a big party and invited us, but she said to me, 'Lou, no party. Let's get out of here.' So we went to this little room with John Harrington and a few others in our group. They brought a drink to us. She said, 'Sit down next to me, Lou.' The conversation was sad. I knew when we left that room, she almost didn't want to come back the next night for game seven."

Harrington, who was also with Gorman and Mrs. Yawkey, remembers, "We were doing everything we could to bring out our superstitions in a positive light. My wife, Maureen, had a finger rosary and was praying. I think Mrs. Yawkey borrowed it. They were really bringing the gods down. When we lost, it was really a downer. I think Mrs. Yawkey was a little angry. She had a temper. We had it in our grasp, and I think she realized a couple of things that could have been done weren't done."

Hmmm. Sounds like even Mrs. Y. was blaming Mac for leaving Buckner on the field.

Ted Williams watched game six from his home in Florida and remembers, "After we won game five I figured, 'Well, we got it now. We finally got it now!' And then, jeez, everything happened again. But that was one of those things that, oh, boy, in fact it did look like the Red Sox were snakebit. Yeah, I thought they were cursed, but I don't even think about that anymore. This is new times."

"There's no curse," Buckner said later. "We just ran into some bad luck. Remember, we were one pitch away from losing the play-offs and won it. . . . But, yes, you think about this curse stuff as a player only because the fans are always bringing it up. And that's because the media is always harping on it."

Dwight Evans said, "If the curse would have affected anyone, it would have been the players from 1918. And they'd be very old players by now. I don't choose to waste my energy on that."

"It's entertainment, like the story of the Loch Ness monster," said former Red Sox pitching coach Rich Gale.

Fine. But the legacy of game six has haunted the Red Sox every day and night since Saturday, October 25, 1986 (starting a record-setting string of thirteen consecutive postseason losses). When the Red Sox were good enough to win the American League East in 1988 and again in 1990, players new to the team were again stunned by the gloom and suspicion that accompanied their success. In 1988, Sox pitcher Greg Harris told *Newsday*, "The past doesn't have anything to do with this ball club. Most of the players weren't even on the team when the other stuff happened. Some weren't even born. I have to be honest. This never comes up unless a reporter mentions it."

Harris's quote can be cut and pasted and applied to just about anyone who's played for the Red Sox since 1946. They ask not to be reminded of the past because it isn't their past. It would be unrealistic for the athletes to have any other attitude. But they fail to understand that the Boston fans see the Red Sox as a continuous entity. Today's ball club is related to the 1946 edition that didn't win the World Series against the Cardinals. They're the RED SOX, not a collection of individuals in Boston uniforms.

After the '86 Series, the *Globe's* Michael Blowen wrote, "Like the generations of actors who played Lear—Barrymore, Olivier, Welles —the cast may change but the play's the same. It's the Red Sox. The Red Sox transcend the individuals who wear the uniforms, the various managers who direct the different casts each year, and even the game itself. . . . The final image of the stoic Wade Boggs, baseball's best hitter, sitting motionless in the dugout with a single tear rolling down his cheek, is surely as evocative as Ingrid Bergman's departure in *Casablanca*. New York can have the Mets. They're just another ball club."

Sox left fielder Mike Greenwell, when the Sox stayed in the race (eventually winning the AL East) in 1990, was honest enough to admit, "The only scary thing about this is the failure side. Then we'll have to hear and answer the questions about how we choked or the jinx. No matter what happens, it's exciting for the players, the fans, the media. Hopefully, we won't look back and say we lost. There's no doubt it means so much for the fans of New England. It we could win a championship, it would be the most incredible thing that's ever happened. I know Boston is a great city with fans of basketball and hockey and football. But I think they're even greater baseball fans. The Red Sox are the talk of the town. I can be at a gas station and the attendant will start talking about whether we can do it. When the Boston Red Sox win the championship, I want to be on that team. Could you imagine being the one who wins game seven of the World Series in Boston?"

Rich Gedman, a member of the '86 Sox, now retired, says, "I'm from Worcester. Can you image what it would have been like for me to be on the team that did it?"

Roger Clemens said, "I tell you, we keep getting to the threshold. We're going to break through one of these years. You can talk all you want about the Curse and all that. But we'll break through one year or another. We're going to win it."

Clemens will forever be dogged by the fact that in the '86 Series he came out of game six when the Sox were leading, 3–2, in the top of the eighth. The circumstances of Clemens's removal from the game remain in question, because immediately after the loss, McNamara stood in front of the national media and said, "My pitcher asked out of the game." When Clemens heard about the remark, he made a rush toward McNamara's office and had to be restrained by Sox pitching coach Bill Fischer.

"I had given up four hits and they were all on sliders. I think only one was hit hard, but they were all through the infield," Clemens remembers. "My finger was bleeding from a blister, but every time we'd put the gauze on for a second, it would stop. Then it would start bleeding again. The only thing I couldn't do was throw the slider, but I'd already given up four hits with it, so it didn't really bother me. After I came off in the seventh [he retired the Mets, one-two-three], there was no conversation. I went to the bat rack and got ready to hit. I pulled my hands out to put my batting glove on and there was blood everywhere. There was blood dripping on the ground. Fish saw it and made a comment about it. I said, 'I'm all right. Let me get into the eighth. I figured Cal [Schiraldi] or Bobby [Stanley] would come in. By the time I went to the on-deck circle, I was pretty sure I was going to hit. Then somebody whistled and I turned around and Greenwell said, 'I'm pinch-hitting.' There wasn't a whole lot said. If it happened now, at this point they would never take me out in the situation I'm in now.

"Once you look back, you just can't believe it. I appreciate it a lot more now because I know how hard it is to do."

Clemens today freely admits, "Whenever we are in Yankee Stadium, I go out to the Babe Ruth monument and wipe my sweat off on the Babe's plaque. I figure maybe that'll help break the Curse."

Most Sox fans are resigned to living with the Curse. The most oft-repeated wish of citizens of Red Sox Nation is, "I hope they win in my lifetime."

Local scribes have been tough on the Curse and its fallout.

In 1993, Bill Reynolds of the *Providence Journal* wrote, "When I was doing a book on the '67 Sox and the Impossible Dream season, while going through the daily newspapers of that year I never saw any reference to it, neither the curse itself nor to the fact that the Sox hadn't won a World Series since 1918. Not one. It was as if it didn't exist, at least not in any overt way that people cared about. When the Red Sox eventually lost the World Series in seven games, it wasn't because of any so-called curse, it was because the Cardinals were better. No more. Now, as soon as the Sox are in any kind of pennant race, references to the curse are dragged out like some old yearbook at a high school reunion, the ghosts of the past that never are allowed to die."

Globe columnist Bob Ryan, tired of the self-absorption of Sox fans, wrote, "In Boston, it's not good enough to have an athletic event. We've got to make it into Hub Mythology, with ghosts and demons and psychoanalysis. . . . At least Red Sox fans have something to suffer on occasion. How would any of them like to live in Cleveland where the Indians have not had a pennant race in thirty-one years? It is, remember, better to have loved and lost than never to have loved at all. I can tolerate no more of this thirtysomething-style whining. Will the Weeping and Wailing Society just shut up and watch the game, please?"

Horror writer Stephen King writes, "There is no Curse of the Bambino. I, who was writing about curses and supernatural vengeance when Mr. Shaughnessy was still learning not to eat the ends of his Crayolas, tell you that it's so. . . . The Red Sox have been victims of an extraordinary run of ill luck, that's all. And bad luck becomes something else when it's put under enough pressure. Push down on a lump of coal long enough and it becomes a diamond. Push enough ill-fated postseason games down on a team and bad luck becomes predestination."

In 1991, when the Red Sox came within one pitch of vaulting into first place in late September (Jeff Reardon surrendered a homer to Yankee Roberto Kelly), keeper-of-the-flame Peter Gammons was forced to write, "The Red Sox serve a purpose to many New Englanders because they give them something to gripe about while the economy is drowning and before the snow comes, but the more one travels around the country, the more one realizes that Red Sox fans are replacing Mets fans as the most unpopular in the country. Mets fans were considered arrogant, but too many nights watching Gregg Jefferies and Vince Coleman in the middle of the field killed the arrogance. Now it's the Red Sox fans who are considered the most insufferable for their droning whine in the key of *me*."

When the April 1995 issue of *Gentlemen's Quarterly* listed "101 Reasons Baseball Is Dead," reason No. 73 was "Self-righteous, self-flagellating, self-aggrandizing Boston Red Sox fans."

When Dave Henderson thought back on his heroic deeds in the hideous postseason of 1986, he said, "I was just trying to be out there doing a job. Everybody else was battling with history. I didn't know anything about Boston history till after the fact—all the so-called jinxes and other crap you guys write about. So it wasn't any big deal to me. Red Sox people can't stomach losing. Sometimes it happens in baseball."

There have been dozens of formal and informal attempts to break the Curse.

In 1991, Sox fan Peter Rayno and his pals took a trip to Baltimore to see the Red Sox play the Orioles at Memorial Stadium. After a grueling Red Sox defeat, the Boston-based fans (season-ticket holders from Fenway's section 40) made a trip to Ruth's birthplace in downtown Baltimore. One by one, they urinated on the brick wall under the commemorative marker. "The Curse had to end and it was up to us," said Rayno, a resident of Haverhill, Massachusetts. "It was no small coincidence that we were in the hometown of the man who had caused so many so much pain over the past seventy-three years. Fate called for us to step up and we did." Alas, the Curse lives and Rayno in 1993 gave up his season tickets as part of a prenuptial agreement.

Paul Brosnan, a Sox fan from northern New Jersey, suggested, "Just like the Phantom of the Opera wanted a seat to be left empty for him in the opera house, the Bambino needs to have an empty locker in the Red Sox locker room with his picture in it."

Dave Albee, a sports columnist for Gannett News Service, wrote in 1990, "After the Bill Buckner Debacle known as the '86 Series, a friend of mine brought back with him a bottle of Samuel Adams beer, Boston lager. I stuck it in the fridge and vowed to him that I would not drink that bottle of beer until the Red Sox finally won another World Series. Very soon I plan to draw up a new will. I'm going to designate that that bottle of beer be passed on to my thirteen-year-old daughter in the event I die before the Red Sox win another World Series."

When the Soviet Union fell apart in the fall of 1991, Red Sox fans found reason for hope. In 1917 an uprising in St. Petersburg forced the czar to abdicate, and a provisional government was formed. Later in that year, the Bolsheviks seized power. The Sox won the next World Series. Boston fans hoped that the 1991 Russian revolution was a harbinger. Wade Boggs believed. Two days before the 1992 Red Sox opener, Boggs said, "The Red Sox always win the World Series the year after the Russian Revolution." Alas, the Sox finished dead last in 1992. Boston fans were Bolshevik.

In September of 1992, Boston FM radio station WBCN ("The Rock of Boston") imported *Saturday Night Live* television star Father Guido Sarducci in an effort to break the Curse. The station produced 104 altar girls, a bucket of holy Perrier water, and a hydraulic cherry picker to hoist Father Guido and a "Rock Babe" named Michelle. The *Boston Herald* reported, "There were two huge posters of the Bambino and a sign that said: 'Forces of Evil, Spirits of the Dark, Get the Heck out of Fenway Park.' Apparently, this is the working title of Dan Shaughnessy's next book."

Globe columnist Ryan, clearly coming to his senses, admitted, "Maybe there really *is* something to the Curse of the Bambino. Perhaps the conventional means of addressing the ball club's problems—new manager, new players, new general manager, new radio or TV station, etc.—have been inherently doomed to a quixotic frustration for a reason that transcends mortal tampering. . . . It should be evident that malevolent supernatural forces are at work."

"This is the first exorcism of a baseball stadium in the history of ever," said Father Guido, sprinkling some sort of water on the Fenway facade. "The Curse of the Bambino is about to hit the road!"

Red and white balloons were released into the air—"symbolic of the Curse going to some other planet, some other ballpark," said Father Guido. "The Curse is gone. Next year, the Red Sox will win the World Series."

The Red Sox front office wanted nothing to do with exorcisms or anything that would legitimize the Curse of the Bambino. The Sox wouldn't let Father Guido into the ballpark, which is why he had to administer his services from a cherry picker.

Father Guido couldn't help. And the mending of fences with the ghosts of 1918 couldn't help. The 1993 Red Sox finished 80–82, tied for fifth place in the American League East.

Ask Red Sox CEO John Harrington if he believes in the Curse of the Bambino and he says, "In a metaphysical way, it can be there. I don't think it affects current players. I think it has more effect on fans than players. There's this superstitious thing that exists in the minds of the fans. Players are oblivious that it would have any impact, but I do believe that maybe it's there with the fans. I think a lot of people out there believe we're cursed, and that's great. That's part of the game. I just don't know how we'll ever get rid of it until we win."

In September 1993, the Red Sox addressed the issue head-on. The ball club invited family members from the 1918 World Champion Red Sox to be part of a weekend celebration in Boston. It was a seventy-five-year-old makeup call of sorts. The 1918 World Series between the Red Sox and Cubs (of course) was nearly canceled because of a dispute about allocation of Series moneys. The ballplayers balked at the new arrangement, claiming it was a 50 percent cut over previous Series shares. Game five of the 1918 Series was delayed one hour, and when the shares were handed out after the Sox won game six, players received just $1,100, the smallest shares in Series history. As another form of punishment, the players never received their championship emblems (the equivalent of today's World Series rings).

Seventy-five years later, the Sox rounded up twenty descendants of ten different players from the 1918 champs and flew them to Boston for the weekend of September 3–5. The Sox imported, among others, the son and great-grandson of Harry Hooper, the daughter of Carl Mays, and Julia Ruth Stevens, Babe Ruth's daughter. Also invited was Max Frazee, the great-grandson of Harry Frazee, the Sox owner who sold Ruth to the Yankees in 1920.

Showing an unusual sense of history and/or humor, the Sox chose to hold the ceremony on Saturday, September 4. The numbers 9–4–1–8 hang over Fenway's right-field grandstand. These numbers signify the four jersey digits retired by the Red Sox—Ted Williams,

Bobby Doerr, Joe Cronin, and Carl Yastrzemski. Quite unintentionally, they also represent September 4, 1918 (9/4/18), the eve of the first game of the 1918 World Series (the Series was played early that year because of World War I).

Saturday, September 4, 1993, Max Frazee got his first look at the ballpark his great-grandfather owned in the 1920s. "I was quite surprised to be invited," Frazee said. "Considering the history of what my great-grandfather supposedly did to the ball club. I think Big Harry's been unfairly hung many times. I don't think they consider the whole picture. From what I've read and researched, I don't think he did much wrong. The act of selling Ruth is probably the biggest question of all time in baseball. He did it either because of financial problems or because he was a businessman and Ruth demanded so much money and was such a tyrant at that time."

Young Frazee was asked if he would have sold a player like Babe Ruth.

"Sell Babe Ruth?" he said. "What, are you kidding me?"

The pins were awarded, the 1918 championship flag was raised in center field, Harry Frazee's great-grandson kissed the cheek of the Bambino's daughter, and 31,223 fans cheered as long-time Sox announcer Ken Coleman said, "The Curse of the Bambino is now officially ended."

Later that afternoon, the Red Sox took a 2–0 lead into the bottom of the ninth against the Kansas City Royals, then lost, 4–2. The macabre defeat was followed by the sound of veteran reliever Greg Harris loudly and angrily negotiating with general manager Lou Gorman on a clubhouse telephone. Harris, who blew the ninth-inning lead when he gave up a two-run bomb to Brian McRae, said his contract negotiations had a direct impact on his pitching. Good thing the Curse had been lifted or the Sox would really have had problems.

Sox fans took comfort when the New York Rangers hockey team won the Stanley Cup in the spring of 1994. The Rangers hadn't won a Cup since 1940, and many New Yorkers blamed it on the Curse of Red Dutton. Dutton was manager of the rival New York Americans and supposedly put a curse on the Rangers when his hockey team went out of business after World War II. Dutton was asked about the curse before he died in 1987 and said, "A lot of that was newspaper stuff, but newspapers can be right sometimes." The Rangers' win in the spring of '94 showed Sox fans that curses can be broken.

In the spring of 1995, the Red Sox made an effort to trade for a Texas minor leaguer named Ted Williams. Unfortunately, the Rangers traded their Ted Williams to the Pittsburgh Pirates. Sox GM Dan Duquette noted, "We'd love to have Ted Williams back in Boston. If we could just get Babe Ruth back, we'd be all set."

Meanwhile, Joe Downey, a Red Sox fan from Dorchester, dedicated a plaque at the Babe Ruth Museum in Baltimore. In exchange for a contribution to the museum, patrons can secure a plaque commemorating one of Ruth's 714 home runs. It's the Museum's 714 Club. Downey's plaque, which is assigned to Ruth home run no. 518 off Jack Russell in Boston, reads, "Please Forgive Boston."

Longtime Red Sox fan Dan Berger submitted a theory as to why the Sox would win in '95:

- In 1918, the last time the Sox won, Babe Ruth collected 95 hits in 95 games. Ruth was born in 1895, emphasizing the importance of both 18 and 95. The 1995 season marked the one hundredth anniversary of the Bambino's birth.
- The 1918 Red Sox had a winning percentage of .595.
- In Ruth's last year with the Red Sox his record was 9–5.
- In Ruth's first year with the Yankees, New York won 95 games. The '75 and '86 Red Sox both won 95 games.
- The 1995 Red Sox won their first spring training game by a score of 9–5.
- The original hardcover price of *The Curse of the Bambino* was $18.95.

Clearly, Mr. Berger is a man with a lot of time on his hands. But it did make one wonder about the Sox prospects in 1995. Boston baseball fans will grasp at anything that gives them hope.

When the 1995 Red Sox bolted from the gate with a 24–11 record and a nine-game lead (the franchise's best start since 1971), once again there was pennant fever in the Hub. Andy Savitz, an environmental consultant and a Red Sox lifer, told the *Globe*, "There's something special every year that makes me believe this year is different. We may need to hire a professional exorcist, and I'm hoping to get ten thousand fans holding hands and completely circling the park. We need to do something to get this curse behind us once and for all."

An editorial in the June 7 *Boston Globe*, "Not since 1918," concluded, "Scientistic spirits cannot blame superstitious Sox fans for believing that forces resembling Zephyr or Athena have intervened on the side of the ball club that has finally earned a surcease from the curse of the Bambino."

It went on like that throughout the summer. In July, the Everett Savings bank took out a large ad in both Boston papers, offering a Curse-Buster CD that would pay .50 percent above the bank's regular CD rate as long as the Sox remained in first place. The headline on the ad was "Announcing the end of the Curse of the Bambino." Rosa Ladd, bank marketing director said, "If the Red Sox get into the 1995 World Series, we'll be delighted. In fact, if that happens, we'll let customers extend the certificate for another six months at the premium rate."

Estimable local author/researcher Glenn Stout came up with his own reasons why the '95 team would be the one to break the Curse. He noted that 1995 was a shortened season, just like 1918 (when the Sox prevailed in a war-abbreviated, 126-game season), that the '18 Sox used a whopping forty-four players (Boston set a club record with fifty-three in '95), and that both the '18 and '95 Boston teams had new managers (Ed Barrow in '18, Kevin Kennedy in '95).

David Rotman, a Worcester native, sold a screenplay, entitled *The Curse of the Bambino*, to 20th Century–Fox, with shooting scheduled to begin in the spring of 1996. Contacted at his home in California, Rotman said, "Nobody out here knows what it's like to be a Sox fan and all the pain and suffering it entails. That's why I thought it would be such a great movie. . . . As Red Sox fans we always have hope, no matter what happens, no matter how close we come to winning it all before getting stung."

New Englanders approached the 1995 baseball play-offs with confidence that was surprising given the Red Sox October history. When the Sox had the misfortune to draw mighty Cleveland (one hundred victories) in the first round of the play-offs, *USA Today* presented a cover story on the dueling curses at stake. Clevelanders have long complained that the Tribe was jinxed when popular slugger Rocky Colavito was traded in 1960. Asked about a Boston-Cleveland play-off, Ohio author Terry Pluto said, "It's kind of like the planets aligning. Which curse gives way first?"

The Babe's daughter, Julia Ruth Stevens, said, "He [the Babe] probably would say that's a lot of baloney. He certainly wouldn't put a curse on the Red Sox or anyone else. This year, I really am pulling for the Red Sox. It's time."

Of course, it was not time. The Curse of the Bambino obliterated the Curse of Rocky Colavito in three straight games.

Game one was the true clincher. It was a rainy night in Cleveland . . . which is as bad as it gets. It was also the night America was reeling from the hideous O. J. Simpson not-guilty verdict. The start of the Sox-Indians game was delayed for an hour. When they finally started playing, it seemed as if the game might not end. The Sox and Tribe battled for thirteen innings, more than five hours. The game did not conclude until Tony Pena cracked a 3–0 Zane Smith pitch over the left-field fence at 2:08 A.M. to give Cleveland a 5–4 victory.

Tony Pena? He was the well-liked former Red Sox catcher who'd been cast adrift by Boston after batting only .181 in 1993. For many Sox fans, a home run by Pena was proof that the Curse lives.

The Sox appeared to have won the pivotal first game when Tim Naehring homered to give Boston a 4–3 lead. In the bottom of the eleventh, Sox manager Kevin Kennedy summoned ace closer Rick Aguilera to finish off the Tribe.

Boston had parted with prospect Frankie Rodriguez to acquire Aguilera in July of '95, and the deal was applauded by Red Sox Nation. The logic was simple: if the Sox got close again, this time there would be no scared kid trying to finish the big games. Boston could turn to somebody who had *been there*. Aguilera saved 184 games with the Twins over seven seasons, and the Sox thought of him as Calvin Schiraldi insurance. In 1991, when the Twins beat the Blue Jays in the play-offs and the Braves in a pulsating, seven-game World Series, Aguilera was almost flawless. He picked up three saves and compiled an ERA of 0.00 in the ALCS. He picked up two more saves in the World Series, giving up just one run in four appearances.

When the Red Sox traded for him, Aguilera already had a special place in Sox folklore. Pitching for the Mets in 1986, he was the winning pitcher of the infamous World Series game six. He'd been rocked for three hits and two runs by the Red Sox in the top half of the tenth inning, but had the good forture to pick up the victory when the Curse of the Bambino reared its huge head in the bottom of the tenth. Nine years later, on July 7, 1995, when he first put on a Boston jersey, Aguilera said, "I tried my best to give the Red Sox a world championship." It was easy then. He was a Met. But attempting to win a championship for Boston while wearing the heavy threads of the Red Sox uniform was altogether different.

Aguilera saved twenty games in less than three months for the Red Sox, but when they gave him the ball in Cleveland after midnight in game one, he failed. He surrendered a game-tying home run to Albert Belle. In an ill-timed act of poor sportsmanship, Kennedy asked to have Belle's bat checked for cork. The bat was sawed in two after the game and no cork was found. Two innings after Belle's blast, Pena won it. Aguilera suffered a pulled hamstring after yielding the homer to Belle. He was finished for the year and so were the Red Sox.

The next night, NBC introduced its game broadcast with the story line of the dueling curses. Boston fans already knew the battle was lost. The Sox were shut out by Orel Hershiser in game two, then came back to Fenway for an 8–2 loss that completed the sweep. Bash brothers Mo Vaughn and Jose Canseco combined to go oh for twenty-seven with nine strikeouts and seventeen stranded base runners in the three games.

Given their horrible 1995 play-off performance, and the franchise's stunning record of thirteen straight postseason losses in only nine years, perhaps Boston's major league baseball team should be placed on October probation. The NCAA has been known to punish rule violators by barring schools from bowl appearances for a specified amount of time. Might the lords of baseball act to stop the Red Sox before they kill another play-off series? Only kidding, folks.

In 1995, in a story in *American Way* magazine entitled "Curse, Again: 20 Sports Foils," writer Steve Pate selected the twenty worst curses in sports. Number one was the Curse of the Bambino. Fortunately, the magazine was conveniently located next to the barf bag in the seat pocket in front of every airline passenger.

Realistically, there is only one way the Curse can end. In the final year of Fenway Park, just before the Sox prepare to move to their new, state-of-the-park facility near South Station, the Sox will play the Chicago Cubs in a World Series. It will be the same year that the Cubs are playing their final games at Wrigley Field. Baseball fans from Boston, Chicago, and everywhere in America will find out what happens when the irresistible force meets the immovable object.

Boston and Chicago. Fenway and Wrigley. There's great symmetry here. Boston and Chicago are baseball's blood brothers. The franchises and cities are intertwined. Like the Red Sox, the Cubs enjoy a huge following outside their region. The Cubs have appeared in seven World Series since 1908 and lost all of them. The Red Sox have appeared in four World Series since 1918 and lost each of them in a seventh game. The last time the Sox won the World Series, it was at the expense of the Cubs. The Sox and Cubs play in baseball's two surviving postcard ballparks. In 1906, the only year in which the White Sox and Cubs both finished first, the Boston Braves and Red Sox both finished last. In 1948, when the Braves and Red Sox both finished first (the Red Sox tied for first and lost a one-game play-off to the Cleveland Indians), the Cubs and White Sox both finished last. Since the Black Sox scandal of 1919 (the first World Series after the Red Sox beat the Cubs), no team from Chicago or Boston and no team with the surname "Sox" has won a World Series. You've got to vault all the way to 1948 (Cleveland Indians) to find the next-longest baseball drought. The New York/San Francisco baseball Giants last won in 1954. No other sport has anything close. In pro football, the Chicago/St. Louis/Phoenix Cardinals (1947) and Los Angeles/St. Louis Rams (1951) have waited longest. In basketball, it's the Rochester/Cincinnati/Kansas City/Omaha/Sacramento Kings (1951). In the National Hockey League, the distinction is held by the Detroit Red Wings (1955).

Red Sox–Cubs would be the Charlie Brown All-Stars versus the Washington Generals, umpired by Harold Stassen. No one would win. The Series would advance to a 3–3 tie, then there would be forty days and forty nights of rain. In the interest of preserving the planet, responsible religious leaders would call for the cancellation of the event. Apocalypse after game six. Mystery novelist King already has

Fenway Park—long on character, short on comforts.
John Tlumacki/Boston Globe Photo

Mayor "Honey Fitz" Fitzgerald throws out the first pitch of the 1912 World Series.
(Rose Fitzgerald is at far right in hat.)
Courtesy Sports Museum of New England

Babe Ruth, who led the Red Sox
to their last World Championship
in 1918.

Courtesy Sports Museum of New England

Fans outside Fenway Park during
the 1918 World Series.

Boston Globe Photo

Duffy Lewis, left fielder, whose
"cliff" preceded the Green Monster.

Courtesy Sports Museum of New England

A groundskeeper climbs the left-field ladder to retrieve balls from atop The Wall.

Bill Brett/ Boston Globe Photo

The Wall giveth and The Wall taketh away: Bucky Dent's home run wins the 1978 Red Sox–Yankee playoff.

Frank O'Brien/Boston Globe Photo

Carlton Fisk waves his twelfth-inning home-run ball fair during game six of the 1975 World Series. The ball hit the left-field foul pole and tied the series.

AP/Wide World

Youthful fans camp in a makeshift shelter waiting for next year's Sox tickets to go on sale, December 1991.

George Rizer/Boston Globe Photo

Loading the Red Sox equipment van for the trip to spring training.

David L. Ryan/Boston Globe Photo

Joe Mooney, head groundskeeper at Fenway, 1987.

Jan Housewerth/ Boston Globe Photo

Elizabeth Dooley throws out the first ball against the Yankees, April 1985.

Frank O'Brien/Boston Globe Photo

Henry and Arthur D'Angelo, in their souvenir shop outside Fenway, November 1977.

AP/Wide World

Peter Gammons.

*Diane Barros/
Boston Globe Photo*

Chuck Waseleski, the Maniacal One.

Boston Globe Photo

Bill Buckner lets the winning run go through his legs in game six of the 1986 World Series— a moment that plays repeatedly, like the Zapruder film, through the minds of Red Sox fans.

*Stan Grossfeld/
Boston Globe Photo*

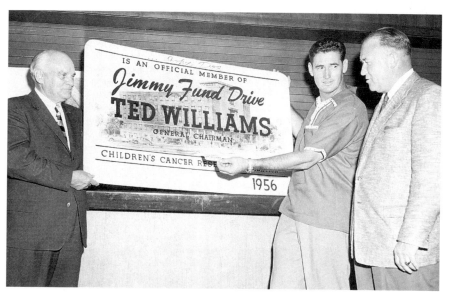

Ted Williams displays a fund drive poster as he is appointed General Chairman of the Jimmy Fund. (Williams is flanked by Massachusetts Registrar of Motor Vehicles Rudolph King and Boston Garden President Walter Brown.)

UPI/Bettman Archive

Former Sox
General Manager
Lou Gorman
welcomes new GM
Dan Duquette,
January 1994.

*Frank O'Brien/
Boston Globe Photo*

Clam chowder in the
stands at Fenway.

*Lane Turner/
Boston Globe Photo*

such a theory. King says that the ultimate Sox scenario would be "one out away from winning for the first time since 1918 and nuclear war is declared."

Cub fans even have their own curse: the Billy Goat Curse. The Chicago Curse goes like this: Sam Sianis, proprietor of the Billy Goat Tavern, claims that in 1945 his uncle bought two Cubs World Series tickets. According to legend, William "Billy Goat" Sianis bought one for himself, one for his goat. The goat was denied admission, and the Cubs lost to the Detroit Tigers in seven games. When the Cubs made the play-offs in 1984, then-general manager Dallas Green allowed Sianis to bring his goat to Wrigley Field. Chicago won two home play-off games, but lost three goatless, gutless games in San Diego (Leon Durham muffing a grounder between the wickets, à la Bill Buckner), and the Padres went to the World Series. In 1989, Sianis called for another goat play-off ticket, but was again denied. The Cubs were wiped out by the San Francisco Giants. Don Zimmer, former Red Sox manager and scapegoat, was managing the Cubs in '89 and took much of the blame for the loss. In 1994, a "ringer" goat was brought to Wrigley and paraded around the field to snap a twelve-game losing streak. The Cubs won the next game, but still haven't won it all.

In the spring of 1995, when the Cubs and Sox both enjoyed first-place starts, the *New York Times* ran a Sunday column headlined, "Looks a Lot like 1918 for Red Sox and Cubs after Early Success." Cubs GM Ed Lynch, a former Red Sox pitcher, said, "The way life is, if we ever get to the World Series, you know we'll be playing the Red Sox. Wouldn't that be something? One of us would break a long drought." Sox GM Dan Duquette countered with, "Bring them on."

Red Sox CEO John Harrington and Cub general manager Andy MacPhail have kidded about the prospect of the Ultimate World Series.

"When I see him at meetings, I say, 'Maybe this is the year for both of us,' Harrington said, laughing. "Of course, we would have to win that one. We could call back Don Zimmer to throw out the first ball. It would be great for the game. Ken Burns wouldn't know what to do."

In the midst of the Cubs' early-season run in '95, former Cubbie

Ron Santo said, "I played fourteen years with this team and unfortunately we never won it, but someday it's going to happen. And, God, I hope I'm there when it does. Wouldn't it be something?"

Santo could be Dwight Evans, Carl Yastrzemski, or Ted Williams. The words and emotions are identical.

Legendary *Chicago Tribune* columnist Mike Royko wrote in 1989 of the mistake his father made: "To this day, I cannot forgive him for taking me to Cubs games at an impressionable age. He didn't tell me I was going to have to live through Smalley, Jeffcoat, Miksis, Chiti, Dave Ding Dong, '69 and '84. That's why, while I've made mistakes as a parent, I did one thing right. I didn't raise my kids to be Cubs fans. When this season ends, they will not shed a tear or lose a night's sleep over a ball game."

Compare this with what *Boston Globe* columnist Mike Madden wrote about his two daughters after the 1986 World Series: "When they were three, I should have trained—no demanded and commanded—them to like the Yankees. I would never have let a friend or a boy do this to them, but I allowed the Red Sox."

Some significant members of the Red Sox Hall of Shame have also worn Cub uniforms. Buckner was traded from the Cubs to the Red Sox in exchange for Dennis Eckersley. Schiraldi—the losing pitcher in the sixth game of the 1986 World Series, the man who could not hold a 5–3 lead with two outs and nobody on base—was traded from the Red Sox to the Cubs after the 1987 season and soon pitched and ate himself out of baseball. Zimmer, the most maligned Red Sox manager of all time (nicknamed Gerbil by Bill Lee), managed the Cubs to the 1989 National League East title.

In 1994, when the great baseball strike wiped out the World Series for the first time since 1904 (which would have been Red Sox–Giants, but New York refused to play the Boston Americans), *Sports Illustrated* ran an August cover story detailing how the season would have ended if the season had run its course. The fantasy issue showed an anonymous Red Sox player sliding into home plate, avoiding the tag of a Chicago Cub catcher. The story, written by Richard Hoffer, detailed a long-awaited Red Sox–Cubs World Series: "David Letterman moves his show to Boston for two weeks; Jay Leno takes his to Chicago. There is only one thing on the country's mind: baseball." In Hoffer's account, the Red Sox take a 3–2 Series lead, then lose the final two games at Fenway. Curses. The Sox could not even win a mythical matchup.

There's even a newspaper connection between the Red Sox and Cubs. The Red Sox were once owned by the Taylors, who owned the *Boston Globe* for more than one hundred years. It was John I. Taylor who named them Red Sox and the Taylors built Fenway Park. In 1981, the Cubs were purchased by the Tribune Corporation, owners of the *Chicago Tribune*. The *Trib* is the paper of record in Chicago, just as the *Globe* holds the distinction in Boston. But there haven't been many banner headlines for either team.

There are other Boston-Chicago sports links:

- Football's Super Bowl has been played since 1967, but teams from Chicago and New England have each made it to the big game only once. Naturally, they made it the same year, and the Bears routed the Patriots, 46–10.

- The best hockey player in the history of the Boston Bruins, Bobby Orr, finished his career by playing twenty-six games for the Chicago Black Hawks from 1976 to 1979. To this day, Boston GM Harry Sinden says letting Orr escape was the worst public relations blunder in franchise history.

- The most celebrated New England college football player in local history, Boston College quarterback Doug Flutie, broke into the NFL with the Chicago Bears and later played for the Patriots.

- Bob Cousy, known as Mr. Basketball in the 1950s, came to the Boston Celtics in 1950–51 and retired after winning six NBA championships. He was the first great player in the long history of Celtic greats. Originally he was the property of the NBA's Chicago Stags, but the Stags folded and Cousy came to Boston in a dispersal draft.

- Steve Lyons played for all three Boston/Chicago baseball franchises. He came up with the Red Sox and was part of the '86 team (the team that should have won the World Series) until midsummer, when he was traded to the White Sox for Tom Seaver. Sox players stiffed him when it came time to vote World Series shares. He played a couple of seasons with the White Sox, where his best moment came when he took down his pants—dusting himself off after sliding into a base —in front of a large crowd and a television audience. He also played with the Cubs during spring training of 1993. His nickname: Psycho. The Lyons-Seaver trade will forever be known as Psycho for Cy Young. This is Lyons's take on Boston versus Chicago as baseball towns:

"Boston's definitely more starved because they only have one team and because the Red Sox are the team for all New England. I think Chicago is a great sports city. The towns are evenly matched as far as having knowledgeable fans and expecting great things. But if Boston ever wins it all, the party in Boston would make any celebration anywhere else look like a third-grade birthday party. The Cubs would have a big celebration, but in Chicago, just as many fans love the White Sox. Boston has tougher fans, I'll say that. And the press is much more intense. When I played in Boston, we had eight or ten writers traveling with us. With the White Sox, it was two. Boston has more media scrutinization. Fans in Boston just want a championship so badly. Those people live and die with the Red Sox."

Lifelong Sox fans are plagued by two unanswerable questions: (1) Is there life after death? and (2) What would it feel like if the Red Sox ever won the World Series?

Ron Darling grew up in Millbury, Massachusetts, and pitched for Yale before becoming a big winner for the 1986 World Championship Mets. Before that '86 World Series, Darling speculated that a Red Sox victory in the fall classic "might alter the way New Englanders view the world."

When the Red Sox were on the threshold of victory, after the fifth game of the 1986 World Series, Ted Williams was asked what he'd do on the night of game six. Williams said, "I'm going to watch the game with some friends, and if we win, we'll raise our glasses and say a toast. It won't be a martini, but it will be a big milk shake or something. Then I'll go to sleep with a warm feeling."

Former Sox general manager Lou Gorman, a Rhode Island native, says, "When the Red Sox win a World Championship, and someday they will, they'll turn this city upside down."

A widespread theory, put forth by many in the 1980s, is that a Red Sox World Championship would ultimately take something away from Sox fans. What, after all, would they complain about if the Sox actually won? And what would be left to look forward to? New Englanders love to grouse about the Towne Team, and if the Sox failed to fail, the team would lose its reason for being.

"You know, Boston has had some great teams and some great players over the years," Buckner said in *One Pitch Away*. "They just haven't made that final step. . . . Now I can understand a little bit of the frustration. If they'd just win that one championship, then that would kind of clear things up. Maybe they wouldn't have anything to talk about then."

Author King writes, "If being just another team is the price we have to pay for finally winning it all, I'm ready to pony up my share. . . . It's important that these jokes should stop, and that we should finally have the pleasure of finding out if we can win as gracefully as we have lost all these years."

Harrington admits, "Clearly, there would be a letdown by everybody. It won't be deliberate, but like any subconscious thing, there will be this collective 'Whew,' and it's going to take some great young minds to keep driving after it happens. I do think us winning would result in a little loss of intensity on the part of our fans. It's like going to see a show for the second or third time. You love it just as much, but the charm and anxiety aren't there."

Charm and anxiety. That's what the Red Sox are all about. Someday they will win it all. And we hope and pray that the blessed event occurs at Fenway—perhaps in the final year of the beloved ballpark.

CHAPTER FIVE

CITIZENS OF RED SOX NATION

THE GOAT

◆ He played in four decades, won a batting title, and hit .300 or better eight times. In his twenty-one years in the big leagues, he played in two World Series and stroked more base hits (2,715) than Joe DiMaggio. But today he is known for one play only. Bill Buckner is the man who let the slow-rolling grounder trickle between his legs in the bottom of the tenth inning on the final play of the sixth game of the 1986 World Series. No less than Harry Frazee, he is the symbol of three generations of Red Sox failure to win a World Series.

Life is not fair. Bill Buckner is part of baseball lore because he failed to field a simple three-hopper off Mookie Wilson's bat. It's been ten years since the grievous error, but time has been cruel to Billy Buck. When author Peter Weiss (*Baseball's All-Time Goats*) polled more than seventy sportswriters in 1991 for a listing of baseball's all-time blunderers, Buckner appeared on 86 percent of the ballots, far more than any other player (Ralph Branca, who gave up the 1951 homer to Bobby Thomson, was second with 63 precent). The video of Buckner's error has been replayed at least as often as the clip of Carlton Fisk's historic homer in the 1975 World Series and there can be no doubt that a reference to the muffed grounder will appear in the first paragraph of Buckner's obituary.

It's all rather silly. From a technical standpoint, there was little remarkable about that single play. Watch any group of major leaguers take infield practice and you're bound to see someone let one slip through the wickets once or twice a week. During the course of a 162-game season, it'll happen at least two or three times to the best major-league infielders.

Technically speaking, it is among the worst of baseball's physical miscues. It is the kind of fundamental error that you're taught to avoid from your earliest days of Little League. *Keep your glove down. Keep your eye on the ball.* At any level, in any situation, the harmless grounder that skips between the legs is embarrassing. It's like shooting an air ball from the foul line. It's like being thirteen years old and having your voice crack in the middle of your church-choir solo. Or standing in front of your peers, bending over to pick up a stick of chalk, and hearing your pants rip apart at the seam.

Removed from the moment, placed in the middle of a humdrum game in late July, Buckner's error would be as forgettable as yesterday's horoscope. But Bill Buckner enjoys no such luck. A rare merger of history, timing, and symbolism have conspired to inflate Buckner's simple mistake and blow it into a gaffe of epic proportion.

On the night of October 25, 1986 (really the morning of October 26), the Boston Red Sox lugged sixty-eight years of heartache, frustration, and angst into the bottom of the tenth inning at Shea Stadium. The Sox led, 5–3, and were within one out (one strike, in fact) of throwing off all the curses and rewarding Red Sox Nation with a World Series championship. When the Mets started their rally with a couple of two-out singles, only the most skeptical Sox fans worried that the unthinkable might happen one more time.

What's conveniently forgotten is that three consecutive singles and Bob Stanley's wild pitch (which really was Rich Gedman's passed ball) took away Boston's lead and gave the Mets a 5–5 tie with the winning run standing on second base in the person of Ray Knight. The Red Sox had already flopped by the time Wilson hit his chopper down the first-base line. Buckner, manager John McNamara, Stanley, catcher Rich Gedman, and other Sox culprits are quick to remind us that *the game was already tied* when Wilson hit his routine grounder toward Buckner. Had Buckner fielded the ball cleanly and run over to tag the bag before Wilson reached it (no sure thing), the Sox would have been out of the inning. Who knows what might have happened in the eleventh? It's also forgotten that the sixth game was not the last game of the 1986 World Series. The Red Sox had another chance to win the Series in game seven and led that game, 3–0, in the sixth inning. But none of that matters when self-absorbed Sox watchers reminisce about the blown opportunity of '86. Buckner's error is the play to remember because its clinical simplicity best demonstrates the ongoing theme of Red Sox horrors.

Buckner grew up in Napa Valley, California, and was recruited to play football at Stanford by coach Dick Vermeil. The Dodgers drafted him in 1968, and he hit .344 in his first season of professional baseball, playing for manager Tom Lasorda in Ogden, Utah. He hit .314 for the National League champion Dodgers in 1974, then was traded to the Cubs in 1977. (Given Buckner's role in Red Sox history, and the double jeopardy that engulfs the Cubs and Red Sox, there has always been some nice symmetry about Buckner's status as a onetime member of both teams.) The Cubs shipped Buckner to Boston in exchange for Dennis Eckersley in 1984, and despite bad ankles, Buckner did a fine job hitting out of the third spot in the order for the Red Sox.

The ankles were really bad in 1986. Buckner knocked in 102 runs, but spent more time on ice than Nancy Kerrigan. Before the Series he admitted, "Some days I feel like I have a piano on my back. I don't run. I wouldn't call what I do running. I'd call it moving. Somewhere between jogging and walking. That's what I do."

Buckner was hit by a pitch in the top of the tenth inning of game six. He took his base and was stranded at first when Jim Rice lined to the outfield for the final out. When Buckner came off the field to get his glove and prepare to go back out for the bottom of the tenth, he made a trip down the dugout tunnel and used the players' bathroom. *Globe* photographer Frank O'Brien was one of the press people assembled near the clubhouse door, waiting to record the long-awaited victory celebration. O'Brien says, "The Sox had the lead and Buckner walked by us and smirked, 'You guys are missing a helluva game.'"

Then it happened. Two easy outs. Three soft singles. A wild pitch/passed ball. Then Wilson, on the tenth pitch of his at bat, hit the slow roller. It bounced twice, then stayed down and scooted under Buckner's glove and into infamy. After the game, Buckner faced the media and said, "I did concentrate on that ball. I saw it well. It bounced and bounced and then it didn't bounce, it just skipped. I can't remember the last time I missed a ball like that, but I'll remember that one."

It was the sports understatement of the decade. Buckner soon found out that he would never be allowed to forget the stupid grounder.

The jokes started immediately. Two days after the Series ended, the day Buckner was set for ankle surgery at the University of Massachusetts Medical Center in Worcester, Buckner turned on his radio and heard, "More than two and a half million people honored the world champions yesterday in New York, and the parade finished with the Mets' team bus going through Bill Buckner's legs." In Wellesley, Massachusettts, a man wore a Red Sox uniform to a Halloween party. From the back loop of his belt, he had a baseball dangling on a string, like a tail. When people asked the man which Sox player he was supposed to be, the man would bend over, look back at the ball dangling between his legs, and say, "I'm Bill Buckner." A year-end network television special cited Buckner's error as the most memorable sports moment of 1986. When *Boston Globe* editor Jack Driscoll toured the People's Republic of China, the Chinese guide, upon learning that Driscoll was from Boston, said, "Ah, Boston Red Sox," then spread his feet and bent over, pretending to watch a grounder squibble between his legs.

In February, a week before the start of spring training, Buckner pledged not to talk about the grounder anymore. He said, "Once I get to spring training, that's it. It's been blown way out of proportion in the first place. This is the last time I'm talking about it, so tell your friends—this is it. I hate to downplay it, but a lot more important things have happened than that. Now that I've seen the films, I know that we were not going to get Mookie Wilson at first anyway. Stanley was not going to be there [to cover first base]. It's just a mistake, and it's still being blown out of proportion. Other people had a tough time in that Series, too. I won't mention names, but other people had as tough a time as I did [in addition to the error, Buckner hit .188 in the Series, stranding thirty-one runners and making the final out in eighteen innings]."

Stanley has never agreed with Buckner's view that he wasn't going to make it to the bag. That kind of finger-pointing typifies the Red Sox personality through the years. Sometimes, even the wives got into it. In a March 1987 *Sport Magazine* article, Stanley tried to get catcher Rich Gedman off the hook for the wild pitch that everybody knows should have been Gedman's passed ball. Stanley told Todd Balf, "Everyone tried to have me blame Gedman. They might as well blame me. They did that all season." Not happy with that statement, Joan Stanley, defending her husband, said, "I mean, he's up there saying, 'I did wrong and I'm to fault,' and here I am saying, 'No, you're not!' For the rest of his career he's going to take the blame for this. And he shouldn't. I mean, I love Geddy, I really do, but he blew it, you know. He blew it."

I love Geddy, but he blew it.

On the first day of spring training, 1987, Sox manager McNamara told his players they would best serve themselves by not thinking or talking about 1986. Don Baylor later said, "We were the first team in history told not to think about getting to the seventh game of the World Series."

Buckner could not put it behind him, and on July 23, batting .273 with two homers and 42 RBI, he was released by the Sox. He said, "I would have to say that things were good for me here, up until the sixth game of the World Series. After that, it just went down. All the bad media and fan reaction. I think everybody in this town, including the Red Sox, holds that against me. I don't think I lost the World Series. There is no guarantee we would have won that game. . . . I think I deserved better. I don't know if the media created or what, but I don't think it all has to be brought up the way it was."

Nobody had to bring it up. It was there. It was everywhere. Stan Grossfeld, a two-time, Pulitzer Prize–winning photographer for the *Globe*, accompanied a New Jersey all-star baseball team to the Soviet Union. One of the Soviet players told Grossfeld, "I want to see two things in my life: this *Natural* movie and the 1986 World Series. Game six, Red Sox–Mets. I have heard about this ground ball."

In July of 1989, the sports world was reminded that sometimes a player is saddled with more than he can handle. Donnie Moore, the man who threw the pitch that kept the Angels out of the '86 World Series, shot his wife, then killed himself with a gunshot to the head. A fine reliever in his day, Moore surrendered a ninth-inning homer to Boston's David Henderson in the fifth game of the 1986 American

League Championship Series. Though many other moments and plays turned the series in Boston's favor (the Sox went on to win games six and seven), it was Moore's gopher ball that became the symbol of defeat. Hours after his lifeless body was found in his Anaheim home, friends and associates talked about the impact of one pitch. Moore's agent, Dave Pinter, said, "Ever since Henderson's home run, he was extremely depressed. He blamed himself for the Angels not going to the World Series. . . . Even when he was told that one pitch doesn't make a season, he couldn't get over it. That home run killed him."

Moore's former teammate Brian Downing added, "He wasn't treated fairly. He was treated like shit. Nobody remembered the great things he did. All they remembered was that one pitch. And it ruined his life. Despite the way he acted, that he didn't care . . . he was a very sensitive guy. No one cared about him after 1986. He was buried. And that's bullshit. No one wants to give him any credit that he got us to the play-offs. Well, that one home run is not the reason we lost. You [reporters] destroyed a man's life over one pitch."

Dave Henderson, learning of Moore's suicide, said, "I don't know. I guess there's a connection. I heard he had a lot of family problems and everything. I'll tell you what—baseball can't be that serious that you'd take your life. There's got to be a lot of other stuff."

The Associated Press story on Moore's suicide led with, "Tormented by the memory of one pitch . . . "

Buckner wasn't about to do himself physical harm, but for a few years he found it hard to have a sense of humor about his place in sports history. In the spring of 1990, at the age of forty, after he'd been released by the Royals, Buckner begged the Red Sox for a spring-training invitation. He said, "The fans realize I have taken quite a lot of grief. They realize it hasn't been easy and that it would take a lot of desire and fortitude to put myself in that position."

In Florida, he slugged his way onto the team, and when the Sox were introduced before their home opener in April against the Tigers, Bill Buckner got the loudest and longest ovation. It was a cathartic moment in Red Sox history, but the healing was only temporary. Buckner was released during the season and hooked on with the Toronto Blue Jays as a minor-league batting instructor. (In December 1995 he became a hitting instructor for the Chicago White Sox.)

On August 4, 1992, actor Charlie Sheen paid $93,500 for the ball that scooted between Buckner's legs. Umpire Ed Montague originally pocketed the ball and gave it to New York Mets traveling secretary Arthur Richman. Mookie Wilson signed the ball for Richmond, and it wound up being auctioned by Leland's in New York.

ESPN's Keith Olberman wanted to bid for the ball, but didn't want to go as high as $93,500. Olberman says, "Myself and a couple of guys here, we were going to rent a storefront in Boston and have Red Sox fans come in and pray to it. We figured we'd clean up on the sackcloth-and-ashes thing. The premise was that there was this quality to it that made it a living piece of history."

A few days after the auction, Buckner challenged the authenticity of the ball, telling a Boston television station, "That ball I got locked up at home in my safe. If he [Sheen] thinks he has something worth ninety-three thousand five hundred dollars, more power to him. But I can tell him, that is not the case."

For a while Buckner stuck to his story. But nobody believed him. Richman says, "If you watch the game on TV now, you'll see Bill Buckner slowly walking off the field. The ball just laid there. But Ed Montague was on the right-field foul line and he picked it up and and brought it into the umpire's dressing room. I usually went around to the umpires' room after the game to see if they needed anything. Montague said, 'Here's the ball.' I said, 'What do I want with it?' He said I should have Mookie sign it and keep it. So I took it to Mookie and he put, 'To Arthur, this is the ball that won it. Mookie Wilson, October 25, 1986.' I took it home and it was in my living room with other baseballs for about six years. A cousin of mine came in one day and said I should auction it. I figured it would only get five hundred dollars, but he wanted to try so I let him. He went to Leland's. Charlie Sheen, the actor, purchased the ball for eighty-five thousand dollars [with another 10 percent going to the auction house]. Now I understand Buckner says it's a phony ball. When they asked him how he had it, he said it was none of their business. Then he wouldn't let anybody see it. I had letters of authenticity from Ed Montague and Mookie Wilson. It was six weeks before Charlie Sheen's attorneys paid. I told my people to tell the lawyers to give me back the ball. I didn't want the money. Then the check came for the full amount."

Richman says he gave the money to charities, including the Steve Palermo Foundation, the Tony LaRussa Animal Shelter, the Association of Professional Baseball Players, the St. Louis Browns Historical Society, the FBI widows fund, and various churches.

"I didn't mean to hurt Bill or anything," says Richman. " . . . Bill's very bitter about the whole thing. I heard he sold his spikes and glove from that game for four theater tickets, so he must have been shocked to see what that ball went for."

Today, Buckner says he was only joking about having the real ball. He must also be joking about his World Series ring, which was reportedly auctioned by Leland's for $33,000, along with a hand-signed letter of authenticity. The ring went to a private collector and the letter says, "Hope you enjoy my 1986 World Series ring. The nightmare of 1986 is over! Your pal, Bill Buckner." Still, Buckner says he has his World Series ring.

As a Blue Jays instructor, Buckner traveled to Europe to conduct clinics in 1993. There he found out that his fame was worldwide. Europeans checked to see if his legs were crooked, and London papers headlined stories "Bill Bucks' Mission Recalls Memories of His Heroic Failure" and "Buckner Batting to Clear His Name." Buckner said, "I've had to deal with this a long time. I can't believe how big it is; it's all over the world now."

It came back home in July of 1993. Buckner was playing catch with his then four-year-old son, a boy who wasn't even born when the Red Sox lost the 1986 World Series. When one of his son's rolling tosses skipped past Buckner, the child said, "That's okay, Dad. I know you have trouble with ground balls." Buckner asked his son where he'd heard that, and the boy reported that an adult had told him about his dad's monstrous error.

There was more. After a minor league game at McCoy Stadium in Pawtucket in 1993, Buckner got into a fight with a fan.

"I was walking out of the park, carrying my bag," said Buckner. "Somebody asked me for an autograph, and another guy said, 'Don't give him a ball, he'll just drop it anyway.' I got to my truck and put my bag inside and I started thinking about it. I went back and found out who said it, and I picked the guy up by the shirt collar. That got his attention."

A week later, after appearing in an old-timer's game during All-Star week in Baltimore, Buckner announced that he was moving his family out of Massachusetts—all the way to Meridian, Idaho, about four miles west of Boise.

"At least once a week during the baseball season I hear something said," Buckner said. "I'm definitely out of there. I don't want to hear it anymore. My kids are getting older now and they're hearing about it. I don't want my kids hearing about it all the time. Why put up with it when you don't have to? People in Boston generally have been pretty good. But people still seem to mention it, and I don't want to hear about it. I'm tired of it. Too many good things happened to me. Playing in a World Series. All-Star game. A batting title. I don't like having to react to the public. For the most part, they've supported me, but I don't want to be a part of it anymore."

Johnny Pesky was sad to hear that Buckner felt he had to move. Pesky was tagged the goat of the 1946 World Series (versions differ, but Pesky may have delayed his relay throw, giving St. Louis its winning run), but he stayed in Boston to serve the Sox as manager, coach, assistant GM, broadcaster, and all-around good guy. When he heard Buckner was moving, he said, "It must have been unbearable for him, but it's something he's got to live with."

Buckner's forced exit to Idaho was national news. *Sports Illustrated's* Leigh Montville (formerly of the *Globe*) wrote, "He is a character from a modern Nathaniel Hawthorne novel about the harshness of village life in New England. A scarlet letter and a scarlet numeral adorn Bill Buckner's chest, the poor man consigned forever to wear the symbol E-3. . . . His image will never be allowed to change. There are people who view him as worse than Sacco and Vanzetti put together, worse than Lizzie Borden and Albert DeSalvo, worse than any and all of the Brinks robbers, and worse than Marky Mark, the pride of Dorchester, Massachusetts, who now poses in his underpants. This is serious stuff. Bill Buckner cost the Red Sox a World Series. This is personal."

Indeed. One Sox fan sent a letter to the *Globe* that read, "Buckner is not being forced to move. He must be aware that media coverage is nationwide. He can run but he can't hide, unless when he moves to Idaho he changes his name to Smith and becomes a cowboy. Everyone knows there's plenty of room between those legs for a horse."

So Buckner moved his family to a 130-acre ranch in Idaho. He still travels around the country with the White Sox, but in his free time he develops housing subdivisions, ranches, hunts, fishes, and drives his kids to school.

ESPN-2 interviewed him in the fall of 1993, after his move, and he said, "I don't really joke about it that much. . . . When that play happened, I'm thinking to myself, 'Oh, blanketyblank.' I was upset we lost, but I was thinking, 'We're going to win tomorrow and I'm going to get to play in the seventh game of the World Series.' I had no idea. I didn't have the feeling that a lot of other people did. The next day, I was asked, 'How are you dealing with losing the game? Are you gonna jump off the Brooklyn Bridge?' I couldn't understand it. At that time, I didn't look at it that way at all.

"I probably shouldn't have read all the stuff. For years and years, every week I could find something in the *Boston Globe* relating to the World Series in '86. I couldn't believe it. I don't even mind talking about it. But does it have to be in the paper every week? Every time somebody screws up? Enough's enough. I try to focus on the positive things and I get offended if people don't let me do that. I don't need anybody to tell me how great I was or how bad I was. Just lighten up on some of these things. It's just something that happened. It was an error, a bad play on my part. But I can live with that. . . . It's harder on my wife. She knows I didn't lose the World Series, and why am I getting tortured because of that?"

A safe 2,200 miles from Boston, Buckner told author Mike Sowell, "It's hard for me to fathom that people really put their whole lives into watching baseball games and being fans."

In 1994, Buckner was profiled in *People* magazine's "Where Are They Now" issue. The article stated, "There are no more cruel jokes, no more pointed remarks about the routine ground ball he didn't field."

In the winter of 1994–95, Buckner attempted to capitalize on his famous gaffe. He filmed a Nike commercial with Spike Lee, Willie Mays, Stan Musial, and Michael Jordan. In the commercial, the baseball greats watch Jordan and comment on his hardball skills. They note that Michael is "trying." When a ground ball rolls between Jordan's legs, Spike Lee says, "He ain't no Bill Buckner," and Buckner replies, "But he's trying."

"Buckner is a class act all the way," Nike PR man Tom Feuer told the *Boston Herald*. "He could have taken umbrage, but didn't. He said, 'I'm way beyond that.' Bill's a very friendly guy, and as far as that incident goes, he's over it."

A *USA Today* review of the commercial stated, "P.S. for youngsters out there: That's a reference to a Buckner botch in the 1986 World Series which left psychological wreckage in the Boston area that bolstered arguments by experts who say society places too much emphasis on winning."

Alas, when Jordan returned to the NBA, Nike spiked the ad. But the commercial represented an important step for Buckner. Ralph Branca, the man who threw the notorious home-run ball to Bobby Thomson in the 1951 National League play-off game, today tours the card-show circuit with Thomson. The two men make money off their historic moment. Branca has a sense of humor about his place in baseball history. It's better than no place at all.

Buckner put out feelers to write his autobiography, but no publisher has expressed enough interest to make the project worthwhile. Certainly as years pass, Buckner will become a bigger part of baseball legend, and fans are going to want a piece of him. But it can't be easy to be asked only about a stupid ground ball after smashing 2,700 hits in four different decades of big league baseball.

But infamy remains eternal. When British actor Hugh Grant was arrested for soliciting a Hollywood prostitute, and *Boston Herald* readers were asked for their reaction, one respondent said, "You screwed up real bad, boy. You had one of the most beautiful women in the world [supermodel Elizabeth Hurley] and you blew it on a fifty-dollar hooker. Real smooth. That's a worse screwup than Bill Buckner."

At the Westwind Florist shop in Saint John, New Brunswick, florist Don Johnson still offers an October special, "Bill Buckner Boot." According to Johnson, the boot includes dried roses, baby's breath, and is decorated with black bows. Attached is a sympathy card that reads, "With Dearest Sympathy to a Red Sox Fan." Johnson says, "Our customers get a big kick out of the boot."

The ground ball between Buckner's legs will continue to be a symbol of Boston baseball. Just when you think it's been beaten to death, something new comes to the fore. Almost ten years after the error was made, a Boston baseball fan called WBZ-TV and asked sports anchor Bob Lobel about a Buckner interview from the 1986 championship series. The viewer swore that he remembered Buckner saying something about blowing the whole thing by letting a grounder go between his legs. WBZ intern Maggie McGrath got on the case and spent two weeks poring over tapes from the station's warehouse in Roxbury. She finally found the dead Sox scroll.

It turns out that on Monday, October 6, 1986, nineteen days before the sixth game of the World Series, Buckner made a prophetic statement. On a sunny, New England fall day, as the Boston Red Sox and California Angels took turns in the batting cage at Fenway Park, Buckner was interviewed by WBZ-TV's Don Shane. Buckner answered questions for about five minutes, finishing with some thoughts on the glories and pressures of postseason play. In his conclusion, he stated, "The dreams are that you're gonna have a great series and win. The nightmares are that you're gonna let the winning run score on a ground ball through your legs. Those things happen, you know. I think a lot of it is just fate."

On the night of February 26, 1995, WBZ dusted off the old tape and ran it again for Boston sports fans. It was eerie. Almost biblical. It was a Red Sox moment.

And people think we make this stuff up. . . .

THE GRANDE DAME

Want to speak to the owner of the Boston Red Sox? You'll have to go through Helen Robinson, operator of the Fenway Park switchboard for fifty-five years and one of the most powerful people at Fenway.

"I sat outside in the lobby one day and I couldn't believe it," says one player agent who must remain nameless or suffer lifetime freeze-out from Miss Robinson. "This was in the days when Haywood Sullivan was in charge, and I sat there listening to her field his calls. She decided who'd get to talk to him and who wouldn't. If she didn't like somebody, Haywood would never even know they'd called."

Robinson came to Fenway in 1941, following up on a tip from a friend who worked at New England Telephone. The friend said the Red Sox were planning to hire an operator. Robinson got the job and has rarely left the building since. She arrives every day at precisely

9 A.M. If she's late, which happens about once every seventeen years, the Sox phone her, then dispatch a ballpark employee to her Milton home. During the season, Helen operates the switchboard until games end. Well into her seventies, she still shows up at 9 A.M. on Saturday after working a late Friday-night game.

"I'll say to her, 'Helen, why don't you come in a little later after those night games. Nobody's going to be calling on a Saturday morning,'" says Red Sox vice president Jack Rogers. "But she won't have any part of it. She's right there the next morning."

"She's a terrific gal," says Ted Williams, who came to Fenway just two years ahead of Helen. "She's a honey. God, I've known her fifty years."

Never married, this grande dame of Fenway had tremendous admiration for Tom and Jean Yawkey and was one of Mrs. Yawkey's closest friends for decades. Gossip around the ballpark was that Jean Yawkey sent Helen on vacations and gave her cars. Miss Robinson still says the busiest day at the switchboard was the day Tom Yawkey died (July 9) in 1976. She told the *Globe*, "He wasn't just a boss, he was also a friend."

In a rare newspaper profile in 1986, she said, "I've never wanted any other job. I've always liked people. I have no plans to retire. What would I do?"

When Yawkey hired her, he gave the order that no direct calls be made into or out of the clubhouse. All calls go through the switchboard, or not at all. T. A. Yawkey is no longer around to rescind the order, and Helen is very selective about who gets through and who gets out. American League managers, both Red Sox and visitors, have made all their phone calls through Helen for fifty-five years. Some suspect she listens to their conversations.

Helen knows where the bones are buried. If a player is trying to hide something from his wife, perhaps leaving tickets for a girlfriend, Helen knows. If the club is worried about a player with a drinking or drug problem, Helen knows. If ownership wants to raise ticket prices or switch spring-training sites, Helen knows. But she tells nothing. She is the guardian at the gate. Discretion is her middle name. She keeps herself out of the newspapers, and she keeps quiet about everybody's business.

She took the calls the day Harry Agganis died, the day Ted Williams homered in his final at bat, and the day Tony Conigliaro was beaned by a Jack Hamilton fastball. She fielded all the calls after the Sox blew the '86 Series and told the *Globe*, "Sure, they take it out on me. Who else are they going to take it out on? You don't really think I can repeat what they said, do you?"

Helen answers each call with a stern, "Red Sox." In fifty-five years, the number of times she's said "Red Sox" would have to number in the millions.

Meanwhile, Helen isn't talking. She refused to be interviewed for this book.

"I just don't want to," she said politely.

A switchboard operator with no comment. Only at Fenway.

THE LAWN-MOWER MAN

Green is the color fans first notice when they enter Fenway. The ballpark facades, including the huge wall in left field, are green, and the playing field is the envied, emerald green of postcards from Ireland. Like every plush lawn in Newport or Wellesley, Fenway's turf requires year-round attention and affection. And for the last quarter of a century Joe Mooney has been the man who protects and defends the green, green grass of Fenway Park.

In or out of season, just about any time of day or night, you can find Mooney at Fenway Park. Deep in the bowels of dirty old Fenway, wedged under the left-field grandstand, Mooney occupies a small office. Outside his office there is a wheelbarrow, which on this day is being used to cart a pile of dirt, a can of insect repellent, and an old Red Sox batting helmet. There's a shamrock on the outside of Mooney's wooden door, and the ceiling of his hut is sculpted in the inverted slope of the grandstand above. The office is cluttered with rakes, clippers, fertilizer samples, paperwork, clipboards, and more dirt. Mooney is the protector of the Fenway sod; dirt is in his blood.

Woeful is the innocent tourist or sportswriter who dares trod on the Fenway lawn without Mooney's permission. Over the years, thousands of naive, well-meaning visitors, salespeople, ballplayers in street clothes, and VIPs have been routed by Boston's lawn-mower man. He doesn't want anyone trampling his perfect grass, and he'll blast trespassers with a high-pressure hose if he must. Ballplayers have come to feel that they are lucky Joe Mooney lets them play on the Fenway green.

Sometimes Mooney doesn't yield the stage, and that's believed to be one of the reasons the 1986 Red Sox stiffed Mooney and his grounds crew when it was time to divvy up the World Series shares. Veteran leaders like Don Baylor and Dwight Evans were said to resent Mooney's reluctance to give up the field when they wanted it, and they took their revenge when it came time to divide the pennant pool.

"It was wrong," says ex–Sox lefty Bruce Hurst. "I say, 'Share the gold.'"

"Aw, that's not true," says the lawn-mower man. "That thing in '86 was just a misunderstanding with two or three guys. Most of the guys on that team were good guys. I let people on the field all the time, unless we're in the middle of doing something. And the players can have it anytime they want. It's just that sometimes the manager gives me certain orders and then the players want to do something different, and I get caught in the middle. But I don't throw people off the field. I get blamed even when it isn't me. Last year, a reporter wrote that I threw some tourist off the field, and I was in Pawtucket that day.

"You can't believe how people will come in here from California, Canada, London. From any place you can think of. And they'll come in the coldest days of wintertime. They all want to touch the left-field wall. I tell 'em, 'go ahead,' if there's nothing here. Sometimes they can't come in because we've got the ramps blocked off because of the ice and snow. But they won't believe you. What happens is, the guy out front at the gate lets them in and then they're all over the place."

A lot of kids who work around the yard live in fear of Mooney's bark, but deep down he's just an Irishman with a green thumb and a soft heart. He looks after his young employees. He has an eight-man crew on weekdays, sixteen on weekends. In the summer, he might have thirty to forty stouthearted men on his payroll. In the winter, the crew is smaller.

With great pride, Mooney talks about past crews, groups who could roll a tarpaulin over the infield in a matter of seconds after the first raindrops fell to earth. "Back in the late seventies and early eighties, the crews were great," he says. "They could get the tarp down in about forty-five seconds. They spoil you."

Mooney was born in Scranton, Pennsylvania, in 1930. Scranton was the longtime home of the Class A Red Sox of the Eastern League, and the ballpark was across the street from his house. When Mooney was nine, his father died, and young Joe went to work for Scranton Red Sox groundskeeper Denny Baskerville.

"I did everything," Mooney recalls. "I cleaned his stands, worked on the field, pushed wheelbarrows. Anything you can think of. When I got out of high school, it was 1946 and I was lucky to be getting eighty cents an hour. I worked from the time the sun come up in the morning until it went down at night. Denny Baskerville was real tough. He was from the real, real old school. They think I'm bad. He was fifty times worse. But he was fair. He was a hard worker himself. He lived to be one hundred and two years old. I worked there until I got out of high school, until the Red Sox sold the team, and then I went on to Louisville."

Mooney went to college for one year at the University of Scranton, but groundskeeping was going to be his life. Following his Red Sox connection, he worked in Louisville (where the triple-A Sox played) from 1952 to 1955. He left Louisville to work two seasons for the San Francisco Seals of the Pacific Coast League, then went to Metropolitan Stadium in Bloomington, Minnesota, where his boss was manager Gene Mauch. While in Minnesota (American Association, 1958–60), Mooney befriended a young Sox prospect named Carl Yastrzemski. Signed out of Notre Dame, the son of a Long Island potato farmer, Yastrzemski was being groomed to replace Ted Williams in left field in Boston. Yastrzemski was always anxious to take extra batting practice, and for a year in the minors young Yaz took batting practice against the pitching of groundskeeper Mooney every morning at ten. Mooney knew the game. He'd played.

"I wasn't as good as the players were, I knew that," says Mooney. "As a kid, I'd played infield. We had a team in Scranton that won seventy-two straight games. We called ourselves the Red Sox Juniors. The minor league club sponsored us, buying us uniforms and everything. When the team was on the road, we played semipro teams and everybody else."

In the winter of 1960–61, Mooney got the break he needed to make it to the big leagues. The old Washington Senators had moved to Minnesota, taking the Red Sox minor league team out of the Met. Newly married, Mooney and his bride, Nancy, moved in the other direction. After a lifetime of working for the Red Sox organization, Joe Mooney took over as head groundskeeper for the expansion Washington Senators in 1961. The new Senators played one year at Griffith Stadium, then moved into the stadium now known as RFK.

In his ten years at RFK, Mooney tended the grounds for both major league baseball and NFL football. By a quirk of fate and location, he simultaneously worked for two American sports legends. In the late 1960s, Mooney kept the grass green for Senators manager Ted Williams *and* Washington Redskins head coach Vince Lombardi.

"How'd you like to work for them both at the same time?" he says, excited at the memory. "They were great. I got along good with both of them. They were two fair guys. Lombardi, after the Redskins got through with practice, would come up and hang around the batting cage. The conversations with him and Ted were great. The worst thing I ever did was not tape them. They were great to work under. You could tell the mood that Vince Lombardi was in when he pulled into the ballpark at eight in the morning. Everybody knew what kind of a day it was going to be. I used to go to mass with him and Edward Bennett Williams."

In 1970, Mooney returned to the Red Sox, getting his first crack at Fenway Park. He was recommended by Ted Williams and hired by Boston GM Dick O'Connell with the blessing of owner Tom Yawkey.

Williams on Mooney: "Everywhere he went, he was the best. That's all there is to it. And everybody acknowledged him. He just had a knack of doing things right more often."

"There were only three drains in the whole outfield when I got here," Mooney remembers. "That first year, whenever it rained in September or October, I put nails in the outfield where the puddles were. That's where we put the drains. It took me about three years to get what I wanted. Now I got fifty-two drains. I also changed the whole dirt in the infield. It was just a powder dirt, and now it's a mix of turf base with a calcified clay and sandy soil and a little clay. The grass is bluegrass, with a little rye. It was grown in Rhode Island."

Mooney and his crew cut the grass every day when the Sox are in season. They keep the turf one inch high for the infield. During a game Mooney walks around Fenway, checking the rest rooms, looking for broken water pipes. He does just about everything except watch the ball game.

A groundskeeper at Fenway deals with a mix of problems relating to antiquity and weather. There's no artificial turf to make life easy. (Just what does the groundskeeper do at the Houston Astrodome?) Fenway's facilities are hopelessly limited and outdated. And New England's unpredictable weather—blizzards, hurricanes, month-long droughts—makes the job challenging and sometimes impossible. It's not like taking care of Jack Murphy Stadium in San Diego. In the winter of 1993–94, the Hub had more than one hundred inches of snow. From November until April, the first-base side of the Fenway diamond gets no sun. Some years, Mooney needs jackhammers to break glaciers covering the home team's on-deck circle. In the late 1980s, he discovered a felt covering to keep the field warm in winter while still allowing air and sun to filter through. The lawn can breathe, even when it's covered.

In addition to keeping the field green, Mooney is in charge of maintaining much of the ballpark. His crew repairs grandstand seats, patches concrete, and attaches the netting atop the left-field wall.

"We've got to have it up there during cutting season because the kids from those nightclubs on Lansdowne Street will throw anything over the wall. We get bottles, nails, car keys. You'd be surprised how many girls' keys you find. They come in here the next day looking for them."

There's an image for you: a young couple staggers out of Mama Kin on Lansdowne Street at 2 A.M. She wants to go home, he wants her to come home with him. They argue, and he chucks her car keys over Fenway's left-field wall.

Mooney's relationship with ballplayers has faded to a point where he has almost no contact with any of today's Red Sox. It was different in the days when he pitched batting practice to Frank Howard, Jim Lemon, and Yastrzemski. In 1983, Mooney bought a house from former Sox catcher Bob Montgomery. He was always close with Jim Rice.

Today, there is no relationship. Mooney doesn't even watch the ball games, unless there's a threat of rain.

"The last few years I have stayed away a lot," he admits. "Overall, I think my relationship with the players has been good. There isn't much now. I think everybody changes. Myself, I think I got a little easier. But I definitely don't pay mind to the game like I used to. I just taught myself to stay away from them."

He has no use for celebrity groundskeepers. Unlike a few lawn men around the league, Mooney has not been accused of doctoring the field to give his team an advantage. He says he's never seen a field win a game.

Mooney's wife passed away in 1993. His daughter, Joanne, graduated from Notre Dame and lives in Houston. Lately Mooney's neck and left shoulder have been bothering him, and too many years of sun have forced him to wear a hat and sunglasses. He hates both. Today his passions are his daughter, his grandchild, and Notre Dame football. The thrill of caretaking Fenway is gone and he plans to retire soon. He is not emotional about the ballpark he's polished for the last quarter of a century.

"I don't think it could go on forever," says Mooney. "It's just like anything else. I think definitely you need a new one. This one is getting there. I think they have to do something because maintaining it and everything else wouldn't be worth it."

Mooney says he'll retire before Fenway is retired. "Nobody goes on forever. Not Fenway. Not me."

THE LADY IN THE FRONT ROW

Elizabeth Dooley has had front-row season tickets (box 36A) since 1944. Except for an occasional wedding or funeral, she hasn't missed a game in more than fifty years. She was there when Ted Williams tossed his bat into the air and inadvertently conked Joe Cronin's groundskeeper in the head. She was there when Earl Wilson homered and no-hit the Angels in a 1962 night game. She was there when Tony Conigliaro homered in his first Fenway at bat in 1964, and when Dave Morehead pitched a no-hitter in front of just 1,247 fans hours before the Sox fired General Manager Pinky Higgins. She was there when Lenny Dykstra led off the third game of the 1986 World Series with a home run off Oil Can Boyd. She was there when Tom Brunansky made a miracle catch to clinch the American League East title on the final day of the 1990 season. She's been to more than four thousand games at Fenway Park.

Incredibly, in a half century of games, she's caught only one foul ball—a pop-up off Carroll Hardy's bat.

"I caught it in self-defense," she says. "Everyone was as surprised as I. Carroll Hardy was at bat in the early 1960s, and he popped one up in my direction. So I braced myself by holding on firmly to a barrier. I fainted and was taken to the hospital, where they discovered I had two broken fingers."

Carroll Hardy, Elizabeth Dooley. It's more trivia for Red Sox Nation. All good Sox fans know Hardy was the one man to pinch-hit for Ted Williams. Now we discover he was also the author of Elizabeth Dooley's only souvenir in fifty years of daily attendance.

Williams smiles at the mention of Dooley's name and says, "Forever, she's the greatest Red Sox fan there'll ever be. She is a sweet thing. I've got a dalmation dog. And he is a honey. And she knows how much I love that dog and she sends me dalmation banks and pictures. Every time I get a chance to get around her, I like to do it because she's really a big-league gal."

She sits in row one, behind the on-deck circle on the first-base side of Fenway. In the old days, it was not unusual for announcer Curt Gowdy to tell the masses, "There's Lib Dooley in her new pink hat."

Elizabeth Dooley's father, John Stephen Dooley, attended every baseball opener in Boston from 1894 until his death in 1970. John Dooley lived to be ninety-seven. He was instrumental in helping the Boston Americans get the Huntington Avenue Grounds for a home field in 1900 and later helped bring Sunday baseball to conservative Boston. He also founded the Winter League, which was a forerunner of Boston's BoSox Club. For several years, Elizabeth Dooley served on the Club's board of directors.

Elizabeth was born a few months after the Red Sox won the 1918 World Series. Her brother John was manager of the Boston College baseball team. She was a redheaded schoolteacher and a Boston College night student when she bought her first season pass in 1944. Better than bridge, better than gossip, attending baseball games was something she could do by herself in the fresh air. In 1956, Dooley moved to Kenmore Square, where she has lived for forty years. She stopped teaching after thirty-nine years in the Boston schools. She never married. The Red Sox stole her heart.

"It was just something I made up my mind I was going to do with my time," she says. "It's a hobby. I thought it was something that would keep me interested in the game. I grew up in a household where baseball was talked about day and night. It was kind of a challenge. I will not play bridge. This was the alternative. I did a lot of traveling through the years. You have to have structure in your life. I used this as the basis of my recreational time. I also figure-skated, played tennis, and rode horses. But this was my choice. And I've met some really nice people."

In 1985, she threw out the first ball for the Red Sox home opener, firing a strike to Sox catcher Rich Gedman. In 1987, team owner Jean Yawkey asked Miss Dooley to hand out the twenty-year commemorative rings to members of the 1967 Impossible Dream Red Sox.

What function do the Red Sox serve in the Boston community?

"I think they keep people's mind on something wholesome," Dooley says. "It's just fun to go. I was there one afternoon when there were four hundred and sixty-one people [September 28, 1965, against California]. We actually did try to count them. I was there for Ted Williams's last home run. All kinds of things. That's what I keep thinking now. These people have missed so many things that I have seen.

"To see a no-hitter is a tremendous thrill, and I've seen five of them. I saw Allie Reynolds throw one against us in New York. Of course, that was when Ted hit a pop-up in the ninth inning and Yogi dropped it. The Fisk home run was a great moment. I saw an unassisted triple play. And to see the four names of those who are in the Hall of Fame [Ted Williams, Bobby Doerr, Joe Cronin, Carl Yastrzemski] and to think there are people who don't know who they are. I do a lot of teaching out there."

After fifty years and four thousand games, does Dooley feel entitled to a World Championship?

"I don't feel entitled," she says. "I think it would be marvelous for the number of years we've been waiting to finally accomplish that. It would be a great achievement. I didn't go to the World Series games in New York in 1986. I felt very badly for Bill Buckner. He wanted to play that day. Some of the others didn't want to play. I have great sympathy for him. They all have kids, you know. The kids have to live with that."

Her favorite ex-players are Ted Williams, Bobby Doerr, Johnny Pesky, and Dom DiMaggio. But she doesn't think of all Red Sox players as "my boys."

"Oh, please," she says. "You can have some of them."

And what about the future of Fenway? It's an emotional issue for Sox fans everywhere.

"I'm not going to worry about it," she says. "I don't think I've got much time left. What they do after I'm gone doesn't matter. But as far as I'm concerned, it's the most valuable piece of real estate in Boston."

THE MAYOR OF FENWAY

Henry and Arthur D'Angelo were born in Orsogna, Italy, on December 12, 1926, and came to America with their brothers and parents in 1938. Their first job was selling newspapers in front of Fenway Park for two cents apiece.

Arthur remembers, "The war was coming and my family felt we would be safer in the United States than in Europe. My three brothers and my parents came over and we settled in the North End. By 1939 my brother and I started selling newspapers—the *Daily Record* and the *Boston American*. You just couldn't go in front of any corner. We used to walk around this city looking for a spot, and there was always a newsboy in front of the train station. But this street [then Jersey Street, now Yawkey Way] was good. There was nobody selling papers here. We just saw crowds and felt we could sell here. We didn't know anything about baseball. We sold our papers in front of Fenway Park, and the only English we knew was "Two cents, mister."

By the time Henry died in 1987, the twins owned one of the largest souvenir shops in the world and the entire block across the street from Fenway Park. Their Twins Enterprises Inc. was selling 20 million caps a year, worldwide. Today Arthur and his four sons oversee the fan-friendly shop, plus the international company that ships baseball caps all around the world. It's a long way from the days of "Two cents, mister."

Arthur and Henry were identical. As teenagers, they would switch dates and young ladies never noticed. The boys were drafted into the United States Army in 1943 and managed to get their high school diplomas while serving their new country. They were discharged in 1946 and immediately took their business back to the streets of Fenway. But this time they were hawking pennants and souvenirs instead of newspapers. Street vendors had sold pennants at college football games for years, but the twins were the first to push pennants during baseball season. It worked. Luckily, 1946 was a magical season in Boston baseball. The '46 Sox, buoyed by the return (from the war) of Ted Williams, Johnny Pesky, Bobby Doerr, and Dom DiMaggio, won their first American League pennant since 1918, went 60–17 at Fenway, and drew a team-record 1.4 million fans.

"Fortunately for us, the Red Sox had their big year in '46, and one thing led to another and that's how we got going," says Arthur.

After the World Series, Arthur and Henry cashed in on America's return from war. They bought an old Greyhound bus and followed a victory train that was touring America, carrying official USA documents. The twins sold pennants with the images of the Constitution, the Bill of Rights, and Japan's official surrender. God bless America.

When the Red Sox returned to defend their American League pennant in the spring of 1947, Arthur and Henry wheeled back to Fenway in their mobile shop, stocked with souvenirs for proud Boston baseball fans.

"We parked around the corner and worked out of the bus, selling our things that way for five years," remembers Arthur. "Then in '52, we rented a small place right near the shop we have now. We rented there until 1965, then we bought the building we're in now. It cost one hundred thousand dollars, and to raise one hundred thousand dollars back then would be like raising five million dollars for us now. You go to a bank and you're just vendors. But we scraped it up and we put up our down payment and bought this building (about twelve thousand square feet). Now we own the whole block. We got lucky. It's all timing."

Timing, indeed. When the twins bought the building, the Red Sox were scuffling through a hundred-loss season. The Sox finished ninth in 1966 and attendance was just over eight hundred thousand. But the twins' gamble paid off in 1967, when the Sox won the most dramatic pennant race in baseball history, doubling attendance and giving birth to a new generation of Boston baseball fans. After 1967, the Red Sox were hot. You could sell anything with Carl Yastrzemski's name on it, and soon there were other hot players and items. Everybody wanted a piece of the Red Sox, and the twins had the posters, T-shirts, caps, and trinkets to make fans happy.

"When the Red Sox won the pennant, we made some good money and that's really when we started rolling," says Arthur. "Because from 1958 to '63, we were ready to go out of business. They used to draw six hundred thousand people and there was nobody buying the stuff. But we battled it out and stuck by it, and it turned out to be a pretty good business for us."

By the late 1980s, the twins had the largest sports store in the nation, carrying 250 different hat logos.

"Now we are probably one of the leaders in the industry in the United States," says Arthur. "We have warehouses in England, Italy, and Germany. We sell baseball, football, basketball hats. We do fairly well. The hats are primarily made in Bangladesh and China. It's shipped directly from there to Europe. Our factory here is for fill-ins. We produce approximately seventy-five thousand dozen per year. But we don't make any money there. Whatever we manufacture in this country, we lose money on. You can't compete with overseas production, but the fill-in keeps our customers happy. Like right now [spring 1995], the Phillies are doing really well and nobody expected it, so we keep filling it in with domestic goods. We have been doing business with Korean and Taiwanese people for the last thirty years. Whatever we do, we need a license for. In the warehouse we employ about sixty people. In the factories another fifty to sixty. It runs into thousands of people."

Arthur's four sons—Robert, Mark, David, and Stephen—run the business with their dad. Arthur's sister-in-law is the family accountant. They lost Henry to lung cancer in 1987.

"We were close," Arthur says, wiping away a tear. "Whatever we've done, we've done together. I'm a workaholic. Eighteen hours a day meant nothing. But since Henry died, I've slowed down. I don't know when the end is going to come."

There have been setbacks, including a fire, some lousy years for the Red Sox, and fallout from baseball's new and never-ending labor crisis. But the twins were most threatened in 1979 when Sox co-owner Buddy LeRoux tried to put them out of business. LeRoux restricted use of the Sox logo and started a ball-club-owned souvenir shop in Fenway Park. This would never have happened in the old days when Tom Yawkey owned the team. More than once, when the late Sox owner had a few too many drinks, Arthur D'Angelo drove the big boss back to his hotel suite. But things changed after Yawkey died.

"They were trying to get us out of the business, but naturally we battled it out," says Arthur. "We bought the old post office on Lansdowne Street in case they changed the entrance to the ballpark. We had to wheel and deal. We have our factory there now."

Today, the D'Angelos are competition for the ball club's official souvenir shop, but there is also subtle cooperation between Twins Enterprises and the Townies. At the ball club's request, Twins stopped selling loud plastic horns and beach balls. And in the new age of licensing fees, Twins must pay a 9.5 percent fee on all Major League Baseball merchandise. It's not like the old days, when they could put Ted Williams's image on everything in the store without having to reimburse Teddy Ballgame. Arthur remembers what would happen when Ted sauntered into the store.

"You guys are making a fortune off me," Ted would bellow.

Arthur would smile and say, "We're making you famous."

It was enough. In 1960, before strikes and lawsuits corrupted baseball, a vendor could satisfy a ballplayer just by telling him he'd make him famous. Now the athlete wants to be rich. Screw famous.

The strike of 1981 cut into business, and it took Twins Enterprises nearly two years to recover, but nothing was as bad as the strike of 1994–95. Crowds returned to Fenway in '95, but they weren't buying in the same numbers. D'Angelo estimates business was off by 15 percent in the first months after the strike ended.

The Great Strike crushed D'Angelo's bank account and his spirit. Although he never played baseball, he's got a front-row seat (box 38, first-base side). From 1946 to 1995 he attended every game at Fenway except the ones during the Rome Olympics in 1960. (He paid for his trip by selling five thousand Olympic banners to the Italians and other tourists.) But in the spring of 1995, Arthur D'Angelo was like a lot of the people who'd stopped walking into his shop.

"Believe it or not, I'm turned off from baseball a little," he admitted. "I'm bitter. Not only financially, but because I'm a sports nut. These guys don't know what the hell is going on in the outside world. . . . It's funny about ballplayers. When they're rookies, they all come in. After they become stars, we never see them again. That's the story."

During the season, D'Angelo arrives at his store at 7:30 A.M. and doesn't leave for home until midnight. He's never in his front-row seat for the first pitch, but he usually makes it by the time the Sox are batting in the bottom of the first. He leaves after the eighth. He's got to be at the store when the customers pour in after the game. When the Sox win, business is up 15 percent.

Stocking the store is risky business. If at Twins they think the Sox are going to the World Series, they need to have T-shirts ready. But they can get stuck with items commemorating events that never happen. D'Angelo still has crates of "Red Sox, 1986 World Champions" pennants and T-shirts. Business was good in the division-winning season of 1995, but strike fallout still cut sales by 15–20 percent.

Bad ideas and bad luck can fill shelves with white elephants. When slugger Ken Harrelson made gold medallions famous in 1968, the twins bought thousands of gold medallions. The Hawk was traded a year later and the medallions are still sagging shelves in the warehouse. Then there was Clyde Vollmer, best known as Dutch the Clutch.

"Oh, he was hot in 1951," Arthur says. "Dutch the Clutch. He had about thirteen home runs in August. We had 'Dutch the Clutch' pennants made up. The pennants came in, and from that day on, he never hit another home run."

The twins have been profiled in the *New York Times* and the *Wall Street Journal*. A year before he died, Henry threw out the first ball before the first game of the 1986 play-offs against the California Angels. It's been a good life for Arthur. He's wealthy, he gets to work with his sons, he makes people happy, and he gets to be around the ballyard.

"A few years back, somebody called me Christmas morning," says Arthur. "They needed a jacket. They promised a sick kid. I came over here and opened the doors and got them a jacket. It was the only place they could get it.

"Today everybody wants wearable stuff. Years ago, if you went to school, you had to wear certain clothes. Now they wear whatever they feel like and they want to be identified with certain teams. People are not afraid to spend money. This has been a great life for us. An enjoyable life. And Boston is still a baseball town. Positively."

He smiles and says, "I walk inside the ballpark and I know all the old people, I know every one of them. I feel like the mayor of Fenway."

THE MAN WHO TRADED JEFF BAGWELL

Affable, cooperative, a great storyteller, and a man with an impressive baseball résumé, James "Lou" Gorman is burdened with a legacy that is both cruel and unfair. Because of the way his career finished—with Gorman blundering through his final seasons as Red Sox general manager—there is in Boston the widely held notion that he is a baseball buffoon. This is simply not true. Like Presidents Johnson and Nixon, Gorman left office under fire, but time and distance should be good for his reputation. When the final box score of Red Sox history is written, Gorman's hits will outnumber his errors.

The Larry Bird Celtics were the top draw in the Hub and interest in the Red Sox had flattened considerably when Gorman first came to the Sox in 1984. From 1986 to 1990 the Red Sox regained their status as New England's top entertainment entity. The Towne Team won three division titles and went to the seventh game of the World Series, while making huge gains in attendance and television/radio revenue. The Sox were more popular than at any time since the pennant-winning seasons of '67 and '75. Presiding over all this bounty was General Manager Lou Gorman, a native of Providence, Rhode Island.

Unfortunately, when things soured in the early 1990s, Gorman was blamed for everything. A sequence of bad trades and free-agent signings buried the team deep in the bottom of the American League East, and Big Lou became the human dartboard of Yawkey Way. Gentle, always available for an interview, overweight, Gorman was an easy target for fans and reporters. His staccato delivery was mocked on sports-radio stations. He tended to be repetitious. His usual response was "Good-good." Throughout baseball, people referred to him as Good-Good. George Brett would spot a writer from Boston and say, "How's Good-Good?"

The constant ridicule started to get to Gorman. In December of 1990, he said, "If I were in Cleveland, they'd build a statue of me downtown. In Boston, they criticize me."

That they did. Columnists and cartoonists had a field day. Gorman became Yaba Daba Lou, a cartoon character, handy for blame whenever the Sox failed to deliver. I contributed to the lampooning of Lou, but the lasting picture of Gorman should be one of a lifelong Red Sox fan who has been a respected baseball executive his entire adult life.

Kicked upstairs before the start of the 1994 season (Gorman's new title is executive vice president of baseball operations), Gorman says he's working on his memoirs. They ought to be good and lengthy. Gorman is a captivating speaker, and anyone who spends time around him will be convinced that Big Lou was responsible for drafting and signing every big league ballplayer in the 1980s. In a variation of *Name That Tune*, Gorman will hear the name of an obscure National League benchwarmer and announce, "I gave him his first job in baseball." Sometimes it seems that Gorman has a relationship and a story to go with every player on every team in the big leagues. His involvement with five organizations over more than three decades gave him thousands of contacts and points of reference. Gifted with selective memory and a knack for hyperbole, Gorman can spin yarns all night long until his audience concludes that Lou must have been there when Brother Matthias delivered twenty-year-old George Herman Ruth to the minor league Orioles in 1914.

James Gorman was born in 1929, the second of five children of Leo and Frances Gorman. Leo Gorman (the original family name was O'Gorman, but the *O* was dropped at immigration) was a Providence fire chief who worked thirty-two years for the department before dying at the age of sixty-one. Young James (his family name was "Buddy") played basketball, football, and baseball at LaSalle Academy in Providence. When he was a junior, Gorman's football team played a game in the Sugar Bowl in front of forty-five thousand people. But baseball was the game James loved, and it was his nifty work around the first-base bag that earned him his lifelong nickname.

Gorman says, "When I played American Legion baseball, I played against Roland Hemond's team for the state championship, and some writer said, 'He looks like Lou Gehrig so we'll call him Lou Gorman.' It appeared in a paper and people started calling me 'Lou' and it just stuck."

After graduating from LaSalle, Gorman went to Stonehill College in Easton, Massachusetts, and graduated in 1953 with a degree in English literature. (Stonehill in 1995 announced that it would name its new baseball field in honor of James "Lou" Gorman.) He had a Navy commitment after graduating and reported to the USS *Hornet*, where he was stationed for twenty-six months. Thirty-four years later, he retired as a captain in the Naval Reserve. It was while teaching at Officer's Commission School in Newport that he met his future wife, Mary Lou, who was working for the Red Cross at the Naval Hospital.

In December of 1960, at thirty-one, Gorman went to the major league baseball meetings at Tampa looking for a job in baseball. It was a bold move.

"I felt I wanted to get into some area of sports," says Gorman. "I made a résumé up and went on my own and stood in the lobby of the hotel. I had a couple of interviews, but I got discouraged toward the end of the week. Now whenever I'm at those meetings and I see kids standing in the lobby, I always talk to them. Because I remember. So on the fourth or fifth day when I'm down there, I got tired and discouraged and went into the cocktail lounge to have a drink. There was only one seat empty at the bar, and it was next to this woman who had her hair all coiffed and the diamonds and everything. She was lighting a cigarette, so I lit her cigarette for her. She said, 'Young man, what are you doing here?' I told her I was looking for a job in baseball and she said, 'My husband just bought a baseball team.' I showed her my résumé and she told me to wait to meet her husband. He was Howard Roth and he'd just bought the Lakeland Giants. They took me to dinner that night, and I sold myself to them. They said if the Giants approved of me, they'd hire me as general manager. The next day I met with Carl Hubbell, who was running the Giants system, and a man named Jack Swartz. They recommended me and they gave me a one-year contract. So that was the beginning of it. I spent the whole year at Lakeland. I had no idea what I was doing."

A year later, Gorman went to Kinston, North Carolina, to oversee a Class A independent team. One of his players was Gene Michael, former general manager of the New York Yankees.

"He was our shortstop," says Gorman. "He was married with a couple of children and came to me and said he was having trouble getting by. He wanted to know if there was anything he could to do make extra money. I said, 'Can you drive the bus?' He told me he never drove a bus in his life. But I put him in bus training school for a week and got him licensed to drive the bus. I paid him one hundred and fifty dollars a month more to drive the bus, and he drove the bus all year. We won the pennant that year [1962] and drew about one hundred and seventy-two thousand people, and I became Executive of the Year in Class A."

At the same time, the Baltimore Orioles were looking for an assistant, and Gorman was hired by Lee MacPhail and Harry Dalton. In 1963, Baltimore was the best possible place to educate any young baseball executive. The Orioles had gone to Baltimore from St. Louis (where they were the Browns) in 1954 and, by the early 1960s, were threatening to break the long, successful run of the New York Yankees. The Baltimore system was put in place by MacPhail, who was followed by legendary general managers Dalton, Frank Cashen, and Hank Peters. Paul Richards was the original Baltimore manager. Richards was the man who, looking at an Arkansas second baseman, recommended that the kid try third base. The kid's name was Brooks Robinson. Richards was succeeded by Hank Bauer, who gave way to Earl Weaver. The Orioles stressed a system of fundamentals that was taught from the lowest level of the minors, straight up through Baltimore. In the years Gorman was in Baltimore's minor league system, he worked with Weaver, Billy Hunter, Cal Ripken Sr., Jim Frey, Joe Altobelli, Darrell Johnson, and George Bamberger. All would go on to become major league managers. Gorman was promoted to director of the Orioles minor-league clubs in 1966. The Orioles won the World Series in 1966 and again in 1970, two years after Gorman left Baltimore for Kansas City.

He joined the expansion Royals in 1968 and was a key player in the experimental "Baseball Academy." The Academy was invented by the late Ewing Kaufman, a multimillionaire who brought baseball back to Kansas City. Ridiculed by many baseball executives, the Academy recruited athletes and attempted to transform them into baseball players. The experiment, largely a failure, was scrapped after five years. The most successful graduates of the Royals Academy were second baseman Frank White (a construction worker who helped build Royals Stadium, now a Red Sox coach and a man who can say that Lou Gorman gave him his first job in baseball) and shortstop U. L. Washington (who was referred by his cousin, an usher at the Kansas City ballpark). By 1976, the Royals were in the play-offs against the New York Yankees. Kansas City made it to the World Series in 1980 and won the fall classic in 1985. Again, Gorman was not around to enjoy the harvest. Kansas City's climb from expansion to championship is considered a baseball prototype, and Gorman gets much of the credit for launching the Royals.

In 1976, Gorman left Kansas City to join another expansion franchise, the Seattle Mariners. (So far he is the only baseball executive to have been at the helm of two start-ups.) This time, the genial executive oversaw a start-up operation that failed miserably. Seattle has never fully recovered from mistakes made in the early years, and Gorman rarely cites his Mariner's experience when he highlights his résumé.

"In the beginning we had the nucleus of a pretty good club," Gorman says. "But it never got to be that way."

In 1980, Gorman left Seattle and took over as vice president in charge of baseball operations for the New York Mets. In New York, he was reunited with Cashen, his first baseball boss in Baltimore. Gorman built the Mets into a World Series winner, but again, he wasn't around to taste the champagne. Even worse, when the Mets finally won, it was at the expense of Gorman's new team, the Boston Red Sox.

The Sox were a dull franchise when Gorman came home in 1984. Gorman was saddled with the task of rebuilding the team and rekindling interest in Boston baseball. The Sox offered little drawing power when matched up against Larry Bird, Kevin McHale, and Robert Parish. In one of Gorman's first deals, pitcher Dennis Eckersley was traded to the Cubs in exchange for first baseman Bill Buckner. Despite Buckner's later infamy, and Eck's emergence as a Cy Young reliever later in the decade, it was a good trade for Boston.

And 1986 was a good year for Lou Gorman. At the end of spring training, he acquired Don Baylor from the Yankees for Mike Easler. Later in the summer, he got Tom Seaver for Steve Lyons, then swapped Rey Quinones, Mike Brown, and Mike Trujillo to the Mariners for Spike Owen and Dave Henderson. When the Sox were desperate for a closer late in the season, manager John McNamara had success with Calvin Schiraldi, a reliever Gorman had acquired in a multiplayer deal with the Mets. All of those deals were instrumental in delivering a World Series appearance to Boston in October of 1986. It was Lou Gorman's finest hour.

In 1994, he looked back and said, "I came home because I wanted to come home, because the Red Sox were my team and I had family in the area and went to college in the area, and I felt I wanted to come back here. One of the things I want is to win a championship, and in '86 we almost did. We did win three division titles. We paid a price for it, but we did win three division titles."

The Red Sox should have won the 1986 World Series, but did not. Things were never quite right for Gorman after that. A lot of his moves backfired, the press slaughtered him, and fans started to think of him as a lovable blunderer. He was Ed McMahon when the Sox needed Norman Schwarzkopf.

The defining moment of Gorman's decline came during the end of the 1990 regular season. The Sox were making a push to win the American League East for the third time in five years. Oakland, which had swept Boston in the 1988 play-offs, was running away with the AL West. When the A's picked up hitters Harold Baines and Willie McGee for the stretch run and postseason, Gorman looked as if he were asleep at the wheel. He was blasted in the Boston papers and on sports talk shows. His response was, "What would we do with Willie McGee?" McGee was a former batting champ who was hitting well over .300. The comment sounded ridiculous. Boston fans were expecting the Sox to make some moves of their own for the September drive, and just a few days after the Baines/McGee fiasco, it was announced that the Red Sox had traded minor-league third baseman Jeff

Bagwell to Houston for veteran reliever Larry Andersen. The trade would ruin Lou Gorman.

There was no way of knowing that Bagwell would become one of the best players in the National League for the rest of the decade. And there is logic in the argument that when you have a chance to win a division title, it's okay to part with a prospect in order to win *now*. But the logic goes only so far. When Gorman traded Brady Anderson and Curt Schilling to the Orioles in exchange for Mike Boddicker in the summer of 1988, he was not criticized when Anderson and Schilling went on to become star players. Boddicker performed for the Sox down the stretch in 1988. He helped deliver a division flag. It was worth the gamble. But the Bagwell deal was a blunder because Sox minor-league personnel were horrified the minute the trade was announced. Gorman hadn't seen Bagwell play. And he got Larry Andersen, a loudmouth middle reliever who pitched well down the stretch, but hardly "delivered" the Sox to the title. It didn't help when Andersen was declared a no-compensation free agent a few weeks after the deal was made.

Still reeling from the trade, and from getting swept by the A's, Gorman committed to helping the Sox via free agency in the winter of 1991. The result was three of the worst signings in baseball history. The Sox signed Matt Young, Danny Darwin, and Jack Clark to multiyear contracts, in each case jacking up the price and adding extra years by bidding against themselves. There was little market for any of the three. It was a disaster.

When the Sox failed to win in 1991, Gorman fired popular manager Joe Morgan, replacing Tollway Joe with Butch Hobson, claiming "a lot of teams want to hire Butch." But of course there was no demand for Hobson, and Hobson himself admitted this. Morgan, who had the sloppy Sox just a half game out of first place with two weeks left in the '91 season, parted with this warning: "These guys aren't as good as everybody thinks they are." The Sox under Hobson finished last in 1992.

Gorman could be hilarious and he could be sensitive. It was not unusual for Gorman to clip negative articles and save them for the day he'd be vindicated. If he heard something negative on a radio or television sports panel, Gorman would often call the program to set the record straight. In the summer if 1993, I did a postgame TV program from Fenway Park and spoke of clubhouse dissension. When I got off the air, there was a message from Lou. Unable to reach him, I drove to Woods Hole to take a boat to Martha's Vineyard. I called home before getting on the ship, and my eight-year-old daughter said there was a message from a man named Lou. Still unable to reach Gorman, I went to Martha's Vineyard and attended a party with friends. At 11 P.M., the party hostess answered the phone and said, "Dan, Lou Gorman's on the line." Lou just wanted to make sure I knew there was no dissent in the Red Sox clubhouse.

But it was the Bagwell deal that crushed Gorman. Bagwell just kept getting better and better, and Gorman was forced to rewrite Andersen's place in Red Sox history. Lou kept saying, "When you have a chance, you have to make that deal. If you're getting a guy who'll give you a chance to win, you have to make that deal every time. I'd do it again today."

Ouch. The Bagwell deal is to Gorman what Al Capone's vault was to Geraldo Rivera.

"It bothers me because it's always brought up," Gorman says. "If someone had said, 'Bagwell's going to be MVP,' I would have said, 'Wait a minute,' but no one said that."

Gorman was typically gracious after he was replaced by thirty-five-year-old Dan Duquette, saying, "I've been through five organizations. Won nine division titles, one American League title. National League pennants. I've had some good years. The last two years, unfortunately, weren't too good. . . . I still think some of the stuff was unfair. I never thought that the game had passed me by. The more experience you have, the more you know about the game. Anybody involved with the club on a daily basis has to be current. The game's not going to pass you by because you put some age on you.

"You always feel it when there's a change made. The first thing that bothers you is you think, 'Gee, they felt I didn't do a good job.' It's normal. But I've been in player personnel for a good part of thirty-two years. Over those years, we've had some good years and some bad years. Some things didn't work out. But in this game, it's not what you did yesterday that counts. It's what you did today. Everybody forgets what you did yesterday."

Sox fans should never forget what Gorman did. He was one of them. He answered his mail. He returned his phone calls. He was never too busy to give a college student a tour around Fenway. For more than a decade he was Boston baseball's goodwill ambassador, cutting ribbons at supermarket openings and spreading the gospel of the Red Sox from Providence to Portland.

THE BOY WONDER

On January 27, 1994, thirty-five-year-old Dan Duquette became general manager of the Boston Red Sox. The appointment was the culmination of a young man's dream and ended a lengthy negotiation during which the Red Sox talked the Montreal Expos into letting Duquette out of his contract. At the time, Duquette was the hottest young executive in the game, and the Red Sox were looking for new direction.

When Duquette was released by Montreal and named to run the Red Sox, his first call was to his mother back in Dalton, Massachusetts. Danny Boy was coming home to do what he'd always wanted to do: the dream job of every New England kid who ever put trading cards on the spokes of his bicycle. When Duquette told her the good news, she asked him the question that was on the lips of every citizen of Red Sox Nation: When he was going to ged rid of manager Butch Hobson?

Hobson, the Forrest Gump of Boston baseball, had led the Sox to consecutive sub-.500 seasons and still had a year left on his contract when Duquette took over. Ma Duquette's question proved that Dan Duquette was a true member of the Red Sox family. He had been brought up right.

For any general manager of the Red Sox, there is an advantage to being homegrown. "I think it helps you understand firsthand what the people in the market like in their ball club and what the young families look for in the ballplayers," says Duquette. "That's helped. As a kid growing up, I went to see the Red Sox every year. I listened to the games. I don't know that I was consumed by them, but both of my parents were big fans. My mom's dad was also a big fan. I've never fallen into the negative thinking that some fans have. The club has had some great moments, but it hasn't had the ultimate moment of winning a championship. I don't think it's got anything to do with anything other than the fact that they didn't make the plays at the time."

Duquette is a young man who dresses like Ward Cleaver and gets "boys' regular" haircuts. His public persona is serious and official. Looking at him, one would be surprised to learn that his favorite song is Bruce Springsteen's "Thunder Road." Privately, he can be quite funny. He was born in Dalton (pop. 6,000) in 1958, the son of Judy and Dennis Duquette. Two hours west of Boston, Dalton is a postcard New England town best known as the home of Crane and Co., a mill where currency paper is printed. Dan Duquette's dad was a lifelong educator, and his grandfather John Duquette worked for Crane and Co. for fifty-three years.

When he played Wiffle ball in his backyard with his brother, Dan Duquette assumed the role of the Red Sox while Dennis took the Orioles. In 1967, when he was in fifth grade, the future GM was reprimanded for sneaking a transistor radio into school; he wanted to listen to the Red Sox–Cardinals World Series. One of his Little League teammates was Jeff Reardon, who went on to become one of the best relief pitchers of all time. Duquette caught Reardon in Little League and Legion ball.

"It was always one of those neighborhood things, but I always said that I wanted to be in sports," says Duquette. "It just seemed natural out there. We all grew up listening to Red Sox games, and that probably had more influence on our lives than anything else."

Quite a neighborhood. There was Reardon, the Hall of Famer–in-waiting. There was Dan's cousin Jim Williams, now assistant farm and scouting director of the New York Mets. And much later there was Turk Wendell, a pitching prospect with the Cubs. Baseball lifers Tom Grieve, Mark Belanger, Eddie Connolly, and Rick Lisi were from nearby Pittsfield. There must have been something special in the Quabbin Resevoir.

"Great Little League programs, great tradition, and of course, the Red Sox," explains Duquette.

He was a catcher and outfielder at Wahconah Regional High School. When he was eighteen, Duquette went to a scouting bureau tryout camp at Pittsfield.

How did his tryout go?

"Good enough to direct me into the front office," says the Sox general manager. "They have you run and throw, and they invite back the better runners and throwers. I didn't make the cut. I took that as informational. I knew that I wasn't going to be able to play pro baseball before that. I just went to the camp to see how they were run.

He was an exceptional young man. Few teenagers can take rejection and make it "informational." So instead of heading to the minor leagues as a no-chance catcher, Duquette went to Amherst, where he majored in English literature and played varsity baseball and football (Duquette chose Amherst over Princeton because he wanted to play football and he didn't think he'd be able to play two sports at Princeton). At Amherst he was a catcher and first baseman in the spring and a linebacker in the fall. In his senior season, the *Boston Herald* named Duquette a College Division All-New England linebacker. When high school pitcher Ron Darling (a native of Millbury, Massachusetts) visited the Amherst campus, Duquette shook the kid's hand and recommended his school. Darling wound up at Yale and later helped the Mets beat the Red Sox in the 1986 World Series.

At Amherst, Duquette had his own radio show, a sports trivia program on student station WAMH. He awarded free pizzas to those who correctly answered questions. His college roommate, Tom Bourque, remembers that Duquette was the first to buy a copy of the *Sporting News* every Thursday.

Bourque says, "We were the types who sat on the bench and watched everything the other teams did in batting practice or infield. We'd go through strengths and weaknesses and talk about everything we saw. . . . I've never known anyone who loved the game any more than Dan. I never knew anyone more analytical. He was never a guy who thought he was smarter than anyone else. Because he loved the game, he respected everything about it."

Duquette's Amherst career counselor, Susan Little, told him, "By the time you've lived your life, you'll have spent forty to forty-five years working, so you'd better do something you like." The words stuck.

Intent on pursuing a career in baseball, Duquette contacted Pittsfield native Paul Ricciarini, who was a scout for the Blue Jays. No luck. Blue Jays team policy dictated that all internships go to Canadians.

"He was always asking questions about the business," remembers Ricciarini. "If you knew the family, you'd never be surprised by anything they did."

Stopped on his first try, Duquette wrote letters to Amherst grads who had jobs in baseball. There were three: Pirates owner Dan Galbraith, Brewers GM Harry Dalton, and Oriole publicist Bob Brown. Duquette got responses from each of them.

Bob Brown was part of the proud tradition of the Baltimore Orioles. He was with the Orioles during the golden years of the 1960s and 1970s and was considered the best public relations man in baseball. Brilliant and often irreverent, Brown was known to have a little fun with his press notes. In 1977, when the Red Sox failed to send Baltimore a probable starter for the final game of an upcoming series, Brown listed the Sox starter as "Carmine Hose, 0–0." A nitwit Baltimore radio announcer fell for it and told his listeners, "On Sunday, the Sox will be calling up a rookie from Pawtucket, young Carmine Hose."

Like everyone else who worked for the Orioles during that era, Brown was a class gentleman, never too busy to help a young college man. Brown contacted Duquette and suggested that Duquette contact Mets general manager Frank Cashen. Cashen had been in charge of the Orioles during their championship reign and was rebuilding the Mets into World Champs when he interviewed Duquette during Duquette's spring baseball trip to St. Petersburg in 1980.

Harry Dalton was equally receptive to the young man from Amherst. Another ex-Oriole executive (Dalton succeeded Cashen in Baltimore), Dalton instructed Duquette to come to New York when the Brewers played the Yankees in April of 1980. Duquette was wide-eyed as he sat in the visitors dugout at Yankee Stadium, talking with Dalton while Lou Piniella and Reggie Jackson took batting practice.

"Bob Brown got me the interview with Frank Cashen," Duquette remembers. "Frank was hiring new staff with the Mets. It was great. He asked me a number of questions to probe my interest. He later told me he had hired Terry Ryan, but said he'd like to hire me, too.

Then I met with Harry in the dugout at Yankee Stadium. It was a thrill. He told me that it was pretty good that this was my first time in Yankee Stadium and I made it to the dugout."

Dalton offered Duquette a job as an administrative assistant in scouting and player development. Duquette had another offer: a chance to serve as Amherst sports information director and assistant football coach. It was no choice. His love was baseball. He went to work for the Brewers and after six years was named Milwaukee's scouting director. A year later, he joined the Montreal Expos as director of player development, and on January 25, 1990, Montreal made him assistant general manager. In September of 1991, when Dave Dombrowski left Montreal to take over the expansion Florida Marlins, Duquette ascended to the position of vice president and general manager of the Expos.

John Cerutti, Duquette's Amherst teammate and a former big league pitcher, says, "We all knew how much Dan loved the game and how much he knew about it. But he was smart, quiet. I think we all figured he'd go on to law school or business school and make a lot of money."

When he got the top job with the Expos, at the age of thirty-three, Duquette said, "I've always felt I could do this and I thought I was prepared."

It had taken only eleven years. Duquette started out as a clerk and wound up running the business. From July of 1980 until September of 1991, he made the climb from the bottom to the top of the baseball ladder.

Duquette: "One of the gifts Harry Dalton has is that he exposes administration people to the entire operation. He really put together a training program. I had exposure to free-agent scouting, the administrative base of the major league team, the minor league system, scouting, and fieldwork. I was assigned to organize tryout camps in Milwaukee. Then they gave me the responsibility of territorial scouting. It was a good opportunity for me to handle the admininistrative work of a major league scouting office."

The key to learning on the job and learning quickly?

"Observation and asking questions," says Duquette. "Veteran scouts in the field were very helpful. They are the people you want to talk to to learn about talent. Those guys love to talk to young people. In this business, I learned you need to be able to evaluate talent, but also you need to be able to evaluate the people that evaluate talent for you. You've got to know what they mean when they like a player."

Bob Brown, Frank Cashen, and Harry Dalton were all schooled in the Baltimore Orioles' system. Speaking of Baltimore's signature manager of the sixties, seventies, and eighties, Duquette says, "I basically adhere to the Earl Weaver model of building a team in the American League. Pitching and power. It's all right there in Earl's book, the diagram for winning in the American League."

The Milwaukee Brewers, because of Dalton's involvement, copied the Orioles system. When Duquette hired his first Red Sox manager, it was Kevin Kennedy, who was drafted by Baltimore and served as a catcher in the Orioles system for six seasons.

"That was a gift," Duquette says of his early exposure to Orioles ways.

In Montreal there was little money, tepid fan support, and no winning tradition. "We have to manage our budget," Duquette said. "But that's okay. It just means we can't make many mistakes and have to work a little harder. We constantly need an influx of young players who are hungry, but we also have spent a lot of time and effort in development."

Development. It is one of Duquette's favorite words. He believes a team should be built from the bottom. Eventually, a strong minor league system will yield a big league winner.

The first manager Duquette hired was Felipe Alou. Later, after much success, Alou looked back and said, "It took a lot of guts for Dan to hire me, to hire someone who hadn't managed in the majors, to hire someone who'd been bypassed, to hire a black Dominican. . . . That took a hell of a lot of guts."

The Sox had kicked Lou Gorman upstairs and were in the middle of a nationwide search in the winter of 1993–94 when John Harrington called the Expos and asked about Duquette. Montreal owner Claude Brochu said, "We have problems with letting him go. We're trying to win this year, the timing is bad, and he is probably the best young executive in the game. But I have never said that I would block anyone from fulfilling his dream."

On the day Duquette was introduced to the Boston media (he signed a five-year, $2-million contract), he said, "Over the next couple of years, we're going to renew the roster with new life. We're going to bring in younger ballplayers, more players in their prime years, between the ages of twenty-seven and thirty-two. We have a number of players on the downside of the curve. We have to bring in more players from our farm system. . . . One of the great things about this franchise is the knowledge of the fans and the knowledge of the press. People are interested in what you're doing. They might not like what you're doing if you trade one of their favorite players, but they understand it."

In Duquette's first year on the job, he inherited a Gormany $40-million payroll, a raft of broken wings, fifteen players over the age of thirty, and a manager who thought that life was like a box of chocolates. The Sox stumbled, and Duquette made the bodies fly. More than thirty players were shipped out and another thirty-five were imported. "We made a lot of changes to get ourselves in a position to win later," said the GM.

When the strike stopped the season on August 12, the Sox were 54–61, seventeen games behind the Yankees. Duquette quickly fired Hobson and replaced him with former Texas manager Kevin Kennedy. New coaches were added and the Sox went about rebuilding.

In the spring of 1995, Duquette was put to the test like never before. Baseball's labor cease-fire gave teams just three weeks to prepare for a 144-game season. When the real Red Sox got to camp, Duquette was looking at a thirty-seven-man roster that had only three pitchers with significant big league experience (Roger Clemens, Aaron Sele, Ken Ryan). Throughout baseball, twenty-eight general managers were scrambling to deal with free agency, arbitrations, tendering contracts, and trades. The old rules were the new rules, and after a winter of thumb-twiddling, front offices were forced to assemble their teams in a couple of New York minutes. Victory would go to the swift and the smart, and citizens of Red Sox Nation were counting on Duquette to stay ahead of the pack. It was Duquette's first big moment in Boston. It was his chance to show Sox fans what he was born to do. There's a lot of Rotisserie League nerd in the Sox GM. Duquette's whole life prepared him for those frenzied hours. At the age of thirty-six, he was holding real-life trading cards. April 3 through April 26, 1995, was a unique period in baseball history, and general managers earned their money as entire teams were reinvented.

Duquette almost made a deal that would have brought Montreal reliever John Wetteland to Boston, but the Yankees came through with extra cash and snatched Wetteland from under his nose. It was embarrassing.

Duquette was more active after the Wetteland fiasco. In a six-day period, he acquired ten new players, while keeping the Sox payroll at around $22 million, down from $40 million in 1994. As of opening day, 1995, only eleven players remained from the Sox 1994 opening-day forty-man roster. When the Sox were introduced to the Fenway crowd, the only pitcher returning from 1994 was Aaron Sele. Roger Clemens was rehabilitating in Florida, and the rest of the '94 hurlers were retired, out of work, or pitching for new teams.

The '95 Sox were hot at the start of the season and had the best record in the American League by May 20. Duquette got a lot of the credit. He'd successfully lopped $9 million off the payroll while putting together a team that was competitive and interesting to watch. For the combined efforts of starting pitchers Eric Hanson, Zane Smith, and Rheal Cormier, Duquette was paying less than Danny Darwin's ($3-million) salary.

"I think that Dan Duquette has done one helluva job," Ted Williams said in the summer of '95. "I've had a chance to talk to him a couple of times. One time I said, 'You need a couple of left-handed pitchers,' and the next thing I knew he had two left-handed pitchers. Now you're not going to get Lefty Grove on every trade. But by God, he's made some damn good decisions.

"He's a man of action, that guy. I call him most of the time. When I see somebody on TV, I might talk to him and tell him I like some guy, and right there he knows all about him. He's a good baseball man. After the first time I ever talked to him on the phone, I said, 'That guy's gonna help the Red Sox.' Just the way he talked. Baseball, baseball, baseball."

The Duke was looking good in mid-June when his Sox were still in first place, far ahead of the favored Yankees, Blue Jays, and Orioles. No-name players like Troy O'Leary (released by the Brewers) and

Reggie Jefferson were doing the job. Knuckleballer Tim Wakefield, who lost fifteen games in the minors in 1994, was signed by Duquette and got off to a 14–1 start, leading the American League in earned run average. In Wakefield, Stan Belinda, Hanson, and Vaughn Eshelman, Boston had four pitchers, rejected by other teams, who started the season an aggregate 17–0 for the Red Sox. All four were Duquette finds. Boston fans were impressed. So was management. All four were bargain-basement acquisitions.

At the All-Star break, the 1995 Red Sox were in first place, three games ahead of the Detroit Tigers, and Belinda, Hanson, and Wake-field were 21–4. O'Leary (discovered by Duquette when he was a high school player in Cypress, California) was batting .345, and Seattle Mariner reject Lee Tinsley was at .295 with five homers and 25 RBI batting out of the leadoff spot. In the first half of 1995, Duquette employed forty-four ballplayers, more than any other American League team (fourteen more than the usually active Oakland Athlet-ics). He wound up using a franchise-record fifty-three players. In late August, he grabbed Dwaye Hosey off the waiver wire for $1. Hosey was Boston's center fielder and leadoff hitter in the 1995 play-offs.

"This is a business where player salaries and revenues are related," said Duquette. "I think the industry is getting back to more and more one-year deals. We estimate what our revenues allow us to spend, and then it's our job to go find the best talent we can for the payroll we can afford. That means looking everywhere and working as hard as we can. The only difference in my job in Montreal and my job in Boston is that here we have more revenue to work with. But it doesn't change the way the job is carried out. The excitement comes in know-ing what the rewards will be when—and if—the Red Sox win.

"That's what we're here for. We talk about it all the time, especially with the people that have been around the club for a long time. Our goal is to be championship caliber year in and year out, and to be knocking on the door and one day go through. We'd like to have the basis and foundation to do this on a yearly basis. And let's face it, anybody associated with the team that finally wins would be canonized in Boston."

THE MANIACAL ONE

The Red Sox are on television today, which means that the stat man is sitting alone in the den of his home in Millers Falls, Massachusetts. A short man with thick glasses, he sits in a room lit only by one naked light bulb, a nineteen-inch TV screen, and a glowing Macintosh PowerPC. His fingers dance across the keyboard each time Sean McDonough says, "That's ball four and another walk charged to Ken Ryan." The stat man is surrounded by clipboards, tattered scoresheets, and leftover pizza. Papers and charts lie all over the room, but the only things left in his refrigerator are a jar of mustard, a slice of cheese, a dozen eggs, and a six-pack of beer. Waseleski can't leave his chair until the game is over, and the Sox bullpen has him working overtime. Again.

Meet Chuck Waseleski, the czar of hardball software. *Boston Globe* readers know him as the Maniacal One.

Maniacal. It's the nickname that fits.

Is Chuck offended by this unusual characterization?

"Sometimes the truth hurts," he says with a laugh. "It's true. I can't refute it."

Waseleski, a forty-one-year-old assistant to the president of an engineering consulting firm, is indeed maniacal in his pursuit of Red Sox statistics. He keeps track of every pitch of the season and can tell you things that nobody else knows. When Sox shortstop John Valentin hits the left-field wall, Maniacal Chuck waits for his phone to ring. He is the one man who can confirm exactly how many times Valentin has hit The Wall during his big league career.

"You hear that so-and-so is a good two-strike hitter," Waseleski explains. "I hate that. I want to know, 'How good?' Be specific."

No one is more specific than Chuck. He knows how Roger Clemens fares against left-handed batters. He knows how many times Mo Vaughn popped up to the infield in 1994. He tracks righties against lefties and lefties against righties—home and away. For three years Maniacal Chuck published a monthly and annual baseball report. Since 1990, each Sunday, in the middle of Peter Gammons's three-thousand-word baseball page, there's a box headlined "From the Maniacal One," which features "this week's offering of obscure but telling Red Sox facts from statistician Chuck Waseleski of Millers Falls."

Low-life sportswriters care deeply about all of this. We know that some *Globe* readers care. So do ballplayers, and ballplayers' agents. The Maniacal One has a small cult following.

Waseleski has converted his hobby into a nice cottage industry. When agents for Boggs and Marty Barrett needed help in arbitration cases after the 1985 season, they summoned Waseleski to New York. Maniacal Chuck, of course, whipped out dossiers that made Boggs and Barrett look like Honus Wagner and Rogers Hornsby. Not all of his data is silly. Ballplayers like to show their employers that they can perform in clutch situations. Waseleski can prove that Mike Greenwell is a better hitter with runners in scoring position in close games. Waseleski compiled negotiation files for thirty players after the 1985 season, and his clientele swelled to seventy after the '86 campaign. He has worked more than fifty arbitration cases and is batting around .600. He also does stat work for the Chicago White Sox.

The Red Sox were a little piqued when this local stat nerd turned on them in arbitration. The Sox PR department has no relationship with the Maniacal One, and it takes great glee in finding an error in his data. "We've never really had reason to deal with one another," says Chuck. "I met Lou Gorman seven or eight years ago. He was aware of who I was. We weren't fighting over doughnuts or anything like that. But the Sox don't need me. They have what I've got. At least I think they do."

Waseleski's compulsion doesn't cost him as much sleep as it once did. This is the nineties and Chuck has cable TV and a VCR. "I'm not anchored to the TV," he says. "I can tape a game and fill in the numbers the next morning if I feel like going out. But I'd rather be doing something than just sitting back with a gin and tonic listening to the game. I'd rather have a clipboard and pen and have the computer on."

Maniacal Chuck was born and still lives in the village of Millers Falls (pop. 1,084), eight miles east of Greenfield. He went to Turners Falls Regional High, where he was class valedictorian in 1972. His father owned a trucking company. Chuck has a younger brother, Joe, who occupies the first floor of the house they share. It's the same house his grandparents lived in. Chuck played sandlot ball, usually second base, but never played organized baseball. He got his Coke-bottle glasses when he was in fifth grade and confesses that he was good at "just about anything except sports."

Like a lot of New England baby boomers, he was a casual Red Sox fan until the magical summer of 1967. "That hooked me for good," he says. The Waseleskis would drive the ninety miles to Fenway once or twice a year, but after '67 Chuck started keeping close tabs on the BoSox. With pal Jim Kopec, he kept scoresheets of every game "just to use for arguments," he says.

When he was attending Merrimack College in Andover ("Yaz's alma mater, and we didn't even have a baseball team," he moans), he started going to Fenway about twenty times a year. He had never touched a computer when he graduated magna cum laude with a degree in English in 1976. Back home, he went to work for Douglas Peterson and Associates. Late in the seventies, the company got a computer system and Waseleski learned to use it. He was still keeping Red Sox scoresheets, but his methods remained archaic and his information incomplete.

In 1982, Chuck began corresponding with national stat king and author Bill James. He provided James with some information for the annual *Baseball Abstract*. James had questions and Waseleski had answers, but never enough. Maniacal Chuck says, "It was then that I realized there was some demand for this material. I started taping games because I realized I had a real life to live. Little did I know that that was when I would lose it.

"People would ask, 'Is Jim Rice a clutch hitter?' That was the question of the eighties at that point. He wasn't. In late innings, close situations, his average would fall off.

"I catalog the games, plate appearance by plate appearance. There's an orderliness to it—knowing that I can get the answer to whatever you ask me or whatever I get curious about. It's great knowing I can find the answer to a question."

Waseleski is insatiable. The more information he gathers, the more he wants. By 1986, he knew there was only one way to go: complete immersion. He had to track every pitch. He had to feed all the information into a computer. He bought his Apple after the '82 season and has logged every Red Sox plate appearance since 1986. The Maniacal One was in on the ground floor of the baseball stat explosion.

"There's so much more of it available now," he admits. "You can get inherited-runners stats in box scores. What people are hitting against left-and right-handed pitching used to be something you'd have to hunt for. Now, you see it every time you turn around. We know what Wade Boggs is hitting on partly cloudy Tuesdays against pitchers born south of the Mason-Dixon Line."

The course of stat history changed when Waseleski met Peter Gammons at a BoSox Club meeting. "Peter was aware of my stuff through Bill James's books," remembers Chuck. "He mentioned to me that there was a lot of stuff you couldn't get other places. I basically told him, 'Whatever you need, I'll have.' I stayed with it ever since. From Gammons to Shaughnessy to Steve Fainaru and back to Gammons [the *Globe*'s Sunday baseball columnists). I've been passed around like an old shoe. The *Globe* has switched off over the years, but who's been the one constant? Me."

His legend has grown. Maniacal Chuck is a cult figure among sportswriters. He's friendly with Al Nipper and Wade Boggs, and he's employed by a lot of agents. He shows up at spring training for a week and has made road trips to Texas, Chicago, Seattle, Cleveland, Toronto, Oakland, and Baltimore. His material has been reprinted in *Newsweek*, the *New York Times*, *The Baseball Abstract*, *The Sporting News*, George Will's *Men at Work*, and most New England newspapers. Every time Wade Boggs flirted with a .400 average, Maniacal Chuck got dozens of phone calls. If Wade had hit .400 with the Red Sox, the Maniacal One would have been a guest on Letterman.

Boggs was a great vehicle for the Maniacal One. "I was glad he was around," says Chuck. "But sometimes I felt that all I did was confirm what he already knew. I could tell him he's eleven for twenty-three against Phil Niekro, but he already knew. He's amazing."

Is is possible to gather any more information on the Sox than Waseleski already has?

"If there's something I'm not keeping track of, I don't know what it is," he says. "Until I get asked a question I can't answer, I'd have to say it's not possible to do more than I'm doing now. You can take that as a challenge, but so far I haven't been asked anything I don't have an answer to."

Would there be a demand for his services in another city?

"I could see this maybe going over in New York, Detroit, Chicago, any of the old-line cities where the fans really care. But I don't think there'd be much call for it in Anaheim."

Waseleski was in Baltimore with the Red Sox when they went on strike in August 1994. Undaunted, he continued the road trip to Chicago before returning to Millers Falls.

"I found out they have theaters in Baltimore and museums in Chicago," he says.

What about that, Chuck. Do you have a life?

"Sure," he says. "I do a lot of this from videotape now. But really, I have no time. I have interests like travel and computers, but really I am maniacal about this. That's the nickname. It works."

THE EYES AND EARS

In New England, the reporter who covers the Red Sox for the paper of record is only slightly less important than Ted Williams, Carl Yastrzemski, Mo Vaughn, or any other star of a given Fenway generation. Boston Red Sox fans know the names of the people who cover the team. Baseball beat reporters are a crucial link between the ball club and the citizens of Red Sox Nation, and in the twenty-five seasons since 1971—a quarter century that produced media stars, tabloid journalism, and the explosion of cable television—Boston's Peter Gammons has been the most important baseball journalist in America. In 1971, Gammons was just a hungry cub reporter out of the University of North Carolina, writing five stories a day for the *Globe* and *Evening Globe*. Twenty-five years later, Gammons is recognized as the best beat man of his generation, a writer who reinvented the way baseball is covered, then went on to become the "commissioner" in his position as ESPN baseball guru and syndicated *Globe* Sunday columnist.

"He's the god of baseball," pitcher Matt Young said sarcastically in 1990.

Young was kidding, but he wasn't far off the mark.

Gammons was born in Groton, Massachusetts, in 1945, one of four children of Edward B. and Betty Gammons. His father designed church organs and taught music at the prestigious Groton School (high school of Franklin Delano Roosevelt and a coterie of Cabots and Lodges). Betty Gammons traced her ancestry back to Ethan Allen, and Gammons claims his great-grandfather, a New Bedford ship-builder, inspired Herman Melville to use the phrase *to gam*. Explaining the euphemism, Peter Gammons likes to say, "It means to bring two ships together and have a cocktail party."

Gammons's first baseball memories: "I was three years old. I was at home and I remember Paul Wright standing outside our house, taunting my mother. He was a big Cleveland Indians fan, and the Indians had just won the 1948 American League play-off game against the Red Sox at Fenway. It was good-natured and everything. He was the assistant headmaster at Groton School and he was also my godfather. There was another baseball memory in my house, one associated with a Red Sox tragedy. My brother, Ned, who's now a minister, drove a compass into my father's desk when the Red Sox lost the World Series in the ninth inning of the seventh game in 1946. . . . The first time I went to Fenway Park was June 28, 1952. The Senators beat the Red Sox, and Walt Masterson beat Dick Brodowski, 5–1. I got to see Dizzy Trout pitch for the Red Sox before he got released. I was seven years old. My brother was supposed to take me, but I wound up going with Bob Moss, and his son. We sat in back of third base in the front row. It's a box seat now, but it was the grandstand back then."

In the acknowledgments page of his first book, Gammons wrote, "My brother, the Reverend Edward B. Gammons Jr., never allowed me to forget the existence of baseball."

Peter Gammons remembers sitting in Billy Sambito's barbershop, listening to Billy Martin's famous catch during the 1952 World Series. Gammons also remembers, "When I got home from school one May day in 1957, my mother, bless her heart, had written down all the names involved in the Dean Stone–Bob Chakales deal with the Senators."

He grew up on the neatly trimmed campus of Groton School and earned money for train trips to the Fenway bleachers by picking apples in one of the many town orchards. Even then, young Gammons was a stat maven, keeping up-to-date records on all the big leaguers. When he wasn't tracking baseball, he was playing the game, often at the Groton field with immortal townies named Dickie Pleasants (now a Boston radio personality) and Bill Shaughnessy (brother of this author). Gammons was a pitcher and still loves to tell the tale of his ill-fated start for Groton against Boston English. English had a tall, left-handed-hitting first baseman named Bobby Guindon. One day Guindon would be a $125,000 bonus baby with the Red Sox, but in the spring of 1961 he was just a menacing slugger waiting for a pitch from a nervous sophomore righty.

"It was the first and last time I pitched all year," Gammons says. "The bases were loaded and we were losing something like thirteen to two. I got the first guy out and thought, 'This is going to be easy. Then Guindon came up. My first pitch was a submarine ball that didn't sink. He hit it out and it broke a window in the schoolhouse in the art room. He went five for five that day and had thirteen hits in three years against Groton."

Besides baseball, music was Gammons's other love, and at Groton he organized two bands—Little Gam and the Athletes, and the Penetrations. Today he has vast knowledge of obscure groups and musicians to rival his baseball knowledge. Gammons says he discovered the music of Delbert McClinton about fifteen years before talk-radio icon Don Imus made McClinton famous.

After graduating from Groton, Gammons went to the University of North Carolina at Chapel Hill, where he met an upperclassman named Curry Kirkpatrick, one of the editors of the *Daily Tar Heel*. (Kirkpatrick later became a celebrated senior writer at *Sports Illustrated*.) Kirkpatrick convinced Gammons to join the paper, and in the fall of 1967, Gammons cut classes and flew to Boston to cover the American League pennant race for his college newspaper.

He dropped out of school during his junior year, moved to Boston, and formed a band that played at bars in Kenmore Square, near Fenway Park. The band was known as Dexter Sensory and the Perceptions. It didn't last. Disillusioned with life in the city, Gammons returned to Chapel Hill and applied for a summer internship with the *Globe*. In the summer of '68, he served as a *Globe* intern and was originally assigned to cover politics.

On his first day at the *Globe*, June 10, 1968, Gammons was approached by Joe Dineen, a managing editor of the *Evening Globe*. Dineen said that the sports department was looking for a hungry intern. Gammons jumped, and it was fast evident that he was doing what he was born to do. Four months after his internship ended,

Gammons was offered a full-time job at the *Globe* (by Fran Rosa), and he left college early to begin a career that will no doubt lead him to the writer's wing at Cooperstown. (Through correspondence, he later earned his degree from North Carolina.)

Early in his *Globe* career, Gammons covered high school sports, particularly basketball and hockey. He can still recite starting lineups of Boston English teams, circa 1969–70. In 1971, he started covering the Red Sox on a semiregular basis, as a backup to veteran reporter Clif Keane. During that time, he started writing a regular feature on the Sox minor-league teams, "Majoring in the Minors." By 1972, veteran Ernie Roberts was running the *Globe* sports department along with a thirty-something assistant sports editor from Ohio named Dave Smith. Smith was a pioneer among American sports editors of the twentieth century. After leaving Boston he worked for the *Washington Star* and today runs the sports department at the *Dallas Morning News*. In the early 1970s, Smith was on the cutting edge, in charge of what many considered one of the best young sports staffs in history. Smith knew he had a rising star in Gammons, and in 1972 he turned the kid loose on the American League.

In the spring of 1972 Gammons started writing a Sunday baseball notes column. It proved revolutionary. Fans loved the tidbits, gossip, and nonstop trade rumors. This hadn't been done before, but today every major paper in the country has its own notes column in every sport. The *Globe* invented the genre with Gammons, Bob Ryan (who started writing his NBA "Round the Rim" column in 1970), and Will McDonough (football) leading the way. I believe the *Globe*'s Sunday baseball column is the best-read item in New England each week. Mail and reader feedback supports this theory. In 1996, a mention in Gammons's (now syndicated) Sunday notes column is like a mention in one of Walter Winchell's columns in the 1950s.

Gammons on the birth of Sunday baseball notes: "One day I just asked if I could write a Sunday baseball-notes column. I just always thought there should be one. We had the Jerry Nason general-notes column on Saturdays, and Dick Young was doing notes in New York. I always thought you should have one on each sport. Ernie [Roberts] was completely receptive. He'd been happy with the 'Majoring in the Minors' column. In those early days, it was a lot shorter, probably ninety to one hundred lines [this would be 1,000 words compared with today's version, which runs about 3,500]. I really believe it's what readers like the most. I've always believed newspapers love awards, so they go overboard on features rather than what people read. People love all that notes stuff."

Gammons requires almost no sleep, and it can be said without dispute that he spends more time on the telephone than any other sports reporter in the country. *Globe* staffers dream of the day that their monthly salaries approximate Gammons's phone bill. In 1994, when Gammons and his wife, Gloria, were in a car crash while driving north on Route 3 from Cape Cod, he carried his cellular phone to the emergency room. They bought a boat later that year on the condition that Peter not bring his phone aboard.

By the late 1970s, just about every major metropolitan daily carried a Sunday baseball-notes column. Unfortunately, too many reporters were simply swapping information instead of gathering their own. It got worse. By the late 1980s, "notes cartels" had formed. Writers were hooking up on Thursday afternoons via conference calls, feeding each other information. The result was that on any Sunday, you could pick up a paper in Atlanta, Dallas, or Baltimore and find almost the exact same notes column. When reporters got lazy, there was a great danger of mistakes getting handed around. In the old days, an erroneous note would run in one city only, be corrected, and be quickly forgotten. Now a mistake gets repeated in just about every paper nationwide. Notes combines have made players supersensitive about their relationships with beat reporters.

Gammons, the godfather of Sunday notes, never subscribed to a notes service because he always did his own work. Still does. He gets his notes from real sources—players, general managers, owners, agents, managers, and coaches. Most reporters have to pad their columns to fill space. Some weeks Gammons will send the *Globe* twice as much material as it needs to fill his page.

The *Lowell Sun*'s Chaz Scoggins, penning a tribute to Gammons, wrote, "Even his renowned Sunday baseball notes column, which fills an entire page, is merely the *William Tell* Overture and leaves us guessing what the rest of the opera sounds like."

From 1972 to 1976, Gammons evolved into the premier baseball beat reporter in the nation. His prose was a little overripe for some readers, and those over forty often did not pick up on his deft use of rock music lyrics, but the new generation of baseball fans thought he was the best baseball writer they'd ever read. Greater Boston is populated by thousands of students from around the country, and Gammons provided the hip voice and the national scope they wanted. When the 1975 Red Sox made it to the World Series, a Series that ranks with the best of all time, the entire American sports press got to read Gammons at a time when he was at the top of his game. Writing under incredible deadline pressure, he could turn out thousands of words in an hour. When Carlton Fisk hit the historic foul-pole homer to climax the sixth game of the '75 Series, Gammons claims to have ripped off eight pages of copy in the fifteen minutes that remained before deadline.

His lead:

"And all of a sudden the ball was there, like the Mystic River Bridge, suspended out in the black of morning.

"When it finally crashed off the mesh attached to the left field foul pole, one step after another the reaction unfurled: from Carlton Fisk's convulsive leap, to John Kiley's booming of the 'Hallelujah Chorus,' to the wearing off of the numbness, to the outcry that echoed across the cold New England morning.

"At 12:34 A.M., in the 12th inning, Fisk's historic home run brought a 7–6 end to a game that will be the pride of historians in the year 2525, a game won and lost what seemed a dozen times, and a game that brings back summertime one more day. For the seventh game of the World-Series."

In New England baseball lore, Gammons's lead is equal to Grantland Rice's famous "Outlined against the blue grey October sky" story about a Notre Dame–Army football game.

A few days later, in a full-page, season wrap-up, Gammons sent the readers into the off-season with, "We have postponed autumn long enough now. There are storm windows to put in, wood to chop for the whistling months ahead. The floorboards are getting awfully cold in the morning, the cider sweet. Where Lynn dove and El Tiante stood will be frozen soon, and while it is now 43 years for Thomas A.

Yawkey and 57 for New England, the fugue that was the 1975 baseball season will play in our heads until next we meet at the Fens again."

Globe insiders will confess that Gammons's copy tends to ramble and lack punctuation, but his disregard for structure only enhances his reputation as baseball's literary genius. When Gammons uses his best fastball, none can touch him. You can look it up. His style spawned a generation of young, workaholic baseball writers. They are Gammons Youth.

Less than a year after the 1975 World Series, Gammons was off to *Sports Illustrated*, where he was wasted as a hockey writer. He starved. There was no daily forum, no feedback from his readers, no freedom to express himself, and no baseball. By February of 1978, Peter Gammons was back at the *Globe*, just in time for the Red Sox–Yankee pennant race that ended with the Bucky Dent playoff game.

By this time, he was a genuine folk hero among Boston's baseball readers. They believed in Gammons and trusted him. He was profiled on the front page of the *Wall Street Journal*. ("I did it for my mother," said Gammons. "She always wanted her son to go into business.") *New Yorker* essayist Roger Angell wrote that in Boston, Gammons was almost "as important to New England baseball as a Yastrzemski or a Fisk." Gammons was profiled in magazines and received offers to do television and radio. And once again he had the daily fix of baseball, a chance to chronicle perhaps the most memorable season in the long, hard history of the hometown team. When the Red Sox tied the Yankees on the final day (Sunday) of the regular season, setting up a play-off game to be played less than twenty-four hours later, Gammons knew what to do. He led his Monday-morning account with a passage from *A Tale of Two Cities*, then wrote:

"And now—after star-crossed seasons of power, Martin, glory, Zimmer, injuries, Lemon, humiliation and redemption—the long, hard summer has come to one heart-to-heart duel.

"Baseball's Athens and Sparta, the teams with the best records in baseball after 162 games and 178 days, have, after it seemed all had been done, been asked to settle it in one afternoon, with Mike Torrez and Ron Guidry.

" . . . It's as if the Lord looked down on all the problems of the world and decided that this is the one thing HE always wanted to see: the Red Sox and the Yankees, in Fenway Park, in the second play-off game in American League history."

In the years after 1978, Gammons grew even closer to his sport. These were years in which the Red Sox were mediocre, even boring. Both of his parents died in the summer of 1981, the summer of the first great baseball strike. Gammons later wrote, "The last time my brother Ned and I spoke to our father before he died in 1981, he said to us, "The Red Sox will win in your lifetime."

In 1984, *Time* magazine called Gammons "that sport's most influential daily chronicler." A year later, he published his first book, *Beyond the Sixth Game*, a 280-page tome detailing just about everything that had happened to baseball between 1975 and 1984.

By 1986, he was restless in his capacity as "eyes and ears" of the fans. Again he left for *Sports Illustrated*, this time with a chance to cover baseball for the magazine. For once, his timing was horrible. Had Gammons stayed around Fenway for one more season, he could have covered the historic ride of the 1986 Red Sox. But there was no way to see what was coming. He was forty-one years old and it was time to move on. Announcing his departure, he wrote, "As for the readership, writing about baseball for any other paper is like Bruce Springsteen playing for the faculty of Liberty Baptist College."

He was not gone from the *Globe* for long. After covering baseball for *Sports Illustrated* for four years, Gammons became a full-time baseball reporter for ESPN and returned to the *Globe* as a special correspondent in 1991. Today he is back on the Sunday page where he belongs, and New Englanders are secure in the knowledge that their hardball hunger will be met over coffee and doughnuts before Sunday mass each week.

In 1986, in an open letter to Sox owner Haywood Sullivan, Gammons best explained what the Red Sox mean to him and to New England: "The Red Sox are not the Red Sox because of Gen. Charles and John I. Taylor, who built Boston's first (and only) great team and Fenway Park. They are not the Red Sox because of Tom Yawkey, who rebuilt Fenway and saved the franchise. Honey Fitz and the Royal Rooters and the New England baseball tradition came before the Taylors and Yawkeys, who returned and built upon what is here. This isn't a franchise like any other franchise, not like the Celtics, Bruins or Patriots, not like the Yankees, not like the Dodgers. New Englanders *care* about the Red Sox in a way Roger Angell so eloquently explained in 1975, and The Olde Towne Team has traditionally been the focus of what is one of our most important emotions. . . . All the people who are the Red Sox really ask is that the caretaker of the franchise *care* as much as they do."

Gammons has become the signature commentator of his sport. When former Green Bay Packer Sterline Sharpe took a job as a commentator for ESPN's *NFL Prime Time Monday*, Sharpe said, "I don't think there are any Peter Gammons–type people in our sport."

Keith Olberman, who works with Gammons at ESPN, submits this account of Gammons's preparation and knowledge: "We [ESPN] did the expansion draft in 1992. We began meetings once a day for several hours in the middle of the summer. We went through every name in the book. We hired consultants on the minor leagues. There were names that no one could identify. There names of players who were about to sign with rookie-league teams. There were names of players who, because they were stuck in a basement in the Virgin Islands for three years, were not known to the public, but would be eligible for the expansion draft.

"We went through something like 1,250 players that might be eligible, and each time with Peter it was . . . 'Well, second base, pretty good bat, good range to the right, they really like him in Colorado.' There was always something about each one of these players until we got to a pitcher named Scott Fredrickson. And Peter said something that froze the room. Peter said, 'I don't know who he is.' That was a moment when I thought I was in trouble because Peter Gammons did not know who he was. But flash forward to the expansion draft. We were on the air for about seven hours. Then the announcement was made that the Colorado Rockies, with the nine-thousandth pick in the expansion draft, select from the San Diego Padres, pitcher Scott Fredrickson. I just turned to Peter and he had the entire history of Scott Fredrickson. That's the breadth of Peter Gammons's knowledge. We refer to him as the man of a thousand phone calls."

When he was honored at the 1995 Boston Baseball Writers bash, in the middle of the baseball strike, Gammons stood at the podium and said, "When I started in this business, much younger than most people covering it, Dave O'Hara [longtime Boston Associated Press sports editor] taught me one of the most important things that I had to know. And that is respect for this business. There isn't a lot of glamour in this business. You are a short-order historian. There are very few times that people remember you. Most of the stories you write are anonymous. And what O'Hara taught me was to be the first guy at the ballpark every day in Florida and be the last guy to leave the press box at Fenway Park after games. Because the mark of people who are great in this business are people who are consistent. You have to come to work and do it every day.

"This winter has distressed so many of us so much and torn so much out of us, and I still have not come to grips with people on either side saying, 'We will shut down this game to prove a point.' Because the people who control the destinies of this game really don't respect what it meant for Tony Gwynn to hit .400, and what it took for Matt Williams to make a run at Babe Ruth's record, and what it takes for Cal Ripken Jr. to show up for work every single day for thirteen or fourteen seasons."

He may as well have been talking about himself. The baseball strike distressed Peter Gammons because he loves the game. His readers have come to trust his words because they know he loves baseball and they know he's out there doing the work. Ripken showing up for work every day for thirteen or fourteen years is no different from Gammons's doing what Dave O'Hara told him at his first spring training in 1972. You get there early, you leave late. And you do it every day. That's baseball.

CHAPTER SIX

THE KNIGHTS OF THE KEYBOARD

Any comprehensive discussion of the relationship between the Boston Red Sox and their fans must acknowledge the role of the Boston press corps. The fourth estate serves as the third corner of the fan-team-media triangle.

For more than a century, major league baseball franchises have depended on newspapers to fuel interest in the hometown team. In the old days, ball clubs had friendly relationships with reporters who covered baseball. Teams would pay reporters' hotel and travel expenses and in some cases even gave writers meal money. It was not unheard of to have a newspaper reporter moonlight for a team as a public relations person. Nobody worried much about conflicts of interest. In exchange for certain hospitalities, teams could expect reams of positive press, designed to inflate expectations and sell tickets. It was old-fashioned trade, and in most towns, it worked.

Boston was a bit different. Year in and year out, the Red Sox were followed by more writers than any other team. The city of Boston had as many as nine metropolitan dailies. Local advertisers wanted their ads placed near the baseball stories, and smaller newspapers from all six New England states found it important and profitable to cover the team. Red Sox players had to answer not only to the *Boston Post* and the *Evening Globe;* they were also queried by the *Providence Journal,* the *Worcester Telegram,* the *Hartford Courant,* the *Springfield Union,* the *Manchester Union Leader,* and the *Portland Press Herald.* As years went by and Boston lost most of its daily papers, the satellite papers and suburban papers multiplied. Today the Sox are trailed by two Boston dailies, plus newspaper reporters from Springfield, Worcester, Providence, Hartford, Portland, Quincy, Lynn, Brockton, Salem, and Framingham. Whether the Sox are at home or on the road, the Red Sox press contingent is often three or four times larger than the group covering the other team.

With these numbers comes competition. A solo reporter in a one-paper town is not going to bother his team as much as a pack of reporters fighting for an exclusive. The competition partly explains why the relationship between Sox players and reporters has historically been strained. Several other factors contribute to the friction. Sports reporters from the Northeast tend to be more cynical and critical. The Sox history of fading in the clutch has further jaded sportswriters and fans. Coverage of the Olde Towne Team tends to accentuate the negative. Over the years, the Boston front office has developed an institutional arrogance and paranoia that reporters find insulting and difficult. The Red Sox public relations staff in the 1980s had a combative reputation, ever likely to tell a complaining scribe, "That's your problem."

A baseball reporter is expected to ask the questions fans want answered. He's expected to take his readers inside the clubhouse and onto the field. His meter is always running. Die-hard baseball fans can recite a game's play-by-play before the next day's paper hits the stands. A baseball reporter must get the inside story to satisfy his hungry readers. He must use his access and tell his readers what he saw and heard.

In 1996, the Red Sox, their fans, and the Boston media enjoy a mostly peaceful and cooperative relationship, one that enables fans to feel informed and included. Under the stewardship of General Manager Dan Duquette, a New England native, the Sox have steered away from the smash-mouth public relations that marked the 1980s and early 1990s. But the situation is still combustible. There are simply too many reporters and too much history.

When we talk about the Red Sox, it's always about history. In the first years of the Red Sox (Pilgrims), coverage was typically positive. Certainly there were few negative stories in the *Boston Globe* during the years when the *Globe* owned the team (1904–12). The *Globe's* Mel Webb gleefully volunteered that when the Boston Pilgrims were preparing to play their first games in 1901, he grabbed a shovel and helped dig into the Huntington Avenue lot. Baseball historian Frederick Lieb wrote, "Mel wasn't overlooked some years later when the Boston Americans celebrated the winning of league pennants and world championships in fitting fashion." One can't be sure if that meant Mel got a share of the winners' booty, but Lieb was a careful reporter and he was telling us that cousin Webb was somehow compensated for his kind words.

In 1901, when Boston's American League franchise was founded, the *Globe's* Tim Murnane, the *Herald's* Jake Morse, and the *Journal's* Walter Barnes were Boston's top baseball writers. Murnane was a former National League player who was offered the presidency of the American League team by owner Charles W. Somers. Murnane opted to keep covering baseball. Clearly that was a different era. In addition to the troika of Murnane, Morse, and Barnes, the new team was covered by *Sporting News* correspondent Peter "Hi Hi" Kelly—a voice of the fans. When the Boston Americans raised third-base bleacher ticket prices to fifty cents from twenty-five cents before the 1902 season, Hi Hi wrote, "This act of the American Leaguers will hurt them here, and cost them many friends."

Always, tragedy surrounds the Red Sox, even in the press box. In the spring of 1907, twenty-five-year-old *Boston Post* reporter Frederic O'Connell developed pneumonia at the club's West Baden Springs training site and died. O'Connell was succeeded by Paul Shannon, who became popular with *Post* readers.

The *Herald's* Burt Whitman was an important writer at the time Babe Ruth played for the Sox. It was Whitman who coined the term "rape of the Red Sox" when Ruth and a hoard of other Sox stars were shipped to New York by Boston owner Harry Frazee.

Purple prose jumped off the page in those early years. When one of the 1918 World Series games (Cubs–Red Sox) was rained out, the *Globe's* Edward Martin wrote this at the top of his page-one story: "When the athletes rolled out of the arms of Morpheus this morning, they observed that the sky was sweating—perspiring torrentially, as they declare in the classiques." When the Sox stuffed the Cubs, 1–0,

Martin wrote, "To be at home when that exacting old codger Mr. Opportunity drops around is not only the proper case in the matter of etiquette, but a swell move from a diplomatic angle. The Red Sox passed up nothing in the way of opportunities. They made hay while the sun was on the job, did not stop anywhere for a drink, and sneaked in the stitch in time while the Cubs threw Mr. Opportunity down flat, turning their backs on him as they would on a professional panhandler."

Martin would have us believe that Mr. Opportunity was the first Mr. October.

There was a great deal of boosterism and exaggeration in those early, innocent days. When the Sox lost, it was because the visitors were lucky or capitalized on Boston's uncharacteristic mistakes. If the Sox won, it was a glorious battle in which the home team overcame enormous odds and beat the visitors with heroism and hard work. Sox players and team publicists would love this type of reporting today. Some baseball fans want only good news. But in Boston, most fans are thankful that the media usually prepares them for this year's letdown.

Between the seasons of 1939 to 1987, the Red Sox had only three regular left fielders—Ted Williams, Carl Yastrzemski, and Jim Rice. It was the baseball equivalent of the Massachusetts Eighth Congressional District, which from 1944 to 1986 was represented only by James Michael Curley, John F. Kennedy, and Tip O'Neill. Through the lengthy careers of Messrs. Williams, Yastrzemski, and Rice, we can trace the evolution of the relationship between the Red Sox and the Boston baseball press.

Reportage of Williams's bombastic Fenway tenure best demonstrates the heights, depths, passions, and exaggerations of the Hub's hardball media. Theodore Samuel Williams joined the Red Sox in 1939 and remained Boston's franchise player until he retired in 1960. His goal was to be the greatest hitter who ever lived, and some would say he achieved this distinction. He may also have been subjected to more pettiness and unfair criticism than any other American professional athlete.

Popular wisdom holds that today's sports coverage is tougher and more intrusive because the new-breed reporters always dig for dirt. Indeed, in the late 1980s, Wade Boggs went through two seasons of embarrassment and ridicule after his former mistress sued him for $6 million. Boggs's public woes served as a vivid contrast to the good old days when "see no evil" sportswriters could watch a knife-wielding woman chase Babe Ruth through a train car—and report nothing. But in Ted Williams's case, all the protocol went out the window. The Kid was too brash, too cocky and rude to Boston scribes.

In his autobiography, Williams wrote, "I was in Boston, where there must be more newspapers per capita than anyplace in the world, with writers vying for stories, all trying to outdo the others, all trying to get a headline, all digging into places where they had no business being."

Today he says, "It was just a matter of a young kid who wasn't careful about what he was saying. I do not think they were very fair and very thoughtful about what they were writing. That disturbed me and I was a little immature and I would show my displeasure, and next thing I know I was saying things that I might not say as an older guy."

When Williams came to Boston, four morning papers, the *Post*, the *Herald*, the *Globe*, and the *Record*, plus four afternoon papers, the *Traveler*, the *Globe*, the *American*, and the *Transcript*, covered the Red Sox. Add the *Christian Science Monitor* and the papers from Providence, Worcester, Portland, Hartford, Springfield, etc. They all knew Williams sold papers.

In 1980, Hall of Fame owner Bill Veeck said, "It used to be that if the Red Sox beat you in Boston, they'd be applauded in two papers and creamed in seven. Then if you beat them, they'd be creamed in all nine. That was always fun."

In 1940, Williams's second year in the big leagues, the great Harold Kaese, then working for the *Transcript* (later of the *Globe*) wrote a column accusing Williams of being jealous of teammate Jimmy Foxx. Kaese blasted Williams for "extreme selfishness, egoism and lack of courage," then added that "it probably traces to his upbringing. Can you imagine a kid, a nice kid with a nimble brain, not visiting his father and mother all of last winter?"

Low blow. Williams was sensitive about his family. His mother was a San Diego Salvation Army worker. His father was an alcoholic who left when Ted was a teenager. Ted Williams's only sibling, brother Danny, was a sickly child who died of leukemia in 1960.

The cheap shot by Kaese cut Williams deeply. (It was uncharacteristic, and legend holds that Kaese tried to have the line deleted but was overruled by a headline-hungry editor. Historian Glenn Stout's research shows that Kaese wrote at least five hundred columns about Williams, all but a dozen of them positive.) It also ignited a flame that burned for the better part of three decades. According to Williams's biographer, Ed Linn, "It was on that day that the carnivorous Boston sports press was born. Until then, it had been the practice of the sportswriters to hold their stories for a gentlemanly three days in order to protect each other. From then on, they were ordered to hand their stories in immediately. Pool reportage was banned. New writers coming in from other cities were astonished to find that they were not only in competition with the other papers, but were also competing with writers from their own paper."

Williams knew how to play the competition. Later in the 1940 season, he committed the unpardonable sin of giving a scoop to Austen Lake of the *Evening American*. Williams told Lake that he'd asked to be traded. He said, "I don't like the town, I don't like the people, and the newspapermen have been on my back all year."

It was a huge story, a coup for the *Evening American*. The rest of the Boston baseball writers, jealous over being scooped and jilted by Williams's assessment of the town, went ballistic. They tore into Ted.

In the words of biographer Glenn Stout: "The writers and Williams fed on each other. Ted gave them material and they made Ted the most talked-about player of his time. In turn, Williams basked in the benefits of such attention and bashed the practitioners. They used each other."

It was open season on Teddy Ballgame. After Williams's second year in the majors, it was wrongly reported that he'd sold his mother's furniture. That was but the beginning. When Williams's draft status was changed from 1-A to 3-A because he claimed his mother as a dependent, one of the Boston papers hired a private investigator to check his story out in San Diego. In 1942 when Williams's daughter Bobby Jo was born two weeks prematurely, Williams was fishing in the Everglades. The Boston press slaughtered him. Kaese wrote, "Everyone knows where Moses was when the lights went out. And apparently everybody knows where Ted Williams was when his baby was born here yesterday. He was fishing."

Oddly enough, the columnist who came to Williams's defense was the *Record*'s Dave Egan—Williams's nemesis throughout his career. Egan constantly degraded Boston's slugger for failing to hit in the clutch and not being a team player. But on the matter of press criticism in the wake of Williams missing the birth of his child, Egan wrote, "This, dear friend, is what is known as yellow journalism at its very dirtiest. It is an invasion of the domestic life of Ted Williams, his wife and his child. It is an action which trifles cruelly with the happiness of a family, just for the sake of a headline. . . . His relations with his mother, his wife and his baby are not the concerns of sportswriters."

Egan had a Harvard diploma and a law degree. He was known as the Colonel. And he made a career out of ripping Williams in the Hearst tabloid. To this day, it bothers the Hall of Fame slugger. On the day that Williams was inducted into the Hall, reporters heard Williams curse Egan from the Cooperstown podium. As ever, it made all the papers.

Williams's feud with the press was a two-way street. The Sox star brought much of it on himself. He would hide some days and could snap at the simplest questions. He enjoyed baiting the writers. He would stand at his locker, sniff the air, and say, "What smells bad in here? Oh, they let the sportswriters in."

After Williams retired, the *Herald*'s Tim Horgan wrote, "He could say *writers* with such honest loathing, contempt and disgust, that it became an obscenity."

In a 1950s *Collier's* article, Williams said he liked just four sports-writers, naming Grantland Rice and Frankie Graham, both New York scribes. Taylor Spink, publisher of the *Sporting News*, wired his Boston correspondent to get the names of the other two, and Jack Malaney wired back, "Joshua and John."

One of Williams's favorite get-even tricks was to grant long, folksy interviews to writers from out of town. He knew this frosted the Boston scribes, so he'd be particularly nice to writers from Cleveland and Detroit. Giving a scoop to a writer like Austen Lake was another way to get back at the pack.

Looking back now, Williams says, "Those things can get out of hand, and I did some things that probably weren't diplomatic, too. But hell, that's fifty years under the bridge. There was a lot of good writers, too, but there were a few editorial writers and those were the bad guys. But you'd have to say in all fairness that they had to eat a lot of crow and I take pride in that."

According to Boston folklore, a Boston writer cheated Williams out of an MVP award. In 1941, when Williams hit .406, he failed to win the Most Valuable Player award. In '42, Williams won the Triple Crown, hitting .356 with 36 homers and 137 RBI, but again failed to win the MVP—it went to the Yankees' Joe Gordon. In the MVP race of '47, Williams and everybody else in Boston was led to believe that a petty old scribe put the screws to Williams and cost him the award. In '47, Williams lost the MVP award to Joe DiMaggio by the slimmest of margins (202–201). That was the election in which it has long been held that the *Globe*'s Mel Webb did not list Williams among his top ten MVP candidates. When asked about his alleged ballot, the writer said, "I don't like the son of a bitch and I'll never vote for him."

Webb was seventy-one years old in 1947. A charter member (1908) of the Baseball Writers Association of America, he'd covered Babe Ruth when Ruth was a teenager with the Red Sox. In spring training of '47, Williams supposedly greeted Webb with, "Why don't you drop dead, you old bastard?" Webb vowed, "I'll fix you for that," and allegedly took his revenge when he got his 1947 MVP ballot. However, historian Glenn Stout researched the situation and concluded that Webb did not have an MVP vote in 1947. According to Stout, the three Boston writers who voted in '47 were Joe Cashman of the *Record*, Burt Whitman of the *Herald*, and Jack Malaney of the *Post*. The records of the persnickety Kaese show all three gave Williams their first-place vote in '47. So the legend of Williams getting screwed out of an MVP by a Boston scribe may be false. But it's served everybody well through the years, and few have bothered to dispute the fable. Whether pettiness got in the way or not, it's indisputable that Williams failed to win the MVP award in both of his Triple Crown seasons, *and* the season in which he made his mark as baseball's last .400 hitter. Maybe he could have helped himself if he'd been a bit more writer-friendly. Cleveland's rude slugger, Albert Belle, learned this when he lost the 1995 MVP to Boston's Mo Vaughn.

In 1956, when Williams hit his 400th career homer, he celebrated the event by spitting toward the press box when he crossed Fenway Park's home plate. The *Herald* published a photo of Ted's expectoration on page one. Three days later, he did it again. Within a week, Williams spit toward the crowd that had been booing him. Egan wrote, "A kid with a small *k* would be spanked and sent to his room for doing the same thing that a man of almost forty has done consistently, and this seems to indicate the man is sick. . . . It will be a good day for baseball when he retires and stays retired."

Owner Yawkey was bothered by all this and once told a reporter, "Listen, you wise guy, I am going to buy your paper just to fire you."

The men from the press never let up on Williams. On the day of his final game, September 26, 1960, the *Boston American*'s Huck Finnegan wrote, "Williams' career, in contrast [to Babe Ruth's], has been a series of failures except for his averages. He flopped in the only World Series he ever played in [1946] when he batted only .200. He flopped in the play-off game with Cleveland in 1948. He flopped in the final game of the 1949 season with the pennant hinging on the outcome. . . . It has always been Williams' records first, the team second, and the Sox nonwinning record is proof enough of that."

In a short ceremony before that final game, after Williams was introduced to the small crowd of 10,453, the slugger turned in midspeech toward the press box, motioned upward, and said, "Despite some of the terrible things written about me by the Knights of the Keyboard up there, and they were terrible things—I'd like to forget them. But I can't."

John Updike was in the stands for Williams's farewell game and wrote about it in his essay "Hub Fans Bid Kid Adieu." His observation on the love-hate relationship between Boston and Williams: "It fell into three stages, which may be termed Youth, Maturity, and Age; or Thesis, Antithesis, and Synthesis; or Jason, Achilles, and Nestor."

There it is again. With the Red Sox, it's always Greek mythology.

Today Williams admits he was a little stubborn in his dealings with the press. Most of the men who covered him have died, and he welcomes phone calls from those who are still around. Asked about Clif

Keane, a crusty *Globe* reporter who was born in 1912, Williams laughs and says, "I thought he was dead. He's not? Well, you tell him I should have punched him in the nose when I had a chance."

Williams on Ed Linn, who wrote a biography of the Kid: "He used to be on my ass all the time. Now here it is twenty years later and he said, 'Ted, do you remember me?' and I said, 'Damn right I remember you.' The last day of the last season, I saw him in the clubhouse. He wasn't supposed to be in there. Well, he started to call me and tell me things I did, working on that book of his. And he's the son of a bitch that was on my ass all the time. But people tell me the book [*Hitter*] is pretty good."

Williams on the late Jimmy Cannon: "He was a little shit. I didn't like him. He liked anything Yankees. He must have thought I could hit, though. I thought, all in all, that the New York press could be very fair. There were a few like Cannon that I didn't like. Arthur Daly was wonderful. God, he was a great guy. His kid was flying a hot, heavy plane going aboard carriers. And of course, Grantland Rice was a great guy."

Williams on the late Harold Kaese: "Harold Kaese was a good writer, but he used to get on my butt. If I spit at anybody, by God, he'd get on me."

They all got on Ted. And it worked out well for everyone.

When Williams retired, it was almost boring in the Fenway press box. A rookie named Carl Yastrzemski took over the left-field position, but in twenty-three Hall of Fame seasons, Yaz never filled the notebooks the way Ted did. Yaz got into a couple of squabbles with his managers, and it was alleged that his relationship with owner Tom Yawkey was too close (Johnny Pesky and Dick Williams wondered if they were "fired" by Yaz), but Yastrzemski's cold demeanor was of little value to a throng of reporters looking for scoops. Yastrzemski did not tell anecdotes, had a poor memory, and little sense of humor. He was rarely good copy.

Keane was involved in a Yaz story that's retold almost every time today's reporters reminisce. In the early 1970s, when Yastrzemski was often portrayed as an overpaid prima donna, Keane found himself in the middle of an unusual controversy. These were the days before computers, modems, and instant transmission of newspaper stories.

These were the days when reporters used typewriters and often handed their copy to Western Union operators, who would wire the stories back to the newspapers. As deadlines neared, dictation was the final resort. Keane was covering a night game in California when Yastrzemski failed to run out a ground ball, then did not report to his position the following inning. Folks back home wondered if perhaps the petulant Yaz was being disciplined by his manager. Keane and others in the press box learned from Red Sox officials that Yastrzemski had hurt his hamstring, which prevented him from running out the grounder and resulted in his extraction from the lineup. When Keane, anxious to make the team's overnight flight back to Boston, dictated the top of his game story, a *Globe* copyboy asked, "What about Yaz? What about him not running out that ground ball?"

Keane, believing the young man in Boston was aware of Yastrzemski's not-so-serious hamstring pull, replied, "Yaz is fine."

Keane hung up the phone and dashed to his flight. When the sports desk asked the copyboy about what they saw as Yastrzemski's apparent malingering and subsequent benching, the copyboy told them that Keane had said, "Yaz is fined."

Fine. Fined. So close. So far apart in meaning. When the boys on the copy desk were told Yaz was "fined," they rewrote Keane's story, highlighting their erroneous interpretation that Yastrzemski had been benched and punished. The headline told readers that Yaz had been fined for not hustling.

Unaware of all this rewrite and misunderstanding, Keane flew home with the team, crawled into bed after sunrise, then was roused by his son later in the day.

Holding a copy of the morning *Globe*, Keane's son said, "Dad, this is some story about Yaz being fined and all."

"Yaz fined?" said Clif Keane, wiping slumber from his eyes. "Who wrote that?"

"*You* did, Dad!"

Today, when Keane tells the story, he affectionately refers to it as "the day I scooped myself."

With the talented, but somewhat taciturn Yastrzemski unable to furnish many colorful quotes or episodes, reporters looked elsewhere for Red Sox characters. This was in the early 1960s, when the team was chronically bad and didn't draw many fans. In 1962, the mysterious disappearance of pitcher Gene Conley and infielder Pumpsie Green gave the press a chance to have some fun. On July 26, after a 13–3 loss to the Yankees in New York, Conley and Green hopped out of a Sox bus that was snarled in traffic. Green was back one day later, but nobody saw Conley for sixty-eight hours. It was almost as good as having Teddy Ballgame around again.

Conley remembers, "It was really hot. I was tired. There were some misplays that day, but that didn't bother me. I'm not a person to blame teammates. I came out of the game and went into the clubhouse and had about four or five beers. The game ended. We lost. And the team got on the bus. I pulled Pumpsie aside and said, 'Pumpsie, let's get off this bus. Let's go inside and have a cold one.' So we did. We told [manager] Mike Higgins we were going to the bathroom. So we got off the bus, and when we came back out, Pumpsie said, 'Hey, that bus is gone,' and I said, 'We are, too.' And we were off. And we were gone for three days. . . . I went first-class. I was staying at the Waldorf, watching the news about me. On the TV, they're saying, 'Hey, this guy is still missing.' I was enjoying it all. Pumpsie stayed with me two days, then said, 'I can't go on more, I've got to get back.' After a couple of days, I went to the airport. I figured I'd go to the Holy Land and solve everything. I called the Shawmut Bank and asked them to transfer the money to the hotel. I had about a thousand dollars. I had been drinking at a place called Al Shacks, plus Toots Shor's and a few other places. Then, when I got to the airport, the guy at the ticket thing said he couldn't let me on because I didn't have a passport."

Instead of flying to Israel, Conley flew to Providence, Rhode Island, and made his way back to his trailer park in Foxborough. The reporters were waiting.

"I couldn't believe all the fuss," says Conley. "I honestly didn't think it had been that big a thing. But when I saw all the media coverage, I thought, 'Oh, wow, what have I done?' "

What he had done was feed the beast.

Reporting on the Red Sox in the 1960s and 1970s was friendly and fun. Williams was gone, the team was bad, and writers tried to keep readers entertained and informed when interest was flat. Dick Stuart, a home-run hitter who could not catch a cold, provided some comic relief for a couple of seasons, and the emergence of local hero Tony Conigliaro (Swampscott, Massachusetts) gave the scribes something to cover, but for the most part it was a chore to make the Red Sox readable.

Everything changed in 1967 when the Sox overcame 100–1 odds to win the American League pennant for the first time since 1946. It was the greatest multi-team pennant race of all time, and the Red Sox finally won it on the last day of the season. For most of the summer, Boston battled Minnesota, Chicago, and Detroit, and one day in August the four teams were separated by a single percentage point. Many forty-something New Englanders still own scrapbooks from this storied season, and a glance at the coverage shows tremendous support and encouragement coming from the suddenly no-longer-carnivorous Boston media. Readers often saw the word *we* in headlines concerning the 1967 Red Sox. They were the cardiac kids, inspiring long-playing record albums, television specials, and fresh-baked loaves of Big Yaz Bread.

Despite their tag as lovable losers, the Red Sox have been competitive almost every season since 1967. From 1967 to 1987, the Sox finished .500 or better every year except 1983. The team was in pennant races in '72, '74, '75, '77, and '78, and this encouraged plenty of readers and a tonnage of excellent coverage. But two things happened to the team-media relationship during the 1970s: (1) several times the Sox came close to winning, only to fold at the finish; (2) a new generation of agressive young reporters displaced the old guard of team-friendly, don't-ask-don't-tell reporters.

The succession of near misses created reader suspicion regarding reports about the Red Sox. For most of this century, Boston scribes have inflated the potential of the hometown team, particularly during spring training. The Sox always look good on paper, and missives from Arizona and Florida usually forecast success in the upcoming season. In most cases, reality has not met expectation. Sox fans came to expect an annual fold in the fall, and coverage reflected this sense of dread. Ball-club officials believed the slant of reporting caused fans' expectations to collapse. It's a chicken-and-egg argument. In either case, after the 1970s, citizens of Red Sox Nation routinely expected losing streaks whenever the Red Sox got rolling. More often than not, the dire prophecies were fulfilled.

Personnel changes in the press box exacerbated the new negativity. Suddenly, writers weren't afraid to hurt players' feelings. Some off-the-field shenanigans became part of the coverage. The scribes and players stopped socializing; little was considered off-limits. This created, at best, a void of trust, and at worst, animosity.

"In those days, I think there was a lot of feeling by people that the writers just wanted to screw us," says Dick Bresciani, a Red Sox employee since 1972 and now vice president in charge of public relations. "I think a lot of it came in the late seventies. Some of it maybe came from a couple of tough years when we lost right at the end. Then people started grousing. A feeling pervaded that you've got to watch yourself with every media guy. It was kind of a blanket feeling about them all, which isn't fair."

In 1975 the *Globe*'s Bob Ryan wrote an early-season column that was critical of several Sox players. As part of his summation, Ryan suggested that relief pitchers Reggie Cleveland and Diego Segui take a transatlantic flight with Amelia Earhart at the controls. Ryan was stunned the next day when Amelia Earhart's sister, then living in Massachusetts, called to complain.

"After thirty-eight years I felt there was a statute of limitation on outrage," says Ryan. "I felt free to make Amelia Earhart jokes. How the hell did I know her sister lived in Squantum?"

The wrath of sister Earhart was nothing compared with what greeted Ryan the next time he went into the Red Sox clubhouse. Ryan was shoved by mediocre second baseman Doug Griffin and got into a screaming match with outfielder Evans.

Years later, Evans admitted, "When a reporter asks me a question, I talk. But I really don't talk. You don't know who to trust."

Orioles coach Elrod Hendricks, who played against the Red Sox for twelve seasons, says, "It's still tough on them because of the media. They beat a team, 20–1, then win 2–1, and everybody wants to know what went wrong. It's tough listening to that day in and day out. Invariably, the media turns the fans on you. By July and August those guys are pissed off at the world. No wonder people don't think they're friendly."

In the spring of 1979, the *Herald*'s Marie Brenner (now with *Vanity Fair*) became one of the first females to cover the Red Sox. By her own admission, she knew nothing about baseball. But some of her observations shed light on the player-writer relationship. In a *Boston Magazine* article she described standing next to veteran beat reporter Hugh McGovern (*Worcester Telegram*) as he said his hellos, one by one, to the Sox cast of stars. The first seven players he addressed said nothing back to him. Brenner asked McGovern how long he'd been covering the team. His answer: fourteen years. He told her he was used to being ignored. Brenner asked coach Johnny Pesky about it, and he told her, "It's a shame. They think if they say 'Hello,' it's a commitment."

As player salaries escalated and travel perks improved, the ballplayers grew further from reality and everyday people. Until the mid-1980s, players sometimes flew on commercial airplanes. When ball clubs flew on chartered planes, writers often flew with the players. The author remembers flying on charters with the Red Sox throughout the 1987 season. One memory lingers: In most cases, there's an unwritten seating chart on team buses and airplanes. In the summer of '87, *Hartford Courant* reporter Steve Fainaru (now with the *Globe*) and I unknowingly beached ourselves in the row reserved for mean-spirited manager John McNamara. Mac said nothing of the grievous offense until the plane landed; then when his thirst was quenched, he turned on us and said, "Don't ever fuckin' sit in those seats again. They are my seats." Mission accomplished, he accepted some congratulatory handshakes from his players ("You showed them, Mac!") and staggered off toward the waiting team bus.

By the late 1980s, teams traveled exclusively on charters, and writers were banned from traveling on team planes or buses. Suddenly, there was little contact. Players and writers saw each other only in the clubhouse, a more formal setting where just about every conversation is an interview. Most players today don't know the names of the writers traveling with the team. And for the most part, they don't care. Why should they? A flattering article is no longer important. In the old days, ballplayers felt they needed good coverage to help their status with the front office and the fans. Today, a player needs a good agent, good stats, ESEN "Sports Center," and little else.

His needs are taken care of. The press is a nuisance and sometimes a threat.

In 1987, struggling reliever Steve Crawford suffered a particularly poor outing in Detroit, prompting me to write, "Crawford was as effective as a sack of doorknobs." It was a throwaway line, tossed into a mundane game story. Somehow, it got people's attention. Crawford's teammates teased him about it, calling him "Doorknobs" and "Knobby." A few days later, when I arrived at the ballpark and stood behind the batting cage, Crawford ran in from the outfield, snorting like a bull. He got in my face, hurled a stream of obscenities, then said, "How could you call me a 'sack of doorknobs'?" I told him, "They won't let us put 'sack of shit' in the newspaper."

A couple of years later, I got into a small jam with Sox reliever Bob Stanley. Stanley was nearing the end of his career, drawing a $1-million salary, out of shape, out of luck, and just about out of the big leagues. At this juncture, he chose to blast manager Joe Morgan, saying, "I hate him." My reaction was a thousand-word rip job on Stanley, written while the team was in Texas. The next night in the clubhouse, Stanley called me over and said, "My wife says that you called me an ape in the newspaper." I told him that I'd torn him to shreds, but made no mention of primates. I pledged to get a copy of the story and show it to him. The *Globe* faxed me one and I soon surmised what had happened. Placing the column in front of Stanley, I said, "Here in the third paragraph, I call you a buffoon. I think your wife saw that, took it to be *baboon*, and said, 'Dan Shaughnessy called you an ape.' But as you can clearly see here, I didn't call you an ape, I called you a buffoon.' The affable Stanley shrugged and said, "Oh, okay. As long as you put it that way."

Bresciani says, "In the seventies, we had guys [writers] who were the primary guys, who traveled, and they were with us the whole year from the first day of spring training. It was almost unheard of for any of them to have a vacation in the middle of the season. They seldom took days off and it became kind of a group. Even though you argued over different things, it was fun. On the road, Jack Rogers (traveling secretary) and I often would get a whole group of the writers and broadcasters and take them to dinner on a Saturday night. That's all changed. Now we have writers come and go. One writer will start a trip, and someone else will replace him after the first city on the trip."

The career of Jim Ed Rice best depicts how the Boston baseball media has changed since 1975. A native of South Carolina, Rice had little to say when he first splashed down on the Boston sports scene. Rice made his initial appearance in the big leagues in the fall of 1974. He was twenty-one years old, inarticulate, suspicious, and no doubt thrown off by the racial dynamics of his new city. In 1974, forced school busing accelerated the ever-tense racial climate in Boston. Police motorcycles rode beside buses of schoolchildren while parents protested.

Rice never commented on the situation, but it might explain some of his discomfort with Boston and the almost all-white Fenway experience. As years went on and Rice became the American League's premier slugger (in 1978 he hit 46 homers, knocked in 139 runs, and became the first American Leaguer in forty-one years to amass 400 total bases), he became more distant and sometimes snapped at reporters. Arguing over a parking spot, Rice got into a scuffle with an elderly Red Sox public relations director. It was the first of several incidents. In Baltimore, when Rice was asked about bumping an umpire, he threatened to deposit the *Washington Post's* Tom Boswell in a trash can. In what should have been a glorious moment, after the Sox won the fifth game of the 1986 World Series, Rice went to the platform and charmed the national media by admonishing a reporter, "Take a hike, buddy!" A year later, during a clubhouse argument in Oakland, Rice tore the shirt off *Hartford Courant* reporter Steve Fainaru. Rice had to be restrained by Dwight Evans while rookie Mike Greenwell carried Fainaru from the locker room.

In a 1987 profile for *Inside Sports*, Ross Wetzsteon wrote that Rice was "the only man in baseball who can make tying his shoes a hostile act." It was Wetzsteon who asked Rice to list his closest friends on the team, provoking Rice to respond, "They're not friends. They're associates."

Rice may, in fact, be the only athlete in history who claimed he was misquoted during a television interview.

"It happened," says WBZ's Bob Lobel. "He said some things and we told him it might get him in trouble, but he said, 'Okay.' Then when things got hot, he denied saying it. We had to keep running the tape over and over to show people that he had said it."

In 1993, on the day Rice turned forty, he looked back (in anger, as always) and said, "I had no trouble with the writers who came down and said to me, 'You fucked up.' 'Cause I did. Now they come down and they make little jokes and little smirks. A lot of guys write stories, they write little things, and they go on TV and it hurts the guy, and then the guy [writer] doesn't show up the next day and that's when a guy wants to kill him. You should go and talk to a guy."

In Boston, it's widely believed that Rice was initially bitter about Fred Lynn's receiving the bulk of credit (and Rookie of the Year votes) when both were rookies in 1975. Lynn was friendly, easygoing—and white. Lynn became MVP and Rookie of the Year. Rice got his hand broken by a Vern Ruhle fastball and missed the greatest World Series of all time.

Asked about the Lynn jealousy theory, Rice says, "That's a lot of crap. I tell you, that's not fair. If I felt that way, you think when I had a chance to go somewhere else—and they talk about the racial thing in Boston—you don't think I would have packed it up and gone somewhere else? I'm from the South. I could have gone to Atlanta. People can spend their money and they can speak for you. And that's unfair. The worst thing about Freddie Lynn that I hated was that he left. Because we had a one-two punch. We could have played fifteen years together.

"When I first came up, the older writers, Jake Liston, Larry Claflin, those guys, they wrote about baseball. They'd ask you about baseball. Then it got different. Now they all want to know what you're doing off the field or how much you weigh or things like that."

When Rice first became eligible for the Hall of Fame in 1994, he received just 137 of 460 votes (30 percent), nowhere near the 75 percent of ballots necessary for induction into Cooperstown. His statistics are comparable to those of Ralph Kiner, Billy Williams, and Joe Medwick. There was every appearance that baseball writers were penalizing Rice because he was surly and uncooperative. It made Rice the perfect bookend to Ted Williams. Rice never was the hitter Williams was, but like Teddy Ballgame his personality hurt him when sportwriters went to the ballot box.

"I was hurt," Rice admitted a month after the vote was announced.

Asked if he felt the vote reflected his poor press relations, Rice answered, "It probably did. But are you basing your vote for a guy on being your boyfriend or are you basing it on his ability to play baseball? If you want someone to kiss you, that's fine. But if you want someone to go put some numbers on the board, that's a different thing."

Does he wish he had been nicer?

"No. I didn't say that. If you want to talk baseball, I talked baseball. That's what hurt me a lot.

"I do not talk about my family, I do not talk about your family. I do not talk about the Red Sox. That was the whole thing. I mean, I wasn't a bad guy. I just didn't take any crap."

It's interesting to note that Wade Boggs, always a headline grabber in Boston, did not make any off-the-field news once he signed to play for the Yankees. During his Red Sox years, Boggs was embroiled in the Margo Adams fiasco, assaulted at knifepoint, and run over by his wife. He feuded publicly with Oil Can Boyd and Roger Clemens. He provided much talk-show fodder. Then he went to New York City, tabloid heaven, and there was never anything about him in the papers. He was just a .320-hitting, Gold Glove–winning, solid citizen. Did Boggs change or is the Boston baseball media tougher and more unfair than the New York press?

In the 1956 official Red Sox program, there is a page devoted to sportswriters. The text, written by the Sox public relations department, states, "Perhaps no other team in baseball receives such widespread and outstanding newspaper coverage as do the Red Sox. These sportswriters are ever-welcome visitors to the ballpark. Their well-written, accurate reports of the games and their talented, interesting descriptions of the many and varied human interest angles connected with the club and its personnel help make the Red Sox truly a part of the household of every New England baseball fan."

It reads like some kind of military propaganda film from 1955.

The Sox PR office didn't think that way in the mideighties. In the first years after the crushing World Series loss of 1986, the perception was that the media was out to "get" the team. The relationship between the club and reporters was downright combative.

Frank O'Brien, a *Globe* photographer who first shot pictures of the Red Sox in 1967, says, "My policy is you never ask the Red Sox for anything. You just do it. If you take the trouble to ask, the answer always is no."

A *Globe* photographer accidently stumbled into a players-only prayer meeting before a Sunday-afternoon Fenway game. The lost photographer was greeted by a veteran Sox outfielder, who snapped, "Get the fuck out of here! Can't you see we're having our prayer meeting!"

Praise the Lord and pass the ammunition. Those were the years when baseball coverage in Boston took on a cold, skeptical, sometimes mean-spirited slant. Contrast the *Globe's* page-one accounts after game-seven World Series losses in 1975 and 1986.

In '75, Gammons wrote, "It was like the death of a favorite grandmother, a season whose life was beautiful and full and gave everyone from Southie to Stonington, Conn., to Groton to Charlestown, N.H., a year they will reminisce about until Olde Fenway calls them back again."

After game seven in '86 I wrote, "The taste is so very bitter. When the Red Sox get to the seventh game of the World Series, the other team uncorks champagne while the Sox uncork wild pitches. What is it like to live in a city that wins a World Series? Call your out-of-town friends and ask. Generations of Bostonians may never know."

The headline over the 1986 story was ". . . And Boston Is Mudville Once Again."

Boston Phoenix media critic Mark Jurkowitz (now *Globe* ombudsman and media critic) digested the 1986 World Series coverage, writing, "If New England sports fans were instantly engulfed in a black cloud of self-pity and recrimination following Game 7, they found kindred spirits in the men who fueled their fires in the pages of the *Globe* and the *Herald* on Tuesday morning, the day after the conclusion of a bittersweet postseason. . . . Should our newspapers become so emotionally vested in the local sports teams that their ability or desire to evaluate and discuss the game dispassionately is hindered?"

Sox players, managers, coaches, and front-office personnel felt the same way, and for several years the club's relationship with the media was strained. "I think it was probably at its worst in the late eighties," admits Bresciani. "I would say that if we would have won that '86 World Series, it would have helped a lot of people. I think that loss and the way it all happened, that sixth game and everything else, kind of got a lot of people because of reading about it and the Curse thing. I think it threw people over the edge. And I think some of our players and coaches came into our organization and because of what other people told them, I think they came in right away being defensive, and it was the worst thing they could have done with the media."

World Series manager John McNamara was especially paranoid, and when most "experts" picked the Sox to finish first in 1988, he said, "A lot of people pick you to finish first just to see you get fucking fired."

At that moment, some writers expected McNamara to start grumbling, in Captain Queeg fashion, about the "Strawberry incident." But the man knew what he was talking about. Mac got the knife on July 14, 1988 (Bastille Day), and was replaced by longtime organization man Joe Morgan.

I was happy to see Mac go. On the day McNamara was fired, I was in a Boston hospital recovering from sinus surgery. Full of pain and drugs, when I learned the Sox had fired McNamara, I vaulted out of bed and went toward my keyboard.

The removal of McNamara and the elevation of Morgan triggered a series of moves that vastly improved the Sox relationship with the press.

Morgan was a certified media darling. He managed the Sox from July '88 until his controversial dismissal after a second-place finish in 1991. During his tenure the Sox started to get better treatment from the Boston sports press. A former Massachusetts Turnpike snowplow driver and a native of Walpole, Massachusetts ("If you don't live in Walpole, you're just camping out"), Morgan charmed the baseball writers with his homespun yarns. He had a million stories and he loved to tell them. He wasn't afraid to tell the truth about his players, and he never lied to protect them. That made Morgan popular in the press box and unpopular in the clubhouse. Writers who covered the Sox during the Morgan years remember the day they went to lunch with him at the Arlington (Texas) Sheraton coffee shop. Surrounded by a pack of thirty-something writers, the sixty-year-old Morgan looked up from his plate and said, "How many of you guys have smoked marijuana?" It was not a question John McNamara would have asked.

Other personnel changes made the Sox more media friendly. Vince Orlando, the ancient, nasty equipment manager, was dismissed after shoving *Hartford Courant* reporter Steve Buckley out of the clubhouse. Trainer Charlie Moss was fired after twenty years of taping ankles. (In 1986, Moss was reprimanded by American League president Bobby Brown after planting a false story about a Roger Clemens injury.) At the highest level, owner Haywood Sullivan, who always believed the press "had it in for us," was bought out by the trustees of the Yawkey estate. John Harrington, much more charming and friendly, became the de facto owner and carried none of the suspicion and distrust that had clouded Sullivan's judgments.

Kevin Shea, a likable young man out of Holy Cross, was hired as Bresciani's assistant. Shea's finest moment came during the fraudulent spring of 1995. A replacement player rushed up to Shea and treated the young publicist with the disrespect that team employees expect only from the real big leaguers. The player pointed to Shea and said, "PR guy?"

Shea pointed to the replacement and said, "Player?"

Butch Hobson and Kevin Kennedy, the managers who followed Morgan, were accessible and friendly and rarely got angry over negative coverage. New general manager Dan Duquette was not as candid as his predecessor, Lou Gorman, but never reacted to criticism. While all this was happening, coverage of the Sox lost the hard edge that had developed in the late 1980s. Reporters did not revert to the boosterism that marked coverage at the beginning of the century, but there seemed to be less delight in the continuing Red Sox woes.

"Sometimes I think the writers might think we're coming up with ideas to hamper them," says Bresciani. "But we really do try to come up with ideas that make it work for everybody. Around the ball club today, I think there's a much better understanding of what the writers are there to do. And I think a lot of it has to do with the support you get from your ownership, general manager, manager, right down the line. I think we've made a big effort in the last few years to help that way. . . . Of course, a lot of people still believe the writers are out to get us."

Even Stephen King believes it. Before the Sox went to the play-offs in 1995, King speculated on the chances of the Red Sox finally winning it all and wrote, "It would be, perhaps, most wonderful of all to watch the New England sports columnists who routinely savage the Sox, from the top management to the lowliest linesman, try to find a way to write pettily about such a triumph. There has been a view among many Boston sports figures over the years that the print columnists in Beantown are the most vitriolic east of the Mississippi, hard-hearted inkhounds who enjoy nothing better than breakfasting on a slow-moving basketball forward, lunching on an overpriced quarterback and dining on a freshly baked DH (did somebody mention Jack Clark?)"

This may never change. The Red Sox, having perfected the art of the near miss, have spawned several generations of cynics. To cover the Red Sox is to hope for the best and expect the worst. Hyperbole is vital. Everything about the Red Sox must be exaggerated. The highs are higher, the lows lower. Reporters will never be neutral about the team. Fans know it, and the players know it. Bombast and sarcasm sell.

CHAPTER SEVEN

THE JIMMY FUND

► ◆ ◆ ◆ ◆ ◆ ◆ ◆ ◆ ◄

◆ As a form of daily entertainment, the Red Sox are hard to beat. Every year of this century they have given New Englanders something to follow, embrace, and debate. The Sox are our sports soap opera, part of every fan's youth, middle age, and golden years. The ball team's struggles and flaws have made it all the more lovable. Nobody roots for Goliath or the phone company. All freethinking New Englanders root for the Red Sox. As topics of conversation, politics, the weather, and the Red Sox never get stale.

Yet the possibility exists that the Red Sox may have been put on this planet to serve a higher purpose. Uniquely positioned to reach the masses, the Boston Red Sox for the last half century have been diligent participants in the fight against cancer in children as the official fund-raising arm of the Dana-Farber Cancer Institute, known as the Jimmy Fund. The ball club's impact on the tremendous strides that have been made is immeasurable.

I hereby forfeit all semblance of objectivity on this one Red Sox issue. My daughter has leukemia. And the long, hard days since Kate Shaughnessy was diagnosed have shed new light on the Red Sox efforts to support the Jimmy Fund.

The following article from the April 18, 1994, *Globe* (reprinted with permission from the *Globe*) serves as both disclaimer and introduction.

► ◆ ◄

My daughter, Kate, threw out a first ball before yesterday's Red Sox–White Sox doubleheader at Fenway Park. Kate has leukemia.

Kate and six-year-old Philip Doyle of Weymouth, another Jimmy Fund patient, were first-ball tossers for the Sox second annual Kids Opening Day. I cannot speak for the Doyles, but I expect yesterday they felt very much like my wife and myself.

Watching Kate walk to the mound, I thought about all the bad times Kate's endured in the last five months. I thought about the spinal taps, bone marrows, MRIs, bone scans, collapsed IV lines, and surgeries. I remembered the empty halls of Children's Hospital when Kate had surgery Christmas Eve. It was a big deal to get Kate home for three hours on Christmas morning. And now she's out there throwing the high heater to Dave Valle in front of 34,501 at Fenway Park.

Life changed for Kate on November 26 [1993]. It was the day after Thanksgiving, the day of the Boston College–West Virginia game. It was the day my wife and I sat side by side on a conference-room couch on the sixth floor of Children's Hospital and heard Dr. Kenneth Cooke say, "Your daughter has leukemia."

Kate has standard-risk, acute lymphoblastic leukemia. I'm told it happens to one out of every 1,580 Caucasian children under the age of fifteen. Kate is eight years old and played her full soccer schedule last fall. At the end of the season, she complained of sharp lower-back pain. We took her to our family health clinic. The doctor ordered a blood test and sent her home with Advil. Then there was a phone call, a trip to the emergency room at Children's, and by nightfall, we knew.

Bad things happen to all of us. This is not fair to Kate, but it's something we've all had to learn to deal with. My wife and I are thankful we live in Boston, thankful it is 1994, and thankful for our families and wonderful friends. December and January were especially cold and scary, but I still get a warm feeling when I remember the love and care showered on our home in the days and weeks after Kate was diagnosed. Ever seen homemade lasagnas stacked like cordwood?

"It's just like the old days," Kate's grandmother would say after another neighbor put some food on our doorstep.

A week after she was diagnosed, Ted Williams called Kate in the hospital. Kate knows nothing about old-time baseball stars. She held the phone a few inches from her ear and said, "Daddy, there's a loud man on the phone, telling me I'm going to be okay."

She passed the phone to me and Ted Williams bellowed, "Dr. [Sidney] Farber used to tell me, 'Ted, we're going to find a way to cure these kids.' Sure enough, he did it. You tell your daughter she's going to be fine. Tell her I'll come visit her."

Ted Williams was the star of the Red Sox when the Jimmy Fund got rolling in 1948. When the Braves moved from Boston in 1953, Tom Yawkey made the Jimmy Fund the Red Sox official charity, and Teddy Ballgame became keeper of the flame. Ted's only sibling, Danny, died of leukemia in 1960. Ted never stopped working for his favorite charity. Meanwhile, Dr. Farber pioneered treatment of cancer in children.

It was the late Edward Bennett Williams who first told me, "The cure is worse than the cancer." In dramatic lore, it is known as chemotherapy, but the real names of some of the drugs are methotrexate, 6 mercaptopurine, vincristine, and dexamethasone. Some of this stuff is administered at home, and its power and potency is underscored by the toxic-spill kit that comes with the medicine. Kate is scheduled to have chemotherapy for two years.

Each Tuesday is Kate's Jimmy Fund clinic day, and the Red Sox are all over the place. John Harrington cut one of the ribbons this winter when the new clinic was dedicated. There's a Carl Yastrzemski treatment room. There's a Ted Williams mural, and one of his silver bats —right next to the Robert K. Kraft blood donor center. Former Sox second baseman Mike Andrews is executive director of the Jimmy Fund, and Rose Lonborg, wife of Cy Young winner Jim, volunteers her time to make the clinic visits less painful and more fun.

One of our lasting impressions of this horrible experience is the innate goodness of people. The nurses of 7-West cared for our Kate as if she were their own daughter. Kate's teachers, coaches, and friends have done everything to make her feel comfortable and included.

Individuals who've been roughed up in this column have called and written to lend support. Dave Gavitt. Lou Gorman. Billy Sullivan. Jim O'Brien. Joe Morgan. Chris Ford. Cam Neely. Adam Oates. Glen Wesley. Mo Vaughn. Larry Bird. Bill Walton. John Blue. In the dugout before yesterday's first pitch, Butch Hobson came over with bubble gum for the whole family. Even me. These sports professionals are fathers and brothers and uncles. They know there is the stuff we do every day . . . and then there is the important stuff.

You should have seen the look on the face of the guy who drives the Federal Express truck when a large package arrived at our door from Katy, Texas. The driver saw the names Clemens and Shaughnessy and suggested we check to see if the thing was ticking. It was a giant white teddy bear. Kate calls her Clementine.

And yesterday she stood on the mound where Roger Clemens stood Friday night.

There are no guarantees. We pray that Kate stays the course and someday is cured. We know many families are far worse off than ours. But most of all we watch Kate and enjoy the good days after so many bad ones. She is strong and smart and—without hair—more beautiful than ever.

She says she plans to be Charlie Brown next Halloween. I love that. Kate and Charlie Brown. Same pitching motion. Same haircut.

► ◆ ◄

If you grew up in New England in the 1950s or 1960s, you knew about the Jimmy Fund from your earliest days. At most candy counters, there was a large piggy bank and a picture of some sad-eyed little slugger asking you to "please give."

The Red Sox carried the torch for the cause—the organization's official charity. As baseball fans, we were bombarded with pitches for the Jimmy Fund. There was a Jimmy Fund Night and a big sign in right field to remind us that Jimmy is watching and waiting for help. Sox play-by-play announcer Curt Gowdy said "Jimmy Fund" as often as he said "Ted Williams" or "Carl Yastrzemski." There was no way to follow the Red Sox and not know that the best cause in the world was the Jimmy Fund's campaign to fight cancer in children. We were constantly reminded that our nickels and dimes mattered. Kids organized neighborhood plays, charged admission, and sent the money to the Jimmy Fund.

An excerpt from a 1960 Red Sox official game program (fifteen cents) reads: "The Boston Red Sox are proud to act as cosponsors, together with the Variety Club of New England, of the annual Jimmy Fund activities in behalf of Children's Cancer Research Foundation. Ted Williams of the Red Sox serves as General Chairman of the fund drive, and under his chairmanship the last four years a total of $2,159,300 has been raised for treatment and research in the fight against cancer in children."

Mike Andrews, a former Red Sox second baseman who serves as executive director of the Jimmy Fund, makes this assessment of the ball club's relationship with the cause:

"I think it goes beyond a partnership. They are synonymous. And as good as the Red Sox have been for the Jimmy Fund, the Jimmy Fund has been good for the Red Sox. Because of the Red Sox, I believe the Jimmy Fund is New England's favorite charity. On the other side, with all the bad times the Red Sox have had, they've always had the Jimmy Fund charity to pull them out of it. You know, it's like the fans say, 'Well, they can't be all that bad.' There is no way to overstate what the Red Sox have done for this cause. Without the Red Sox, it's hard to imagine where it would be in terms of fund-raising."

The Red Sox were not the first Boston baseball team to support the Jimmy Fund, however. It was the National League Boston Braves who got the campaign rolling along with the Variety Club of New England.

The Variety Club is a charitable and social club established by show business people in greater Boston. When the Club decided to select a charity in 1947, it helped Dr. Sidney Farber—"the father of modern chemotherapy"—establish the Children's Cancer Research Foundation, in conjunction with Children's Hospital of Boston.

A native of Buffalo, Dr. Faber earned his M.D. from Harvard and survived a bout with cancer in the 1950s. "Cancer has been the one great mystery of the ages," he said in 1971. "The children—I was always interested in them because when I was young, I was deeply disturbed by the little white caskets leaving homes, with tiny victims of diphtheria and scarlet fever. Working with children and wanting to help them was natural for me."

In 1947, Dr. Farber developed a treatment that enabled some of the cancer-stricken children to go into temporary remission. Dr. Farber's breakthrough inspired renewed effort to raise money for the cause.

The Variety Club in '47 raised $47,000 for the Foundation. Early in 1948, members of the Club and the Boston Braves, under the direction of the late Lou Perini, orchestrated a mass-media event to create the Jimmy Fund.

Billy Sullivan, former owner of the New England Patriots, was publicity director of the Braves in 1948. He says, "There was a man named George Swartz who was a member of the Variety Club. He knew a lot of people in Hollywood. The Variety Club decided they wanted to do something to help Dr. Sidney Farber. At that time, Dr. Farber had a small basement apartment on Longwood Avenue near the hospital. It was very unimposing. There dwelled Dr. Farber and an assistant and ten thousand mice. The Variety Club went to George Swartz and asked him if he could get any Hollywood people to help Dr. Farber."

Swartz flew to Hollywood and made his pitch to Ralph Edwards, host of radio's popular *Truth or Consequences*. A coast-to-coast radio fund-raiser was scheduled for May 22, 1948.

The program was broadcast live from Hollywood, starting at eight-thirty on Saturday night. In the middle of the show, Edwards said, "A part of the function of *Truth or Consequences* is to bring this old parlor game to people who are unable to come to the show. And tonight we take you to a little fella named Jimmy. We're not going to give you his last name because he's just like thousands of other young fellas and girls in private homes and hospitals all over the country. Jimmy is suffering from cancer, but he doesn't know he has it. He's a swell little guy, and although he can't figure out why he isn't out with other kids, he does love his baseball and follows every move of his favorite team, the Boston Braves, the great National League team only two or three games from the top of the League.

"Now by the magic of radio, we're going to span the breadth of the United States and take you right up to the bedside of Jimmy in one of America's great cities, Boston, Massachusetts. And into one of America's great hospitals, the Children's Hospital in Boston, whose staff is doing such an outstanding job of cancer research for the cause of not only Boston children, but children in every city in the world. Up to now, Jimmy has not heard us. And now we tune in a speaker in his room in the hospital. All right engineers . . . give us Jimmy, please."

Edwards: "Hello, Jimmy."

Jimmy: "Hi."

Edwards: "Hi, Jimmy. This is Ralph Edwards of the *Truth or Consequences* radio program. Well, I heard you like baseball, is that right?"

Jimmy: "Yeah, that's my favorite sport."

Edwards: "It's your favorite sport. Who do you think is going to win the pennant this year?"

Jimmy: "The Boston Braves, I hope."

Edwards: "Which one of the Boston Braves is your favorite player?"

Jimmy: "Johnny Sain."

It was a setup. Johnny Sain entered Jimmy's room and greeted Jimmy. Edwards asked about more Braves players, and one by one, they walked into Jimmy's room just after Jimmy mentioned their names. The players came with T-shirts and autographed baseballs, bats, mitts, and tickets to the next day's doubleheader. Braves manager Billy Southworth said that Jimmy would be the team's guest at the twin bill against the Cubs. Southworth promised at least one victory.

Edwards said, "Oh, man, you'll be the envy of every boy in America having all those big-league baseball players in your one room at one time," then got Jimmy and his new friends to sing "Take Me Out to the Ballgame."

Jimmy signed off saying, "Thank you very, very much, Mr. Edwards."

After the connection was severed, Edwards addressed his coast-to-coast audience: "Now, folks, listen. Jimmy can't hear this, can he? Now, look. Really, let's make Jimmy happy. Jimmy doesn't know . . . he has cancer. And we're not using any photographs of him or giving his full name so he will know about it. But let's make Jimmy and thousands of other boys and girls happy who are suffering from cancer by aiding the research to help find a cure for cancer in children. Because by researching children's cancer, we automatically help the adults and stop it at the outset. Now we know that one of the things little Jimmy wants most is a television set to watch the baseball games as well as hear them. Now if you friends will send in your quarters, dollars, tens of dollars, tonight to Jimmy, for the Children's Cancer Research Foundation, and if over twenty thousand dollars or more is contributed for this most worthy cause, we'll see to it that Jimmy gets his television set. Now here's the address for your contributions for Jimmy and the boys and girls of America. Here it is: Jimmy. Children's Hospital. Boston 15. Massachusetts. That's all. Now this isn't a contest where you'll win anything, folks. This is our chance to help little boys and girls, such as Jimmy, win a greater prize, the prize of life. Give from the heart for a cause so worthy it's impossible to describe. I hope the total is over twenty thousand dollars so little Jimmy gets his television set. I know you folks, grown-ups, schoolchildren, all of you won't let Jimmy down."

Dr. Farber also appeared on the program. After the broadcast, Edwards told the doctor that Variety Club of New England Children's Cancer Research Foundation was too long a name for a charity. Farber suggested they go with "The Jimmy Fund."

Back in Boston, things were moving quickly. Before the Braves players left the hospital, people began arriving at Children's with money for Jimmy. More than forty thousand letters and telegrams poured in from all over the country.

Jimmy went to the next day's doubleheader and the Braves won both games.

The ball club made no announcement regarding the presence of the now-famous patient. Meanwhile, Boston newspapers did a masterful job of concealing the boy's identity. In some photographs, he appeared with his back to the camera. In others, several children are present and the cutlines cite Jimmy with his "pals," identifying neither the patient nor his friends.

In the news accounts, Jimmy is described as a "typical American boy with tousled hair and blue eyes."

In 1971, Dr. Farber told writer Ann M. Bierfield (*Boston Sunday Advertiser*), "I was careful then, as I am now, about the exploitation of sick children—I don't permit their names or faces used if there is a chance they may not survive. I don't think the child or his parents should be put through that.... The program representative went through our little clinic and chose a fine-looking twelve-year-old boy. Then they insisted they needed a name. I said, in desperation, 'Well, call him Jimmy!' And that's how the title came about—'Jimmy,' you see, is any child with cancer. But let me tell you about that boy. He was actually one of the first children to respond to the new chemical treatments we developed here in the laboratories. And today he is in his middle thirties, the father of a fine family, and has required no treatment for years."

A few days after the original "Jimmy" broadcast, Jimmy got his television set. Braves players donated the money themselves. Swartz delivered the set to Jimmy's room at Children's, accompanied by Braves players Tommy Holmes, John Beazley, and Phil Masi. The final result of the initial fund drive was $231,485.51 cash. On top of that, the Braves went on to win the 1948 National League pennant.

Sullivan recalled, "After the broadcast, there were hundreds of people that came by the hospital to give money. That night we raised twenty-six thousand dollars in change, just people giving a dollar here and there. A few days later the Massachusetts mayors had a convention. I spoke to them about the Jimmy Fund and they joined the cause. Then we got the chiefs of police. Sidney Farber was the glue to the thing because there was no one who ever met him that didn't love him. And so the Braves carried the ball until they left town. It was the baseball that did it." (On September 4, 1981, Red Sox announcer Ken Coleman chaired a reception and luncheon for Ralph Edwards. The retired broadcaster got his first look at the abundant fruit from the first seed he planted in 1948.)

The original Jimmy Fund building opened in January 1952. On March 18, 1953, the National League voted to allow the Braves to leave Boston for Milwaukee. It was the first time any franchise had moved since 1903. Braves owner Lou Perini said, "The country has changed in the last seventy-five years." In Boston, Perini was portrayed as a civic traitor, but Richard Cardinal Cushing came to his defense, reminding Bostonians that Perini was the Jimmy Fund's best friend.

With the Braves gone, it was left to the Red Sox to pick up the ball.

Sullivan says, "When the Braves left for Milwaukee, there was a league meeting in St. Petersburg and I spoke with Mr. Yawkey. He was reluctant at first. He said that he didn't really like it when he was listening to a Braves game and he heard the broadcaster interrupt by saying, 'And Joe so-and-so, the Pontiac dealer, just gave a thousand dollars to the Jimmy Fund.' But he agreed to take on the cause, and when he embraced it, he did it all the way."

April 10, 1953: "The Boston Red Sox Baseball Club officially announced today they have accepted the invitation of the Variety Club's
Chief Barker Walter A. Brown (owner of the Boston Celtics) to join
with the motion picture industry as cosponsors of the Jimmy Fund. In
making the announcement, Tom Yawkey revealed that the Red Sox
organization and the sponsors had been interested in this great charity
ever since the founder of the Jimmy Fund, the Variety Club of New
England, first sought the aid of the general public."

This is how the Jimmy Fund became the official Red Sox charity.
And Ted Williams became the keeper of the flame.

Johnny Sain won twenty or more games in a single season four
times and pitched in four World Series. Billy Sullivan became an NFL
owner and watched the team he founded go all the way to the Super
Bowl. Curt Gowdy became one of the most famous broadcasters of
his time, and Ted Williams staked a claim to being one of the greatest
hitters who ever lived. But their professional contributions paled
against their efforts on behalf of the Jimmy Fund.

"It was great that Perini and the Braves had started it during the
war," says Williams. "And then Mr. Yawkey took it over. Our club was
the big club in Boston then. And it was perfect that that happened,
and he got to be the most devout Jimmy Fund supporter."

Crude, vulgar, hot-tempered, and sometimes mean, Williams has
been the patron saint of children with cancer. He abhors taking credit
for charity work and won't discuss the roots of his compassion. It's
been suggested that he may have followed the lead of his mother, a
lifelong soldier of the Salvation Army. More likely it was the plight of
his brother, Danny, that hit Williams hardest.

"My brother had cancer of the bone marrow or some damn thing,"
says Williams. "He threw a ball or an orange at somebody and broke
his arm. Ah, shit. Could have been me, you know?"

The late Tom Dowd, longtime Red Sox traveling secretary, told of
getting a letter from a young boy dying of leukemia. The boy requested an autographed baseball from Ted Williams. Dowd went to
the Sox clubhouse and read the letter to Williams. According to
Dowd, Williams signed the ball, then said, "Let me see that letter
again." He read the letter, then told Dowd he wanted to go to the
hospital to see the boy. He fingered Johnny Pesky and Joe Dobson

and said they'd be going, too. Dowd took them to Children's, where Williams presented the ball to the dying boy. Dowd's recollection: "In those moments, the kid was whole again. He was one of them, there with his heroes, in a beautiful world."

Pesky remembers, "Ted got very deep into it. When he was a player, he used to go to the Children's Hospital, and when he would come back, he'd get very quiet. Finally, he got talking to Bobby and Dom and myself about this. He was always concerned with the Jimmy Fund. He's got a lot of sentiment in his soul. Ted was always worried about people who were sick. He's been that way since I've known him."

Williams says, "Of course, Mr. Yawkey was the one, and after the Braves left town, Mr. Yawkey took it over from the Braves. When he did that and I happened to be there, of course it was just a natural thing for me to be in there. And if I have to say anything for myself, and I hate to say it, but I am kind of a very compassionate fella. And I could see how important it was. And then you got to bring up the fans and they were showing it every day by contributions. You know, in the old days, raising money was a lot tougher than it is now. Between the Red Sox and the fans, all of a sudden it was one of the biggest things in America."

It matters not why. What matters is that Ted Williams has used his celebrity to generate millions of dollars for cancer-stricken children. When he returned from Korea, the Red Sox and the Boston Chamber of Commerce feted him at a $100-per-plate dinner at the Hotel Statler on August 17, 1953. All proceeds went to the Jimmy Fund, and Williams insisted that all members of the head table pay their share. The toastmaster was a New York newspaperman named Ed Sullivan. Wearing a necktie for only the second time in his Boston career (the first was in '47 when he picked up an MVP award at a writers' dinner), Williams told the audience, "I have had a chance to see for myself some of the sick children who are suffering from cancer, as well as the wonderful work that is being done by this great and kind man, Dr. Sidney Farber, and that staff at the Jimmy Fund Building. . . . The way I look at it, there is always something we can do for some youngster somewhere. Here, we don't have to look any further than the Jimmy Fund. Somehow, it strikes me that a dollar tossed into this drive is the whole American way of life in a nutshell. All the bullets and all the bombs that explode all over the world won't leave the impact, when all is said and done, of a dollar bill dropped in the Jimmy Fund pot by a warm heart and a willing hand. . . . You should be proud and happy to know that your contribution will someday help some kid to a better life."

After Williams spoke, Dr. Farber spoke and said, "Ted Williams is not a new friend. And may we through him welcome the Red Sox into our fold. I'd like to say just two things about our foundation. We've never turned away a child. As long as a child is alive, the term *incurable disease* may not be used."

More than $125,000 was raised, including a $50,000 gift from the Joseph Kennedy Foundation, presented by twenty-one-year-old Edward Kennedy, brother of Sen. John F. Kennedy.

It was just the beginning for Williams. In a kind and generous way, he became the first professional athlete to "sell" his autograph. Send Ted Williams a check and he would sign your check over to the Jimmy Fund. You'd get a canceled check with Ted's autograph and the Jimmy Fund would get a contribution. Red Sox secretary Barbara Taylor posed for a photograph headlined "Ted's Exchange Bureau."

Over time, Williams and Dr. Farber became friends. When the great Sox slugger was elected to baseball's Hall of Fame in 1966, he posed for a picture with Thomas Yawkey, Richard Cardinal Cushing, and Dr. Sidney Farber. When Williams was enshrined in Cooperstown, the Jimmy Fund received thousands of dollars in his name.

In 1969, the institute's charter was expanded to provide services to patients of all ages. In 1976, the Children's Cancer Research Foundation was renamed the Sidney Farber Cancer Institute. In 1983, it was renamed again, this time the Dana-Farber Cancer Institute in recognition of longtime support from the Charles A. Dana Foundation.

A 1990s marketing survey indicated that 90 percent of New Englanders know what the Jimmy Fund is. That recognition factor runs ahead of any elected official, and only slightly behind the Red Sox themselves. Today the Jimmy Fund is the prime fund-raising arm of the Dana-Farber Cancer Institute, supported by thousands of individuals, groups, members of the media, and corporations throughout New England and beyond. Ninety cents of every dollar contributed goes to cancer research and treatment at the Institute. In 1993, the Jimmy Fund raised more than $10.5 million for cancer research and treatment programs. The Dana-Farber Cancer Institute is one of twenty federally designated regional cancer centers and gets $35 million in annual federal funding, plus $25 million in charitable contributions. About $11 million of that $25 million comes from the Jimmy Fund.

Red Sox CEO John Harrington, who came to work for the club in 1972, says, "It was Dr. Farber who was the heart and soul. He had such a vision. He was determined to come up with a cure, and as you know, they did. When I met him, he was sick, but even then you could capture the determination the guy had. I think that was Tom Yawkey's link. The Yawkeys were youth-oriented. They'd started an orphanage in Carolina. They really thought that the Jimmy Fund was where their money could be used best."

In 1973, Thomas A. Yawkey received the Dr. Sidney Farber Medical Research Award for being a guiding spirit of the foundation. Yawkey died of leukemia in 1976. The pioneer of chemotherapy, Dr. Farber, died of cancer in 1973. Dr. Farber would not be the first or last Jimmy Fund patron to die of the disease he spent his life battling. Sox manager Joe Cronin, club attorney Jack Hayes, and Bill Koster, the first director of the Jimmy Fund, all died of cancer. In 1993, Sox legal counsel John Donovan died of cancer.

At one time, the Jimmy Fund paid for the entire research budget of the Dana-Farber Cancer Institute, but an infusion of government money has dwarfed the Jimmy Fund's percentage. In 1995, the Jimmy Fund accounted for about 15 percent of Dana-Farber's budget, and the clinic was curing (cure is defined as five years of uninterrupted remission) some 80 percent of young patients with standard-risk, acute lymphoblastic leukemia.

Former Red Sox second baseman Mike Andrews had been executive director of the Jimmy Fund since 1978. Andrews was a rookie on Boston's Cinderella pennant-winning team in 1967 (the team voted to give a full World Series share to the Jimmy Fund) and became involved with the Jimmy Fund almost immediately.

"I can't remember what day or how it happened," Andrews says. "But the day it really hit home with me was the day that Bill Koster [former executive director] came around the park and asked me to help him out. He usually lined up things for you ahead of time—a check presentation or to say hello to somebody. On this particular day, whoever he asked was in the trainer's room. Bill came up to me right before game time and said he was in a jam. I'll never forget it. I was actually irritated. I said, 'All right, but we got to make it quick.' So I threw on a sweatshirt and we went out into the dugout and I met a twelve-year-old kid who was ill and had missed his last year of Little League. He was looking forward to playing Babe Ruth baseball and was all excited. I wished him well. As I'm walking back in, I say, 'Bill, he seems like a really good kid. I hope he does well.' And Bill told me that they had sent the boy home because the doctors already had done everything they could do for him. The boy wasn't going to make it. All of a sudden, I had all this guilt. Here I was worrying about a potential oh for four or upsetting my routine. After that, I was much more sensitive to the Jimmy Fund. I did check presentations during the winter and things at the park. Then, when I was out of baseball, Ken Coleman [longtime Red Sox broadcaster] was working as executive director and asked me to help out. I was in the life insurance business and I said I would love to."

And that is how Mike Andrews left life insurance and went about the work of saving lives.

Bob Stanley pitched in more Red Sox games than any other player who ever wore the uniform. He was part of the Boston baseball saga for thirteen seasons, always available (starting, middle relief, closing), often effective, sometimes cannon fodder, and too often unlucky.

Off the field, Stanley spread what luck he could. He walked the corridors of Children's Hospital, signing baseballs and visiting children with cancer.

"I was lucky," he said. "I felt I was lucky to have three healthy children, and if I could help a kid and cheer 'em up a little, I'd do it. I just love kids. I still think of myself as a big kid."

When young Red Sox ballplayers complained about their troubles on the field, Stanley would take them to the Jimmy Fund Clinic for perspective on their batting slumps. In the late 1980s, Andrews called Stanley and asked the Sox reliever to speak to a young patient who was despondent. The boy had lost one of his eyes to cancer and wasn't speaking to anyone, not even his parents. Stanley brought the child a bat, a ball, and one of his No. 46 uniform jerseys. "It was unbelievable how that boy responded to Bob," says Andrews. The doctor couldn't believe it, and neither could his parents. That jersey became the most important thing in his life." The child died a few months later and was buried wearing Stanley's jersey. Then in January 1990, Bob and Joan Stanley learned that their nine-year-old son, Kyle, had a large malignant tumor in the sinus area behind his right eye. It was a case similar to that of the young boy who'd worshiped Bob Stanley. After years of visiting Children's Hospital, Bob and Joan Stanley moved into a room on 7-West, where they lived with their son while he went through the rigors of early treatment.

Stanley said, "This is no time to feel sorry for ourselves. Sometimes you wonder, 'Why me?' But you shouldn't say that. We're not the only ones going though this."

One of three Stanley children, and the only son, Kyle was familiar to plenty of Sox fans and sportswriters because the Stanley family made it a habit to live at the club's hotel headquarters in Winter Haven each spring. Bob and Kyle Stanley broke the silence in the Holiday Inn courtyard on many a March evening with their Wiffle-ball games. It was not unusual to hear the Steamer tell his son, "Okay, Kyle, bottom of the ninth, two outs, seventh game of the World Series. The bases are loaded, we're up one run, and there's a pop-up to the infield. Can you catch it?" The next sound would be Stanley yelling, "Don't dive, Kyle! Those are your good pants and we're going to dinner."

After his diagnosis, Kyle Stanley endured a year of chemotherapy and radiation treatment. He underwent eight hours of surgery at Children's in January 1991, and by the end of 1992 was cancer free. Parents never relax, and Kyle will have checkups for the rest of his life. But technically, he is cured. He is one of thousands of children who've been saved by the Jimmy Fund.

For Bob Stanley, there was new perspective. The Steamer had felt the pressure of standing on the mound, trying to close out a World Series, and failing. But it was nothing compared with what later happened to his son.

My Kate, who has hair again, reminds me of that every time she turns her smile on a Red Sox player working for the Jimmy Fund, then says to me, "Daddy, be nice to this guy. Okay? Just try."

"God had something else in store for me," Stanley told author Mike Sowell. "When my son got cancer, He answered my prayers that way. Instead of being a hero, I got my son's health. You can throw the 1986 World Series right out the window."

In the Red Sox clubhouse, there is a large plaque that every player walks past every day. The plaque is from the Jimmy Fund, Dana-Farber Cancer Institute, and the inscription reads, "To all of the players, coaches, managers, trainers and clubhouse staff past and present. Whose unselfish support of the Jimmy Fund has made a significant difference in the battle against cancer, we salute you one and all. From the children and adults who have benefitted through your kindness and the clinicians, researchers and staff who care for them. Cancer, it's too big a battle for a kid to fight alone."

Red Sox CEO John Harrington says, "Our relationship with the Jimmy Fund is a marriage. Everybody here is in it with both feet. The Jimmy Fund people love the Red Sox and cheer us up when we're down. I get a little choked up thinking about it. It stems from Yawkey's commitment. He wasn't first, that was the Braves, but when asked, he jumped in. Nothing was ever expected in return. We give what we can give. I call it our real world."

On December 15, 1995, forty-two years after the Hotel Statler fund-raiser, Ted Williams was honored at a Park Plaza dinner celebrating the kickoff of the .406 Club. The Club consists of individuals who've pledged at least $5,000 to the Jimmy Fund over a five-year period. The .406 Club will raise more than $2 million for the Jimmy Fund and is named in honor of Williams's .406 batting average in 1941. It will stand forever as Williams's lasting gift to his life-long charity.

The final speaker of the evening was my daughter Kate. She read a poem that she had written herself for the occasion.

> *Ted Williams is a really, really great guy,*
> *He really likes kids, but he hates wearing ties;*
> *He won 2 Triple Crowns and was the MVP twice,*
> *He feuded with sportswriters, but to kids he was nice.*

521 homers, he's in the Hall of Fame,
He's the Kid, the Thumper, and Teddy Ballgame.
He would do anything for the Jimmy Fund,
And I'd like to say thank you, for all that he's done.

For most of this century, the Red Sox have entertained New England without winning a World Series. But since 1948, when a little boy at Children's Hospital told the country that his favorite sport was baseball, Boston's Olde Towne team has won a lot of battles off the field. And so have the children.

CHAPTER EIGHT

SAVE FENWAY

► ◆ ◆ ◆ ◆ ◆ ◆ ◆ ◆ ◄

◆ Call me a traditionalist. Call me a man from the wrong century. Call me someone who still likes to ride trains even though airplanes are so much faster. Call me a cab and lock me away. I do not want to bear witness to the final days of Fenway Park.

It's not easy to hold one's ground against the avalanche of contrary evidence. Cleveland's Jacobs Field and Baltimore's Camden Yards, baseball's best new ballparks, truly are crown jewels on the urban landscape. They are baseball-only parks, artfully carved into old neighborhoods, made to look as if they've always been there. They offer the asymmetry of old Fenway. They are hitter friendly, with giant scoreboards, kiddie playgrounds, and row elevation that allows your seven-year-old son to see over the head of the man in front of him. These new ballparks offer breathtaking views of city skylines. They're made of exposed steel and brick. They offer acres of horizontal space. They've got adorable nooks and crannies, DoveBar stands, luxury suites, in-house hospitality rooms, and restaurants. They offer spacious walkways where fans can peer homeward from beyond the outfield grandstands. They've got picnic pavilions. There are no poles to impede your view. The walls of the men's rooms are not lined with those disgusting, unsanitary troughs. There is no century-old flattened gum on the ramps that lead to the grandstand. The new ballparks always are full. They are a license to print money and assure that the Indians and Orioles can compete for the top talents. They are spacious yet intimate. They have real grass. They borrow gracefully from Fenway, Ebbets Field, Shibe Park, Crosley Field, Forbes Field, Wrigley Field, and the Polo Grounds. They are near subway lines and major highways, surrounded by ample parking.

But I'm not going to let go easily. I live in a ninety-five-year-old house, grew up in another just like it, and I know what feels like home.

Save Fenway.

Fenway has the aforementioned gross bathrooms, no parking, cramped seating, and a dearth of luxury boxes. It has antiquated facilities for fans, players, and media. But it's still the most beautiful ballpark in the world, and it'll always be the place where our fathers and grandfathers watched games. It's the place where Ted Williams took batting practice. It'll always be home.

By now, even the hard-core traditionalists know that Fenway Park is a moribund baseball theater. Local politicians and businessmen assault us with nonstop babble about megaplexes and bids to lure the summer Olympics to Boston. It is to laugh. Meanwhile, Red Sox ownership talks about structural problems, the expense of maintenance, and the inevitability of a new baseball park.

Sox fans were first confronted with Fenway's mortality in the late 1950s. Those were years when other cities were building new parks, and Boston officials wondered how long the Olde Towne Team could play in an antique facility. In February 1960, House Bill No. 1850—a bill authorizing the construction of a new park in the Fens—was introduced in the Massachusetts State Legislature. Predictably, it failed. But the notion never fully faded. In 1966, veteran Sox chronicler Al Hirshberg wrote an essay entitled "Why Boston Needs a New Stadium." Hirshberg stated, "Fenway Park is no longer suitable for major league sports. Furthermore, because of its strange proportions, it has almost ruined the Red Sox. The park is so lopsided that the Red Sox must constantly seek ballplayers peculiarly suited to it."

In 1967, Red Sox owner Thomas A. Yawkey told the *Sporting News*, "My position is the same as it was six months ago. I feel the [new] stadium is necessary for Boston, this state, and all of New England."

That was the mind-set thirty years ago. Fenway had to go. Boston's baseball park was old in a time when everything was new again.

In the chrome-and-glass 1960s, Cincinnati's Crosley Field, Philadelphia's Connie Mack Stadium, and Pittsburgh's Forbes Field were demolished and replaced by circular, dual-facility, artificial-turf, concrete stadiums. Today, Riverfront (Cincinnati), Veterans (Philadelphia), Fulton County (Atlanta), Busch (St. Louis), and Three Rivers Stadium (Pittsburgh) stand as monuments to the unimaginative thinking of that era. They are ugly, and their configurations, while ideal for football, are ill-suited to baseball. They will never be ballparks. They are tacky sports warehouses, rendered old and obsolete within two decades of construction.

But nothing is forever, and Red Sox ownership knows that something must be done about Fenway. In 1989 the Sox commissioned the Boston engineering firm of Howard Needles Tamman & Bergendoff to study the ballpark. It was determined that Fenway was structurally sound for another twenty years.

By the mid-1990s, when Mrs. Yawkey had been dead for three years, Red Sox management was comfortable talking about the inevitability of a new park. Across Baseball America, there was a new mentality, one fostered by the tremendous aesthetic and financial success of Baltimore's new baseball park. The Ballpark at Camden Yards opened in 1992 and has been touted as the greatest baseball park ever built. Almost immediately, Cleveland and Texas produced similar parks. In Baltimore and Cleveland, the downtown ballparks were hailed as city saviors. Meanwhile, the poor folks in Chicago were mocked for building new Comiskey Park. The new Comiskey was opened in 1991 and serves as a perfectly suitable modern facility. But it lacks all the old-timey charm and ambience of Camden Yards, Jacobs Field, and the Ballpark at Arlington (Texas).

Larry Lucchino, a former Orioles executive who came to baseball under the tutelage of owner Edward Bennett Williams, was one of the spiritual architects of Camden Yards. He says, "Ballparks have become vital parts of the economic vitality of a baseball team. They do more than simply serve as a place to play. They provide huge income streams. They become part of the reason people go to the games."

Citing the civic treasures of Fenway Park, Detroit's Tiger Stadium, Chicago's Wrigley Field, and New York's Yankee Stadium, Lucchino says, "Most of the parks now being built are simply copies of those parks, updated by a century."

In this spirit, the Sox addressed their needs and hopes without fear of backlash or hysteria. On January 18, 1995, Red Sox general manager Dan Duquette told the Boston Chamber of Commerce, "We're going to need a new ballpark in the next five, six, eight years. I'd like to build that [Camden Yards] type of facility. If you've seen it, you know it's an old-timey ballpark with all the charm of the old stadiums, but also with the amenities of the modern-day baseball facility. The time is coming from a competitive and practical standpoint where we're going to need a new ballpark."

In April, the week the Sox opened their 1995 season, club CEO John Harrington addressed a special state commission reviewing convention center and sports team needs. Harrington said it was his hope that the Red Sox could host the 2001 All-Star game in Boston at a new ballpark.

"We'll take the risk, but we need your cooperation," Harrington told the group. "It might cost us one hundred and fifty million dollars to finance a stadium. We don't really want to leave Fenway Park. The spirits that are there are great. The problem is this eighty-three-year-old stadium has become obsolete."

Economically obsolete. It is the phrase that the Red Sox use to brace fans for old Fenway's inevitable closure.

"We started calling the park economically obsolete a few years ago," says Harrington. "Our fans are so good, but they're not able to get quality seats. There is a significant demand, and the only way to meet it is to expand and reconfigure. As we went through the revenue-sharing proposals, we became more aware of this. We finished renovating our bathrooms and it still is not pleasing to our fans. You can spray with perfume and put powder on it and it's still unacceptable to some of our people. All of that wears on us. We're spending more on maintenance than other clubs."

"I think it would be a great thing if they got a new park," says Ted Williams. "I think there are some inequities in this park. When you've got to build yourself for your home park, you're going to suffer a little in some other place, and I think that's been the case for some time. I think you can improve the park and the dimensions of the ballpark.

Anytime you favor the pitcher or the hitter, you're hurting the game. It's a game that's so standard. I think a fair ballpark is an awfully important part. They've tried to repair Fenway a couple of times, but if they do it right this next time, boy, it would be a good thing. I would not be sentimental about moving into a new ballpark."

Boston sports fans know a little bit about romantic attachment to ancient sports palaces. In the spring of 1995, the Boston Bruins and Celtics played their final games in the Boston Garden. The Garden was built in 1928, fashioned after New York's Madison Square Garden. The National Hockey League Bruins moved in immediately. When the Boston Celtics were born in 1946, part of the Basketball Association of America, they, too, played their games in the Garden.

More than Fenway Park, the Boston Garden was the scene of hundreds of nonsports events during its sixty-six-season run. The Garden featured ice shows, circuses, rock and roll (including the Beatles in 1964), book shows, a Shriners ball, political rallies for the likes of FDR and JFK, and in 1953 a Catholic mass offered by Bishop John J. Writer. Winston Churchill and Elvis both worked the Garden. As a sports theater, the Garden showcased Boston's college and high school sports, boxing, bike races, auto races, ski jumping, and a Notre Dame football game. But the Celtics and Bruins were the primary tenants. The Celtics won sixteen championships under the Garden rafters, the Bruins five. Like Fenway, the Garden housed a championship team in its first year. The Garden opened in November of 1928, and the Bruins' first Stanley Cup was won in the spring of 1929. But on the national level, it was the Celtics who made the Boston Garden famous. Basketball fans from Miami to Seattle are familiar with the Garden's parquet floor. When the NBA was coming of age in the 1960s, the Celtics were pro basketball's centerfold team. Fans across the land saw coach Red Auerbach lighting his cigar when the Celts clinched another victory. Bob Cousy and Bill Russell changed the sport in the 1950s and 1960s, and two decades later, a young man named Larry Joe Bird did it all over again.

In New England, the Boston Garden was the house of the B's and C's, a warm old barn where we could watch Bobby Orr skate and John Havlicek run the fast break. Like Fenway, everything about the Garden was old and inconvenient. The arena/train station was shoehorned into an area filled with tobacco shops, newsstands, cleaners, tailors, and dark saloons. Outside, the nonstop screech of steel wheels assaulted our eardrums. There was no place to park your car, and sports fans had to sidestep ticket scalpers, newspaper hawkers, and sidewalk salesmen. Inside, the ramps smelled of stale beer and urine. There were no escalators and no elevators. More than a thousand of the fourteen thousand seats were obstructed views. If you didn't pay top dollar, you were in danger of sitting where you couldn't see either the scoreboard or a portion of the playing surface. The concession stands were small and limited, the bathrooms gross and grossly inadequate, and more than a few rats were sighted over the years. Climate control depended on what you chose to wear to the game. The arena smelled like the bottom of your popcorn bag.

In its final winter of 1994–95, the Garden stood as the oldest functioning indoor pro sports arena in the country. Celtic fans said good-bye on the night of May 5, when the Green Team lost a play-off game to the Orlando Magic. After the game, more than a thousand fans swarmed the court, many refusing to leave until police intervened. Fans wept openly as they walked out of the Garden for the last time.

The new Garden, the FleetCenter, opened in the fall of 1995. There was plenty of celebration, but some of us missed the old Garden. It just wasn't the same when we had to go to a shiny new arena with no stench and no obstructed views. Going to the new Garden for the first time felt like the year Grandma sold her house and had us over for Christmas at her new condominium with the fake-log fireplace. Somehow, Christmas was more fun in the drafty farmhouse, where we could point to the floorboards worn from Grandpa's rocking chair and the storm window we'd cracked with a snowball back in '55. The old Garden was a place where things had *happened*. It was where Sam Jones picked up a chair to defend himself against an enraged Wilt Chamberlain. It was where Orr flew through the air after winning the Stanley Cup with an overtime goal against the St. Louis Blues. It was the last place in Boston where all the men smoked cigars and wore hats. The new Garden was just new. It reminded us of a shopping mall. Once inside the new arena, we lost all local bearings. There was nothing to remind us that we were in Boston. Watching a game at the FleetCenter is like watching a game at Market Square Arena in

Indianapolis or at the America West Arena in Phoenix. Trading in our old Boston Garden for a new one proved to be a loss of soul in return for air-conditioning.

Traumatic as the death of the Boston Garden was, it will pale in comparison to the end of Fenway Park. Many New England baseball fans have an almost irrational attachment to Fenway. In the spring of 1995, Lisa Pincus, a graduate student at Columbia University, set out to have Fenway declared a landmark. "Fenway Park represents the golden age of baseball," said Pincus. "It's Boston. It's important to preserve this American icon." According to the Boston Landmark Commission statute, a landmark is a "physical feature or improvement which in whole or part has historical, social, cultural or aesthetic significance to the city, and the commonwealth, the New England region or the nation."

Unfortunately for Pincus and other do-good fans, when a property is declared a landmark, all future physical alterations must be reviewed and approved by the Landmark Commission, and the Red Sox don't want the headaches that would come with the distinction. In May of 1995, Pincus received her master's degree in historic preservation from Columbia's Graduate School of Architecture, Planning and Preservation and continued to push Fenway toward landmark status . . . without much success or encouragement from Red Sox management.

On March 16, 1995, the Boston Redevelopment Authority (known to all headline writers as the BRA, much to the delight of adolescent boys throughout greater Boston) unveiled a plan to rebuild and expand Fenway over three years. The proposal called for an expansion of the grandstand along the first-base line and the addition of skyboxes and upper-deck seats. The Sox rejected the plan instantly, with Vice President Lou Gorman quipping, "Why would we want to add seats to a ballpark that's ninety years old? We have to move forward and consider the future. We need a new ballpark in Boston."

Fenway was built in 1912. The seats are small and hard. There is no legroom. When a row is full, it's nearly impossible to get to a center seat. It's like having a window seat on a DC-9 aircraft and climbing over other passengers to get to the aisle that leads to the bathroom. And like a 1950s kitchen, with bad paneling and lumpy linoleum, Fenway is almost impossible to clean. Even when it's thoroughly washed and vacuumed, it looks dirty. The team spends $1 million a year on maintenance, repairs, and cleaning. When the Red Sox were swept out of the American League play-offs in three straight games in October of 1995, *New York Times* columnist Harvey Araton wrote, "It's time to realize that it's the beloved little ballpark up here that has become the curse. It's time for the Red Sox to get the heck out of Fenway, and fast . . . more than anything, this team and its fans need a different look, a fresh approach."

The Sox say they'd like to build a park with about forty-nine thousand seats, 15 to 20 percent of them premium boxes. The team would like to build within three-quarters of a mile of Boston's South Station.

In May 1995, Red Sox executive vice president John Buckley said the ball club was ready to build a new stadium for $150 million either independently or in conjunction with the city's special convention-center commission. Buckley said the rebuilding option was "on the back burner. We can still play in this ballpark for another ten or twelve years. But our construction consultant said it would cost thirty to thirty-five percent more to completely reconstruct Fenway Park on its current site."

WEEI sports-talk host Dale Arnold devoted three hours to the hot topic the day Buckley's quotes appeared in the *Boston Herald*. Casting votes for, and against, Fenway, seventy-one fans called or faxed Arnold. Thirty-six listeners wanted to keep Fenway at any cost, while thirty-five voted for a new ballpark. Some of the faxes were quite passionate:

- "Forever Fenway! If your can is too big for the seats—stay home and exercise. I've been to several other parks (including Camden Yards) and there is no better place to see a game than Fenway."
- "Would you like to fly in an airplane made in the 1950s, with seats that are too small, springs coming through, and engines that are over forty years old? No way! I love Fenway but it has to go. Make it a museum.'
- "Those poles will never get thinner and neither will I."
- "Creature comforts and amenities are for yuppies and wussies, of which I am neither. Be a man, whizz in the horse trough."

- "Viva La Fenway! Viva La State House. Viva La Old North Church, snow shovels, and all the rest."

A week after the radio show, the Sox held their first ever Friendly Fenway Family Festival, and more than twenty-five thousand fans turned out on a rainy Monday afternoon for a tour of the park. Passion was plentiful.

"I was able to touch The Wall," said forty-two-year-old Dana Jones of Conway, New Hampshire. "That's something I've been dreaming of doing since I first took the mound in Little League. It was like seeing Moslems making their pilgrimage to Mecca. That's what Fenway is . . . a shrine."

Arthur D'Angelo, owner of the Twins Enterprises souvenir shop across the street (a man with a huge financial interest in seeing the park preserved) says, "People can say new Fenway Park, but I think they'd be making the biggest blunder in the world. Even if they got rid of Fenway Park, ours would be a valuable piece of property. I'm almost seventy years old and it doesn't really matter to me. But this is the best area. They could never get another ballpark like this. Never, never."

Steve Sheppard counts himself among the most loyal of Sox fans. He says, "Most people talk about how the upper grandstand in right field are the worst seats in the house, but during a nothing game I still enjoy sitting up there. It's the only place in the park where you can't see the 600 Club or the electronic scoreboard over the bleachers. They still have the old hanging lightbulbs suspended from the roof. I know when I'm there that I'm getting the same view my grandfather would have gotten fifty or sixty years ago. There aren't too many places left that are evocative like that—Durgin Park, maybe, but that's about it."

Trash Fenway? Sheppard's cousin, superfan Paul Comerford, says, "It's what the other ballparks aspire to. I see that in Pittsburgh they're trying to build Forbes Field again. You can't get a better seat in baseball than a third-base box seat at Fenway. It's where baseball was meant to be played. The expressway is an inconvenience, too, but we all drive on it. There's nothing any nicer than an early April day, walking up the ramp between home plate and first base, and seeing the greenest grass you're ever going to see. It's like home. You have a connection to the game when it's an old ballpark. This is where players have been. A new ballpark makes it seem like a new sport. We like Camden Yards, but it was like Disneyland. It was a nice place to be, but it wasn't the same."

Meanwhile, some Fenway traditionalists are making their voices heard, and not all want to keep the old yard. The *Globe*'s Marty Nolan, first to note that "the ballpark is the star [1986]," wrote, "Fenway seems like home to many, but economics is making home into a ghostly mansion on Sunset Boulevard. The ballpark has become Norma Desmond. . . . In 1992, postmodern architecture produced Camden Yards in Baltimore. Eli Jacobs, the [Newton, Massachusetts, native) financier who then owned the Orioles, transformed his boyhood memories of Fenway into wider seats, better food, and an urban tourist attraction. Fenway's uniqueness slowly dissipated amid the intimate feel of Jacobs Field in Cleveland, the old-timey reproduction of The Ballpark in Arlington, Texas, and the coziness of Coors Field in Denver. . . . Fenway's future is safe in its storied past. The future of baseball in Boston needs a new ballpark."

Red Sox slugger Mo Vaughn was more to the point. After a Sox loss in July of 1995, Vaughn told the *Herald*'s Joe Giulotti, "Blow it up. Blow the damned place up. . . . We need a new place to play. We need a new stadium."

On May 24, 1995, Massachusetts governor William Weld and Mayor Thomas Menino announced the convention-center commission's selection of a Summer Street (South Boston) site for a proposed megaplex. The proposal called for a domed football stadium, a convention center, and an outdoor baseball park to be built by the Red Sox on land donated by the city (predictably, the megaplex proposal died at the State House, but the Sox still want to build on the site). A Summer Street location would offer baseball fans a view of the Boston skyline and waterfront beyond the new left-field wall. John Buckley said, "We're elated the commission selected Summer Street. It is with much enthusiasm that we look forward to further progress in the ultimate achievement of building the best baseball facility ever constructed. . . . If it sits the way we think it will, it will be about four hundred and fifty feet from home plate to the waters of the channel.

So instead of Mo [Vaughn] hitting one onto the Turnpike, it'll be into the channel."

Harrington says, "If we can take the left-field wall, we'll take it. We could make it sort of a wailing wall. But I also think we could build a new wall and get it to thirty feet high. We might have some seats and make the top transparent. The league has some rules about dimension and we may have to conform, but I think we'd ask for some exceptions."

Will the word *Fenway* be part of the name of the new ballpark, even though it's not going to be located anywhere near the Fenway section of Boston? Harrington says, "It would be nice to do that, but I have the feeling we may have to have some sponsorship and naming rights."

Sponsorship. Ouch. That hurts. In 1995, the mayor of San Francisco sold the name of Candlestick Park to a Silicon Valley computer company. After thirty-five years, Candlestick became 3Com Park. Imagine Red Sox fans watching American League baseball games in the USAir/Pizza Hut/Weed Eater Ballpark at Summer Street. Say it ain't so.

Sox management uses every opportunity to talk about a new ballpark. When the team was swamped with requests for 1995 postseason tickets (40,000 applied for the available 2,800 tickets per game), Gorman said, "This just shows what support we have. With a new stadium, we can easily draw more than three million fans."

The Sox want to be in their new park by the year 2001, the one hundredth anniversary of the franchise. The Red Sox know that no matter how much they celebrate the opening of their new ballpark, most of the emotions will be felt when they close down old Fenway.

Anticipating the emotion when the Red Sox finally move out of Fenway Park, Harrington says, "I envision the ceremony. You know how much ceremony is related to tradition. With Fenway, I think we will have an appropriate ceremony to capsulize the spirit of Fenway and transport it to where we go. And I think the traditionalists will have to understand that the tradition will go with us. It's going to be difficult for all of us. We'll try to make it joyful, but there will be a little bit of solemnity for something that's been great for all of us for so many years."

It's still great. It could always be great. Save Fenway.

BIBLIOGRAPHY

Balf, Todd. "The Mourning After." *Sport*, March 1987.

Bauer, Douglas. "The Prime of Miss Jean Wilson." *Esquire*, June 1985.

Baylor, Don, and Claire Smith. *Don Baylor—Nothing but the Truth: A Baseball Life*. New York: St. Martin's Press, 1989.

Beierfield, Ann M. "Dr. Sidney Farber." *Boston Sunday Advertiser*, February 28, 1971.

Booth, Clark. "Faithfully Fenway." *Boston Magazine*, April 1987.

Boston Globe newspaper articles, 1901–1995.

Bryan, Mike. *Baseball Lives*. New York: Pantheon Books, 1989.

Cataneo, David. *Peanuts and Crackerjacks*. Nashville: Rutledge Hill Press, 1991.

Clark, Ellery H. *Red Sox Forever*. Hicksville, N.Y.: Exposition Press, 1977.

Denison, D. C. "Soxology." *Boston Phoenix*, June 19, 1979.

ESPN-2, Dan Patrick segment with Bill Buckner, 1993.

Gammons, Peter. *Beyond the Sixth Game*. Boston: Houghton Mifflin, 1985.

Golenbock, Peter. *Fenway*. New York: G. P. Putnam's Sons, 1992.

Hirshberg, Al. *The Red Sox, the Bean and the Cod*. Boston: Waverly House, 1947.

Johnson, Dick, and Glenn Stout. *Ted Williams: A Portrait in Words and Pictures*. New York: Walker and Company, 1991.

Lieb, Frederick G. *The Boston Red Sox*. New York: G. P. Putnam's Sons, 1947.

Linn, Ed. *Hitter*. New York: Harcourt Brace & Company, 1993.

Lowry, Philip J. *Green Cathedrals*. Reading, Mass.: Addison Wesley, 1992.

Mann, Jack. "The Great Wall of Boston." *Sports Illustrated*, July 28, 1965.

Rosen, R. D. "Portrait of a Ball Park." *Boston Magazine*, June 1978.

Ruth, Babe, and Bob Considine. *The Babe Ruth Story*. New York: E. P. Dutton, 1948.

Bibliography

Shaughnessy, Dan. *The Curse of the Bambino*. New York: E. P. Dutton, 1990.

Sowell, Mike. *One Pitch Away*. New York: Macmillan, 1995.

Sullivan, George. *The Picture History of the Boston Red Sox*. New York: Bobbs-Merrill, 1979.

Walton, Ed. *Red-Sox Triumphs and Tragedies*. New York: Stein & Day, 1980.

Wetzsteon, Ross. "What's Eating Jim Rice?" *Sport*, June 1987.

Zingg, Paul J. *Harry Hooper: An American Baseball Life*. Chicago: University of Illinois Press, 1993.

INDEX

DT#920125
8/1/96

BALDWIN PUBLIC LIBRARY

3 1115 00406 2260

796.3576 Shaughnessy, Dan. 24⁰⁰
S
         At Fenway.

NO LONGER THE PROPERTY OF
BALDWIN PUBLIC LIBRARY

DATE		

BALDWIN PUBLIC LIBRARY
2385 GRAND AVE
BALDWIN, NY 11510-3289
(516) 223-6228

14
DAY
OOK

This book ma
for 14 days on
It cannot

BAKER & TAYLOR